TRANSITION

Renewing Old Concepts,
Be Renewed In the Spirit of Your Mind

DORY ROBERTSON

WESTBOW
PRESS®
A DIVISION OF THOMAS NELSON
& ZONDERVAN

WestBow Press books may be ordered through booksellers or by contacting:

WestBow Press
A Division of Thomas Nelson & Zondervan
1663 Liberty Drive
Bloomington, IN 47403
www.westbowpress.com
1 (866) 928-1240

ISBN: 978-1-9736-8775-7 (sc)
ISBN: 978-1-9736-8774-0 (e)

Print information available on the last page.

WestBow Press rev. date: 3/19/2020

'Restoration of Original Sacred Name Bible'.
First Assembly of Yahvah
806 RSCR 3330
Emory, Tx 75440

The Amplified Bible Copyright 1987 Zondervan

The Passion Translation by Brian Simmons
BroadStreet Press

.

Proverbs 19:25 *He who has understanding will discern knowledge.*

Hebrews 5:14 *But solid food belongs to those who are of full age, that is, those who by reason of use have their senses exercised to discern both good and evil.*

Proverbs 25.2 God conceals the revelation of His Word in the hiding place of His glory, But the honor of Kings is revealed to all by how they thoroughly mine out the deeper meaning of all that God says.

The Passion Translation by Dr Brian Simmons BroadStreet Press.

All emphasis is by the author with underlining except in the Amplified Bible verses. I just want to point out crucial information for my readers to ponder more closely.

Transition - Renewing Old Concepts 2020
Ephesians 4:23 *Be renewed in the spirit of your mind*...Dory Robertson, Ocala, Florida

The cover image is from Marybeth Karsteadt
A dear friend from Beloit, Wisconsin.

All the Poetry Written Herein Is from My Book
<u>Poetry and Prose</u> by Dory Robertson.

We are God's 'workmanship' [means poiema] - His poetry. His Word sings to His bride as we respond in worship.

These poems were given to me over many years from the heart of God, as He sought to deposit within me, His love and peace, and all glory goes to the Lord of my life.

Some things you know
Some things you don't know
Some things you wish you knew
Some things you want to know
Some things you will investigate
Some things will surprise you
Some things will change your life
BUT IF...Some things don't matter
Then some things you don't want to know.

Transition

According to the Way,
The Truth and the Life
A New Way of Thinking
A New Way of Discerning
A New Way of Researching
A New Way of Finding Truth
A New Way of Trusting Scripture
A New Way of Trusting God.

Dedicated to The Body of Christ That Living Organism Though Whom Jesus Shows Forth His Love to The World - God's Witness. For God has brought us out of darkness into the Kingdom of His dear Son. The battles we fight are prevalent in the Body of Christ. *No temptation has overtaken you except such as is common to man.*

To you, the Lord would say
Ye shall not need to fight in this battle;
set yourselves, stand ye still,
[stand in the position of faith]
and see the salvation of the Lord with you.
Be not afraid nor dismayed
by reason of this great multitude;
for the battle is not yours but God's.
(2 Chronicles 20.15&17).

Contents

MEET THE AUTHOR

Dory Robertson is a Minister of Pastoral Counseling; Ordained in Ocala, Florida, in June, 2008. Now a member of One Foundation Ministries, Ocala, FL

Born again in 1972, I began to read the Bible with Genesis. It seems I was taken into another world as I read of creation and the Creator. I couldn't get enough. Hours every day I spent seeing a God of love but also a God Who understood what He had created.

Psalm 8:4 *What is man that You are mindful of him, And the son of man that You visit him? .*

2 Chronicles 16:9 *For the eyes of the Lord run to and fro throughout the whole earth, to show Himself strong on behalf of those whose heart is loyal to Him. .*

Oh yes, He sought me and brought me out of dread darkness into His glorious light [Colossians 1.12-14].

We have the opportunity now, to explore God's truth, to search it out. It's there plainly for all to see, to not be seduced by the evil one, and we all have the same choice. The truth of God's Word will come to you as you read it. But the reality of God's Word comes from studying it, comparing Scripture with Scripture. There are words in the Bible spoken by man, much of it questionable. But the true Word of God will have 2 or more witnesses, Old and New Testament. A Concordance will help you search. God has given us a wonderful resource of wisdom; that is His Holy Spirit.

John 14:26-*27 But the Helper, the Holy Spirit, whom*

the Father will send in My name, He will teach you all things, and bring to your remembrance all things that I said to you. . I am totally dependent on all the help He will give me So, I encourage you to research and compare as I have done in all my books. It is very rewarding; and please don't take my word for it, study and compare, and take nothing out of context.

The Father of Glory Has His Eye on You
And Loves You Dearly.

MY STORY

I was gloriously saved in 1972. I had just given birth to my 5th child and my 3rd husband gave all the signs of going out the door. I was saved 3 months after she was born in March. He did leave 15 years later. Out of this fire came a book called 'He Never Came Back'. It took a long time for me to realize he wasn't. God gave me an unconditional love for him in the middle of his unfaithfulness; so I really thought... but he didn't. He died 10 years later.

My greatest stronghold was the fear of abandonment, so I also knew that if I did anything wrong God would also leave me. I tried to 'follow the leader' and began to believe everything that I was told. I also read The Late Great Planet Earth in 1972 and I went along with what everyone else believed.

When I opened the Bible, I could see and read about Life, the one thing that I was so starved for. So, I just began to devour the Word. One day I opened it and there on the page printed was Jeremiah 15.16.

Your words were found, and I ate them, And Your word was to me the joy and rejoicing of my heart; For I am called by Your name, O Lord God of hosts. Oh, how that blessed me. I didn't know it then but God had a plan for my life and it was to devour His Word. .

Now at the age of 88, my own memory sometimes doesn't recall as I want, but between God's words and His Word, I will continue to write what He tells me. [John 10.27;15.14-15]. I don't speak of these things to make myself important, but as other writers and speakers share their credentials, and where they get the authority to speak on any subject, well, even Jesus was questioned.

Matthew 21.23 When He came into the temple, the chief priests and the elders of the people confronted Him as He was teaching, and said, "By what authority are You doing these things? And who gave You this authority?" He didn't answer their arrogance but the people who He was teaching, who wanted truth, He said, *John 12.49 For I have not spoken on My own authority but the Father who sent Me gave Me a command, what I should say and what I should speak. .*

We should never speak 'in the name of Jesus' unless He has given us the words. Certainly, I do not think I have the authority of Jesus, but He has promised to lead us into all truth. So I admonish my readers to do your own research instead of taking the word of others.

I share what's next as for my credentials even as other writers and even Paul shared his.

In October 1996 I was at a prophecy convention; Pastor Bill Hamon's Church. During a time of worship, I had a vision of a tool box much like the big red ones mechanics use. God said, 'I have given you a chest – a power chest and the keys to every drawer. You will open them one at a time and use them as I direct. The first will be the Word'. He pointed me to -

Proverbs 2 The treasures of wisdom and understanding are found in the Word for the Lord gives wisdom. From His mouth comes knowledge and understanding. He stores up sound wisdom for the upright. Then He said, 'I have planted a seed in you and I want to see My harvest. You are my seed'. (I'm so glad He caused me to keep a journal). Maybe you could also.

Jesus is the power chest. More drawers were opened down thru the years, but the first key opened the drawer to The Word. This should always be first. The Living Word and the written word; *come to the laver - be washed by the water of the word*. The treasures of wisdom and understanding are found in the Word. The second key was a deeper understanding of the Word.

Does the Word inspire or incarnate? The key to the Word of God is being able to relate personally to what it is saying. A relationship between you and the written Word brings about a relationship between you and the Living Word (John 1.1); to become flesh in you. There comes understanding the Word with your whole being; drawn into experiencing the reality of what it is saying. Relationship is experienced in body, soul and spirit.

That's how the Word ministers to the believer; when truth - understood in the mind and heart becomes reality, it is a living thing that involves our whole being. Then came: Visions and Prophecy 8/07;

Deeper Understanding 9/02;

Discipline/ Intimacy 10/05; Love 10/07;

Revelation 12/07; Hope 12/15 and some others.

These things were in my life [in part] but on these dates they were accelerated.

Now please know my heart. I am not anyone special, only that God has claimed me as His own. God's people have the same gifts, perhaps used in some different ways. These gifts are to equip anyone who will listen to the Spirit. Each one of us has an anointing to walk the path God has chosen for us.

Some gifts were made available to me in the ministry of counseling others as the Lord led me, to help them overcome many of their issues [1Cor 12.1-10]. It is wonderful to keep a journal to remember what God has done for you and in you; to remember. He gives to His people the keys of the Kingdom to open the doors that were meant for your life.

In 1987, God prompted me to begin writing what I realized were chapters of a book; 19 chapters in all. I never published this one. In 1992 He told me to begin to edit these chapters because they were really only an outline of what it would be. It was all about how God had changed my life; the book was named 'Our Inheritance'. Transition came almost every day in some form; and I was so glad to be set free.

For 15 years after I was saved, God had been delivering me from the fears that taunted me all my life; and the deception I had lived under, as to what life was really all about and how God was restoring me into His image; foremost of how much He loved me. Then He had me to compile these chapters into several books; for instance, one book 'The Love of Jesus' has the chapters on love - 1. The Beginning; 2. What He did for me; 3. Teaches us to love our enemies; 3. His Love and ours [conditional and His unconditional]; and finally, 4. The love of Jesus brings us from law to grace.

All these from my original book. Several of my books were written and completed before the year 2000; but not published until 2010. That year I found CreateSpace, a publishing Company. It is now owned by Amazon.

One night I had a dream that Jesus stood before me and gave me a ring of keys. Some years later in 1988 someone gave me a big brass ring of 'skeleton keys', five in all [brass for judgment and five for grace]. I believe it was for God to open new doors in my life.

In 2006, God had me to write a book; A Word on Wisdom and Knowledge. He gave me a clear exegesis of what it was saying, If you are interested in having it, see the back of this book.

Revelation knowledge is available to all who will seek and search for truth. God warns us to not be deceived [James 1.16; 1 John 4.1]. Because of the insight, understanding and the leading of the Holy Spirit, I began to gather notes for my first book, 1996, The Temple of God Restored. It compares the rebuilding of the 5th century temple by Zerubbabel, and How God restores us to be His temple. It was completed but not published until 2010. This was the first book I published. Since then I have written and published 15 books besides this one. Remember Ephesians 4.11-16. Some of us are teacher/ writers.

Even though God was working in my life during those years; except for God, I had no ambition to do much of anything. But after Mike left it seems I was alive again. God told me He was delivering me from a dead marriage and it seemed like I felt a coffin came off me; and as the years went by, there came a lot more deliverance from my painful past.

Changes Made - Transition
Into What God Created Me To Be.

2 Corinthians 5:17-18 *Therefore, if anyone is in Christ, he is a new creation; old things have passed away; behold, all things have become new. .*

Psalm 84:11-12 *For the Lord God is a sun and shield; The Lord will give grace and glory; No good thing will He withhold from those who walk uprightly. O Lord of hosts, blessed is the man who trusts in You! .*

The Bible is not a 'To Do' list – its purpose is as Jesus told us. In the Gospel of John, Jesus shows us His Father over 100 times. And throughout the Bible, many more times. Jesus said, John 20.17 *'I am going to my Father and your Father.* Yes, He wants us to know Him. Read John 14. 20-23. God's love for us is incomprehensible. We may not understand it, but we can experience it to its fulness.

In all my shattered brokenness A heart that never knew
A revelation comes to me, the experience of You
A moment when I couldn't speak -
relations with another
Came to bring an emptiness, such shame,
Such guilt, to gather a broken soul into the depths
Of hell - that could only throw me into a well
Of self-hatred, grief and pain
But then there shown within my heart
A glorious light of truth
There really is a path to life
Redeemer, Lover, Friend - You
Healing there it came to me.
In brokenness I sing
Into the arms of faithful love
My Father - My Savior - My God
My King.
And You Will Share in My Glory
For as Long as I Am Your God.

INTRODUCTION

In The Beginning - God... All Things Begin With God,
The Lord of Life.

You have in your hand, a book that I hope will lead you to study THE BOOK. Confirming all these references will lead you to understand that God means what He says, because all this was and is - His Idea. This is how I learned the truth of His Word after I was born again 48 years ago, when I began to read the Word for myself. When I read any other book; and I've read a lot of books by Authors I believed I could trust to share the true Word of God; I did research to see if all was truly His Word, and where else can the Word of God be confirmed? Nowhere but the true Word of God.

ow it is vital to your spiritual health to get into the genuine Word of God, not the compromised bible that the cults have printed to keep their followers in deception and controlled by their leaders. God will always lead His people into truth, ask Him which Bible You should read [2Timothy 2.15;3.16,17].

You must Know There Is No Other Gospel but The One That Has Been Preached since the Beginning, the Words of the Apostles and Prophets, As Given to Them by the Holy Spirit.

Galatians 1:6-10 *I marvel that you are turning away so soon from Him who called you in the grace of Christ, to a different gospel, which is not another; but there are* *some who trouble you and want to pervert the gospel of Christ. But even if we, <u>or an angel from heaven</u>, preach any other gospel to you than what we have preached to you, let him be accursed. As we have said before, so now I say again, if anyone preaches any other gospel to you than what you have received, let him be accursed. For do I now persuade men, or God? Or do I seek to please men? For if I still pleased men, I would not be a bond servant of Christ. .*

It behooves us all to follow Paul's instructions as we become a witness to the Kingdom of God [Acts 1.8].

There are some controversial subjects written herein that must be inquired of; subjects that one view of them is stuck in people's head and won't give place to investigating. I am an archeologist digging into Scripture, for Jesus said,

John 8.32 *You will know the truth and the truth will make you free. .* I believe we must not continue to take other people's word for anything pertaining to the Word, if it does not agree with the true Word after much investigation.

Proverbs 25:2 *It is the glory of God to conceal a Smatter, But the glory of kings is to search out a matter. .*

God may hide His word but revelation is given those who will seek and search until he finds. Be careful that you don't mistake your opinion for truth; or especially the opinion of others for revelation knowledge. God expects us to search out truth for ourselves. If we do, God will cause us to understand even the deeper things.

John 16:12-15 *I still have many things to say to you, but you cannot bear them now. However, when He, the Spirit of truth, has come, He will guide you into all truth; for He will not speak on His own authority, but whatever He hears He will speak; and He will tell you things to come. He will glorify Me, for He will take of what is Mine and declare it to you. All things that the Father has are Mine. Therefore, I said that He will take of Mine and declare it to you. .*

Do You Have the Spirit of Truth Living in You?
If You Don't Know - Ask God. He Will Show You
And Lead You to What You Need.

God never leaves us alone, He is constantly drawing us closer to His heart as we will allow Him; and as long as we desire to know Him, He will reveal Himself through His Spirit to grow us up to follow the plan He has for us. Please read Romans 8 - God's Holy Spirit will explain it.

We are responsible for what we believe, so we must know what the Word is really saying, for God promises us that we can ask for wisdom and it will be given freely to those who are sincere in their asking [James 1]. I strive to give the witness of the Word for all I have written. Feel free to give your witness... email in the back of this book.

Romans 12:2 And do not be conformed to this world, but be transformed by the renewing of your mind, that you may prove what is that good and acceptable and perfect will of God. Trust God - Prove all things. .

Please know that all I say herein, is backed up with the immutability of the Word of God. If it can't be proven as His truth, I will not print it. His Word is confirmed by an oath.

Hebrews 6.17-18 *This was so that, by two unchangeable things [His promise and His oath] in which it is impossible for God ever to prove false or deceive us,* [Amplified Bible] [Even God has His two witnesses].

So, if we want to understand the Word of God as He reveals Himself, we must not be satisfied with 'junk food', a little here and a little there; but God has delivered to us a banquet - all of it to feast on. Reading and researching the New Testament that is verified in the Old Testament will satisfy your appetite for real truth.

We must Learn to Prove the Word By the Mouth of Two or Three Witnesses and Taken in the Context of Which it Was Written.

Deuteronomy 19:15-16 *By the mouth of two or three witnesses the matter shall be established. .*

2 Corinthians 13:1 *By the mouth of two or three witnesses every word shall be established. .*

And where would we find a witness to the Word in the Bible Paul and the other Apostles preached from - why of course it was the Old Testament; the supporting frame for the New Testament. AMEN.

It's Too Bad That Many People Don't Think the Old
Testament Is Relevant for Today, Not Realizing
It Is the Foundation for Our New Testament.

I am taking on a tremendous opportunity to resolve some of the madness that has been promulgated throughout the Christian world that sorely needs another look; but I don't do so arbitrarily; there is already much too much transcribed in our Bible that testifies to truth.

Our magnificent God and Lord of the universe desires our presence into His Kingdom. SO...

. Psalm 99:8 *Exalt the Lord our God, and worship at His holy hill; For the Lord our God is holy .*

This book is founded on much Scriptural exegesis. I pray you will seriously do your own Bible Study to see if all is correctly laid down.

Deuteronomy 4:2 *You shall not add to the word which I command you, nor take from it. .*

Deuteronomy 18:21-22 *How shall we know the word which the Lord has not spoken? — when a prophet speaks in the name of the Lord, if the thing does not happen or come to pass, that is the thing which the Lord has not spoken; the prophet has spoken it presumptuously; you shall not be afraid of him. .*

The Scriptures I use herein are proven by comparison. The word of two witnesses; the Old and New Testament.

2 Sam 22:31 *As for God, His way is perfect; The word of the Lord is proven; He is a shield to all who trust Him.* .

Jesus is the Word [John 1] and the Word can be trusted if it is translated from the original Scriptures, not the corrupted Bible of the cults.

Matthew 13:18-19 *Therefore hear the parable of the sower: When anyone hears the word of the Kingdom, and does not understand it, then the wicked one comes and snatches away what was sown in his heart.* .

This is why we must get understanding of what the Word is saying; and we do this by the counsel of God's Holy Spirit and by researching. Too many verses are taken out of context to say what someone wants it to say, thereby misleading others.

Mark 7:13 *making the word of God of no effect through your tradition which you have handed down. And many such things you do.* .

Spreading false ideas to many people too often becomes tradition and Jesus said it would make the Word of God of no true value. We must get understanding. Only God can give it. Ps 119.103-5; Proverbs 3.5; Col 2.2; 1Co 14.20.

1 John 4:17 *Love has been perfected among us in this: that we may have boldness in the day of judgment; because as He is, so are we in this world. There is no fear in love; but perfect love casts out fear, because fear involves torment. But he who fears has not been made perfect in love. We love Him because He first loved us.*

The Joy of Knowing His Love
Fills My Heart to Overflowing.

Michael Jr. is a well-known comedian and an awesome evangelist. He's on YouTube a lot. Besides being very funny, he shares some great facts about being a Christian. Tonight, he spoke to our deepest heart.

"We have to let go of what we want
So we can receive what we need.
And Study The Art Of Listening".

How Do I Love Thee Lord?
Let Me Count the Ways,
So Many in the Book You Wrote -
That Says
I Love You Because You First Loved Me
I Love You Because You Hung on That Tree
I Love You for the Mercy and Grace You Extended
For the Broken Heart Which Your Love Mended
Thank You Lord That You Died in My Place
Your Righteousness Now
Lets Us Meet Face to Face
How Do I Love Thee Lord, Now Let Me See?
I Love Thee Because You First Loved Me.

JESUS - THE SON OF MAN

God delights in revealing Himself to His creation, that's us, because He wants us to know Him; He wants relationship with those He loves -

John 20.2 *Then she ran and came to Simon Peter, and to the other disciple, whom Jesus loved... .*

This was obviously John, the one who wrote the gospel, three love letters and the Revelation of Jesus Christ; and saw himself as one who Jesus loved. We can very well say that about ourselves as lovers of God [1Jn 4.19]; so here is a breathtaking visual of Jesus, the Son of God, Savior and Redeemer, manifested in all His glory. And so, He stands before John, the Apostle.

This Is What John Was Looking At.

John the Apostle was on the Isle of Patmos. He saw Jesus, the embodiment of the entire promise of God in the plan of our redemption. He is revealing to John His Character, His Personality, His Nature. From Revelation Chapter one - have you ever looked at it this way? John walked with our glorious Savior, Lord and King, as King/Priest and Bridegroom. He is searching for the overcomer, His priest/bride, in the midst of His Church body (Revelation 2&3). Jesus will speak to His people through these seven Churches. Many are called but who will answer?

1. HE IS THE ALPHA AND OMEGA -
The First and the Last - the Beginning and the End.
THERE IS NO OTHER GOD BUT HIM.
2. SEVEN GOLDEN LAMPSTANDS -
The Church complete, His body. He is the Head,
and He is standing in her midst.
HE HAS THE FINAL WORD FOR ALL WHO EVER LIVED.
3. IN HIS HOLINESS AND GLORY
Hair white as snow [wisdom], Eyes a flame of fire [discernment], Feet like bronze burned in a furnace [judgment]. He has come to judge His people.
HE IS SEARCHING FOR HIS BRIDE!
4. HIS VOICE IS LIKE MANY WATERS;
He speaks to every kindred and tongue - people and nation.
NO ONE IS OVERLOOKED.
5. SEVEN STARS - He will judge especially, the leadership. Are they in that position [Rev 1.20]?
FOR HIS GLORY - OR FOR THEIRS.
6. WITH HIS MANIFESTED POWER, He sends forth His two-edged sword to divide soul and spirit.
HIS WORD - HIS TRUTH! [Hebrews 4.12].
7. AND HE HOLDS THE KEYS OF DEATH AND HELL!
SEVEN JUDGMENTS - GOD'S PERFECT WILL.

Revelation 2.8 *Fear not; I am the first and the last; I am he that lives, and was dead; and, behold, I am alive for evermore, Amen, and have the keys of hell and death. And, behold, I come quickly, and my reward is with me, to give every man according as his work shall be. Blessing, and glory, and wisdom, and thanksgiving, and honor, and power, and might, be unto our God forever and ever. Amen. .*

The Kingdom of God came to us in the person of Jesus. Every word He spoke showed forth the Kingdom of God. He is the Word become flesh. The Kingdom of God invites us to partake; invites to know God as Father;

to inherit all there is in Christ, the living witness of a Kingdom outside ourselves that it becomes OK to leave all behind us and pursue this new life in Christ. It will always be safe to reach out to this Redeemer of our soul, to hide ourselves in Him.

[Excerpt from <u>The Holiest of All</u>, by Andrew Murray] 1996 by Whitaker House Publishers.

God Has Spoken in His Son, The Word Came Forth
from the Fiery Furnace of God's Holiness,
From the Burning Glow of Everlasting Love,
He Himself Is the Living Word. He is the Outshining of
God's Glory and The Perfect Image of His substance.

WHAT IS THE SACRED NAME?

We are so used to using the Name Jesus, but it's also good to know what is God's original Name. Scriptures from ROSNB

Isaiah 52.5 *Now therefore, what do I hear, demandeth Yahvah, that my people have been taken away for nought? They that do howl, declareth Yahvah and continueth all the day is my name brought into contempt. Therefore, shall my people acknowledge my name.*

2 Chronicles 7.16 *Now therefore have I chosen and hallowed this house, that my name may be there unto times age-abiding.*

Revelation 14.1 *On Mt Zion, 144,000 having His Name and His Father's Name written on their foreheads.*

So, do we know the Name above all names?

Proverbs 30:4 *Who has ascended into heaven, or descended? Who has gathered the wind in His fists? Who has bound the waters in a garment? Who has established all the ends of the earth? What is His name, and what is His Son's name, if you know?*

Exodus 3:13-14 *The God of your fathers has sent me to you,' and they say to me, 'What is His name? what shall I say to them? And God said to Moses, I AM WHO I AM.*

'I AM' Literally - I Continue to Be, and Will Be
What I Continue to Be, and Will Be.

Deuteronomy 6.4 Hear oh Israel: YAHVAH is our
ELOHIM, YAHVAH alone.

Elohim is plural, compounded of words that mean -
'THESE ARE GOD'.

There is no difference of will or purpose among them.

Deuteronomy 6:4-*5 Hear, O Israel: The Lord our God,
the Lord is one!* Not just '*Hear oh Israel*', but -

'*Gather together, unite under this one truth*'.

YAHVAH	Our ELOHIM	Is One YAHVAH
GOD	These are GOD	GOD
Father -	Son -	Holy Spirit

That the inherent Ones are so united together - One in
the Other without end, They being the exalted God. Three
exalted original One's, Trinity in unity; unity of essence,
each exists of Himself.

JUST WONDERING

Too often the suppositions of men take precedence over reality. Most men and women of God read the Word of God, but too often don't take the time to really study it and research any referring Scriptures.

2 Timothy 3:16-17 All *Scripture is given by inspiration of God, and is profitable for doctrine, for reproof, for correction, for instruction in righteousness, that the man of God may be complete, thoroughly equipped for every good work. .*

Profitable for - *correction, reproof, instruction to thoroughly equip the 'man of God'*; yet too often I hear statements [supposedly Bible truth] from Scripture taken out of context.

2 Peter 1:19-21 *we have the prophetic word confirmed, which you do well to heed as a light that shines in a dark place, until the day dawns and the morning star rises in your hearts; knowing this first, that no prophecy of Scripture is of any private interpretation, for prophecy never came by the will of man, but holy men of God spoke as they were moved by the Holy Spirit.*

One meaning of this verse is that every man shall not interpret Scriptures out of their own imagination. Another is that the truth always confirms itself; two witnesses.

God will always confirm His Word By the power of two or more witnesses. He wants us to be sure that we understand.

If what we think may be an essential doctrine in the Bible is not confirmed with other Scripture, we may have to think it over and talk to God about it. Here is a good example taken out of context; is in 1Corinthians 15.29. There is no efficacy in baptizing people for the dead as some Churches believe. There are no other verses that would confirm this as truth. It is not baptism that saves anyone, we are saved by grace through faith.

Ephesians 2.8-9. Yes, it is our own faith that saves us, not from someone else. In this Scripture, Paul was teaching them about the resurrection - not baptism. We are baptized into Christ when we are saved and then water baptized; and this takes place when we are alive. But here, Paul was reassuring them of the resurrection.

1 Corinthians 15:29 *If the dead will not be raised, what point is there in people being baptized for those who are dead?* Holy Bible, New Living Translation,

1 Corinthians 15:29 *Why do you think people offer themselves to be baptized for those already in the grave? If there's no chance of resurrection for a corpse, if God's power stops at the cemetery gates, why do we keep doing things that suggest he's going to clean the place out someday, pulling everyone up on their feet alive*?

THE MESSAGE: © 2002 by Eugene H. Peterson.

1 Corinthians 15:29 *Otherwise what will become of those who got themselves baptized for the dead? If the dead do not rise at all, why are these baptized for them?* .

This is a futile ceremony.

2 Tim 2:25-26 *in humility correcting those who are in opposition, if God perhaps will grant them repentance, so that they may know the truth, 26 and that they may come to their senses and escape the snare of the devil, having been taken captive by him to do his will.* .

Acts 4:12 Nor *is there salvation in any other, for there is no other name under heaven given among men by which we must be saved.* .

7

Hebrews 9:27 *It is appointed for men to die once, but after this the judgment. .*

There is no interim baptism.

1 Timothy 2:3-6 *For this is good and acceptable in the sight of God our Savior, who desires all men to be saved and to come to the knowledge of the truth. For there is one God and one Mediator between God and men, the Man Christ Jesus, who gave Himself a ransom for all. .*

The dead cannot come to any knowledge. If Any die without Christ, *nothing*, including baptizing in their name, will save them. The whole matter of this Scripture concerns resurrection. We must be very careful of how we handle The Word of God. Just remember, Paul and the apostles taught out of the Old Testament as they wrote the New Testament with Holy Spirit wisdom.

Inaccurate Information from Movies or TV
Can Also Corrupt the True Word of God.

So, Stick with the True Word of God,
The Original Word of God.
Not a version printed by counterfeit christians.

TRANSITION:

A movement, a passage. a change from one position, stage, subject, concept - to another. A transfer, conversion [Webster's Dictionary].

This is what we do when we choose to come out of darkness into the glorious light of the Kingdom of God; and every time we choose to change our life style; our ideas about sin and the righteousness of God that has been transferred to us [2 Corinthians 5.17-21]. Yes, it is a reconciliation. Reconciling truth for error. There is much we have to change to have *the mind of Christ.*

Yes, our sin nature was taken to the cross, but now we have to change our old habits that seemed to suit us well, but in reality, many of them gave permission for the evil one to maintain a place in our lives to keep us in deception. Oh yes, when we don't walk in truth, that's what happens. Revelation letters tell us we can be overcomers if we pay attention to God's Holy Spirit Who will lead us. Transition from darkness to light is a gift from Father God.

John 14:15-*19 If you love Me, keep My commandments. And I will pray the Father, and He will give you another Helper, that He may abide with you forever — the Spirit of truth, whom the world cannot receive, because it neither sees Him nor knows Him; but you know Him, for He dwells with you and will be in you. I will not leave you orphans; I will come to you.*

John 14:25-27 *These things I have spoken to you while being present with you. But the Helper, the Holy Spirit,* whom the Father will send in My name, He will teach you all things, and bring to your remembrance all things that I said to you. Peace I leave with you, my peace I give to you; not as the world gives do I give to you. Let not your heart be troubled, neither let it be afraid.

Jeremiah 31:31 *I will put My law in their minds, and write it on their hearts; and I will be their God, and they shall be My people. [All .]*

The Things God Said Are Written in His Word,
Old and New Testament. They Have a Habit
Of Agreeing with Each Other.

*It May Be a Long Road
But We Are Transitioned
At the Foot of the Cross.*

GOD'S WISDOM OR MAN'S

Paul's world consisted of people who worked hard at living their life from their own senses. 'What I think for myself is the best way to live'. [*In those days there was no king in Israel; every man did that which was right in his own eyes.* [Judges 21.23]. . . And This Generation????

So, he had to show grace and compassion to those who would listen. It's not easy to change the mind of another, bent on living their own life. Only the Holy Spirit in Paul could change their way of thinking. It was a challenge to the heart and mind to alter their goals; so, he went about showing where they were, in opposition to God's wisdom and way. God asked Adam, Where Are You?

And Isn't This What the Believer in Christ Is also Called to Do? Where Am I? Is Jesus Really My Lord or Am I Playing Games. Do I Really Want to Change?

WITNESS #1:

1 Corinthians 1:17- *For the message of the cross is foolishness to those who are perishing, but to us who are being saved it is the power of God. For it is written: I will destroy the wisdom of the wise, and bring to nothing the understanding of the prudent.* .

HERE IS WITNESS #2: Isaiah 29:14

Therefore, behold, I will again do a marvelous work Among this people, A marvelous work and a wonder; For the wisdom of their wise men shall perish, And the understanding of their prudent men shall be hidden. .

Now back to: 1 Corinthians 1:20 *Where is the wise?*

Where is the scribe? Where is the disputer of this age? Has not God made foolish the wisdom of this world? For since, in the wisdom of God, the world through wisdom did not know God, it pleased God through the foolishness of the message preached, to save those who believe; but we preach Christ crucified, to the Jews a stumbling block and to the Greeks foolishness, but to those who are called, both Jews and Greeks, Christ is the power of God and the wisdom of God. . .

Because the foolishness of God is wiser than men, and the weakness of God is stronger than men. For you see your calling, brethren, that not many wise according to the flesh, not many mighty, not many noble, are called. But God has chosen the foolish things of the world to put to shame the wise, and God has chosen the weak things of the world to put to shame the things which are mighty; and the base things of the world and the things which are despised God has chosen, and the <u>Things Which Are Not</u>, to bring to nothing the things that are, that no flesh should glory in His presence. But of Him you are in Christ Jesus, who became for us wisdom from God and righteousness and sanctification and redemption — that, as it is written, He who glories, let him glory in the Lord. .

I'm So Glad I Was an 'Are Not'
That God Would Come after Me.

I wrote a treatise in my Book <u>A Word on Wisdom and Knowledge</u>, as God brought me through understanding. No, I didn't know how to apply it all but God does. He is so gracious as we ask [James 1.5]. God gives revelation wisdom and power to those who will pursue to know the deeper things of the Spirit; not to rely of what others may believe - those of whom will not seek and search for themselves but to rely on others whether they be right or wrong. We must know, are we hearing the voice of the Lord or being deceived by the voice of another? Make Jesus the cause of all you do. The Bible is blatantly accurate to reveal more than we can possibly imagine. Revelation partners with Wisdom so that we will know truth [John 14.17].

I've done things to my regret because I didn't ask God for His wisdom. It behooves us to know that God so loves us that He offers us His Kingdom, to walk the path, the journey into God's peace. Our Father's love and concern for His children is so great that He sent His only Son to free us from the captivity of the evil one.

Acts 17:24-25 *God, who made the world and everything in it, since He is Lord of heaven and earth, does not dwell in temples made with hands. Nor is He worshiped with men's hands, as though He needed anything, since He gives to all life, breath, and all things.* .

James 4:6 And *He gives more grace. Therefore, He* says:

God resists the proud, but gives grace to the humble.

James 1:5-6 *If any of you lacks wisdom, let him ask of God, who gives to all liberally and without reproach, and it will be given to him.* .

Colossians 2:2-3 All *riches of the full assurance of understanding, to the knowledge of the mystery of God, both of the Father and of Christ, in whom are hidden all the treasures of wisdom and knowledge.* .

Proverbs 1:2-8 *To know wisdom and instruction, To perceive the words of understanding, To receive the instruction of wisdom, justice, judgment, and equity; To give prudence to the simple, To the young man knowledge and discretion — A wise man will hear and increase learning, And a man of understanding will attain wise counsel, To understand a proverb and an enigma, The words of the wise and their riddles. Fear of the Lord is the beginning of knowledge, But fools despise wisdom and instruction.* .

Proverbs 2:1-11 *My son, if you receive my words, And treasure my commands within you, So that you incline your ear to wisdom, And apply your heart to understanding; Yes, if you cry out for discernment, And lift up your voice for understanding, If you seek her as silver, And search for her as for hidden treasures; Then you will understand the fear of the Lord, And find the knowledge of God. For the Lord gives wisdom; From His mouth come knowledge and understanding; He stores up sound wisdom for the upright; He is a shield to those who walk uprightly; He guards the paths of justice, and preserves the way of His saints. Then you will understand righteousness and justice, Equity and every good path. When wisdom enters your heart, and knowledge is pleasant to your soul, Discretion will preserve you; Understanding will keep you.*

"The writer's great discovery...To seek God does not narrow one's life, but brings it rather, to the level of highest possible fulfillment". The Pursuit of God, A.W. Tozer

Make Jesus the Cause of All You Do
That He Lives in the Very Center of Your Being.
Treasure God's Wisdom,
It Will Lead and Guide You on Your Road to Life.

WHERE IS WISDOM?

Job 28 Job's Discourse on Wisdom.

Surely there is a mine for silver, and a place where gold is refined. But where can wisdom be found? And where is the place of understanding? No mention shall be made of coral or quartz, For the price of wisdom is above rubies. From where then does wisdom come? And where is the place of understanding? Then He saw wisdom and declared it; He prepared it, indeed, He searched it out. And to man He said, 'Behold, the fear of the Lord, that is wisdom, and to depart from evil is understanding. .

The possession of wisdom is far above rubies or pearls. Shall I be afraid of God? NO! He has declared me His child. But He is awesome and holy, and I will reverence and worship Him because He is God. I'm so grateful He has bestowed on me His love, and made available to me - His wisdom (Colossians 1.9).

Job 28.16 *It cannot be gotten with gold, neither can silver be weighed for the price thereof. It cannot be valued...precious onyx, or...sapphire. It cannot be exchanged for jewels, not to mention coral or pearls, For the price of wisdom Is above rubies. .*

There's Only One Place to Find Wisdom
And God Doesn't Tease Us; He Tells Us Plainly...

James 1.2-8 *My brethren, count it all joy when you fall into various trials, knowing that the testing of your faith produces patience. But let patience have its perfect work, that you may be perfect and complete, lacking nothing. If any of you lacks wisdom, let him ask of God, who gives to all liberally and without reproach, and it will be given to him. But let him ask in faith, with no doubting, for he who doubts is like a wave of the sea driven and tossed by the wind. For let not that man suppose that he will receive anything from the Lord; he is a double-minded man, unstable in all his ways. .*

Can We Count it All Joy? Well Yes, If We Are Sure
That the Lord Who Loves Us So Much Is on the Job.

Whence then cometh wisdom? Where is the place of understanding? God understands And He knows the place thereof. He who sees under the whole heaven, Who measures the weight of wind, unto men He saith, Behold The fear of the Lord— That is wisdom. To depart from evil— That is understanding. .

Romans 5.1-12 Therefore, having been justified by faith, we have peace with God through our Lord Jesus Christ, through whom also we have access by faith into this grace in which we stand, and rejoice in hope of the glory of God. And not only that, but we also glory in tribulations, knowing that tribulation produces perseverance; and perseverance, character; and character, hope. Now hope does not disappoint, because the love of God has been poured out in our hearts by the Holy Spirit who was given to us. .

Jesus Christ Took Our Place.

For when we were still without strength, in due time Christ died for the ungodly. For scarcely for a righteous man will one die; yet perhaps for a good man someone would even dare to die. But God demonstrates His own love toward us, in that while we were still sinners, Christ died for us. Much more then, having now been justified

16

by His blood, we shall be saved from wrath through Him. For if when we were enemies we were reconciled to God through the death of His Son, much more, having been reconciled, we shall be saved by His life. And not only that, but we also rejoice in God through our Lord Jesus Christ, through whom we have now received the reconciliation. And Ultimately

Proverbs 1.7 *The fear of the Lord is the beginning of knowledge, but fools despise wisdom and instruction. .*

Psalm 111.10 *The fear of the Lord is the beginning of all wisdom. He who would have wisdom, let him in love, Fear God And forsake his sins. .*

To Be Wise With God's Wisdom
Is in the Bible Hundreds of Times.
Do You Think It Is Wise
To Use God's Wisdom?

17

WHOSE TEMPLE ARE WE?

The spirit of antichrist has been in the world since Adam believed the lie. Perhaps called by another name but has been against all that is God. He has led nations into darkness, caused malicious hatred among men, and captured the souls of the unwary to feed his lust for power [Revelation 18.13].

How prophetic was Paul that he knew there would come doctrines of demons that would lead God's people into lies, whose agenda would be to rob Jesus of His rightful position and identity; ones who would change the Word of God to suit their own beliefs, or add their own interpretation; even as Daniel 7.25 reveals,

He shall speak great words against the Most High and shall wear out the saints of the Most High and think to change the times and laws. .

Knowing the Truth Will Also Define Your Identity; Who You are in Christ?

*To wear out...*used only in a mental sense [Strong's Concordance] ... Oh yes, the devil tries to do a job on our mind. We must stay alert and know what says the Word of God, the Word of Truth. *Renew your mind* [Eph 4.23-24] *for we have the mind of Christ* [1Cor 2.16]. His Holy Spirit will teach us and bring us into all truth [John 14].

Perhaps this was Paul's thorn; the torment that many of his converts would deny the Lord who brought them [Galatians 1.6-9], and give in to deception and heresies;

or even agnostics, denying Jesus is God [Romans 9.5; 2 Timothy 3]; or that no one can have a relationship with God.

But this Is the Core of True Christianity; That Is, to Be Sons and Daughters of the Most High God, His Family, In Relationship with God and One Another in Love.

2 Corinthians 6.17 *Come out from among them and be separate, says the Lord. Do not touch what is unclean, And I will receive you. I will be a Father to you, and you shall be My sons and daughters, says the Lord Almighty.* .

Reading John Chapter 17 will clarify and bring truth and reality to any who doubts; especially verses 17.20-23. I do not pray for these alone, but also for those who will believe in Me through their word; that they all may be one in us, as You, Father, are in Me, and I in You; that they also may be one in Us, that the world may believe that You sent Me. And the glory which You gave Me I have given them, that they may be one just as We are one, I in them, and You in Me; that they may be made perfect in one, that the world may know that You have sent Me, and have loved them as You have loved Me.

That they may be one just as we are one... This is certainly not saying we would be *in* one/another person; rather that we would be of the same mind concerning Jesus and the Kingdom of God; after all, He has given us *the mind of Christ* [1 Cor 2.14-16]. *The things of the Spirit are foolishness to the natural man*, and it's hard to find two people who would agree on anything; but find a Christian, a like-minded one who lives for the truth. The glory that Adam cast off for what he believed was better than the presence of God with him; well, that's what Jesus came to restore; our covering of glory so that we may fellowship with God just as Adam once did. One man brought us sin and death, the Second Man brought righteousness and life [1 Corinthians 15.47; 2 Corinthians 5.21].

Zechariah 2.8-*10 For thus says the Lord of hosts, after the glory He sent Me to the nations which plunder you; for he who touches you touches the apple of His eye. For surely, I will shake My hand against them, and they shall become spoil for their servants. Then you will know that the Lord of hosts has sent Me. Sing and rejoice, O daughter of Zion! For behold, I am coming and I will dwell in your midst.* [Yes, the Lord did come to us]. .

It is God's mantle over us, that we know we belong to Him; it is a cloak of *righteousness in Him* [2 Corinthians 5.21].

1 Peter 4.13-*14 If you are reproached for the name of Christ, blessed are you, for the Spirit of glory and of God rests upon you.* .

2 Corinthians 5.17-21 *Therefore, if anyone is in Christ, he is a new creation; old things have passed away; behold, all things have become new. Now all things are of God, who has reconciled us to Himself through Jesus Christ, and has given us the ministry of reconciliation, that is, that God was in Christ reconciling the world to Himself, not imputing their trespasses to them, and has committed to us the word of reconciliation.*

For He made Him who knew no sin to be sin for us, that we might become the righteousness of God in Him. .

1 John 2.20-23 But *you have an unction from the Holy One, and you know all things... and that no lie is of the truth. Who is a liar but he that denies that Jesus is the Christ* [the only Savior, Redeemer]. *He is antichrist that denies the Father and the Son. Whoever denies the Son the same has not the Father, whoever confesses* [believes] *the Son, has the Father also.* [Amplified Bible]

To deny Him means to contradict, disavow, reject, and refuse to acknowledge that He is our Sovereign God.

Even as this New Testament was being written, John would come to know centuries of millions of true believers subjected to massive torture and murder for their faithful

20

stand on the true Word. This vicious demonic force tip-toed into the Roman world unnoticed, until it was able to conquer and possess the minds of countless lost souls. Any that disagreed would be put to death.

I'm sorry to say that mankind is so easily taken by deception, that even millions on earth today are deceived by false religions; or, think they don't need any religion. *If we say we have no sin, we deceive ourselves and the truth is not in us, and we make Him* [God] *a liar.* [So, no need for God and no promise of salvation]. ['I need to be saved?? - from what!!'] And so, Babylon has captured the souls of men [Revelation 18.13]. Of course, please understand that Christianity is not a religion; true Christianity is being in relationship with the God Who created you, and lives in the temple of born-again believers.

It's not hard for satan, the master deceiver, to get your mind on other issues when that annoying thing about getting saved comes up in your life [he did it to me]; or that someone is explaining to you the truth about Who Jesus really is, and that truth is, He wants a relationship with you. He wants to set you free from the evil one and bring you into His family. God's love for you drove Him to the cross for your salvation.

Colossians 1.12-14 *Out of darkness into His light.* .

Deuteronomy 11.16-17 *Take heed to yourselves, lest your heart be deceived, and you turn aside and serve other gods and worship them.* .

We must realize that religion is manmade, that is, God's creation is creating their own god; whereas what the real God wants is to touch us with His love, to have relationship with each individual. He is our Father. We were created to be His children; to be His temple for Him to abide [John 14.21-23]; and it is for us to have intimate relationship with Him. He loves us so much, remember....

Romans 5.8 *But God demonstrates His own love toward us, in that while we were still sinners, Christ died for us. .*

God's Creation Was Brought Forth for the Purpose of Habitation, His Glory Living in Us and Around Us.

Yes, Man Was Created to Be a Temple,
But Whose Temple Are We?

The devil is alive and lives on planet earth. He also lives in the hearts of his followers, his temple. He darkens their mind so the light of the true gospel cannot enter.

Job 38.2 *Who is this who darkens counsel by words without knowledge*? .. See, he's been doing this for a long time. That one who is a pretender to usurp the throne of God, has convinced those dark minds that he is the true God; and so he has marked them as his own. He lives in their temple. They will do as he proposes, and they will sink deeper into his lies until he is finished with them; then he will cast them into his reward.

Man was created to be the temple of God. Going back to the meaning of Adam's lamb, to the sacrifice of the Lamb of God, the whole reason for it all; that each step in the Word of God reveals our journey into God to acknowledge that we are a temple of flesh; but that God may live in us is revealed in John 14; *and the glory you have given me, I have given them.* And finally, *who has known the mind of the Lord that he might instruct him, but we have the mind of Christ* [1Corinthians 2.16]. .

We Are to Know Him Intimately.
This Has Always Been His Purpose for Creation.
It All Began in the Garden.

In the early, beyond creation
Lives a God and King
And all the angels worshiped

Continued their hearts to sing
But He desired a people
For love and for peace
So He created them
And then released
The grace that reigned forever
Was a product of His love
Spread out before His people
From His Kingdom above.
But then there came one forever dissatisfied
And gathered a multitude, to them he lied
Dishonor and grievances was his accusation
For this God and King Who ruled their nation
Rebellion was the answer
To make him lord of all
And those who lived beneath his lies
Responded to his call
Such cunning and deception
Created his crown
For he would have his nature
Ring with renown
But this glorious God and King
Would not be cast aside
For He was loved and worshiped
Far and wide
His power, grace and mercy
Far outweighed
The usurper who thought he could win
A war with just one raid
He didn't know his plans were known
That he was far outnumbered
And those whose 'legience to faith and truth
Were more than he could plunder
Thrown out of the Kingdom
To create his own
He thought he'd won at last

He was blinded by his arrogance
Cause victory would not be shown
Many who would bear their sin
He denied them will to live
He drove his victims to their death
For that's all he could give
But this King watched
With grace and love
For the perfect time to act
And when it came, He stepped aside
From His glory - to renew His pact
He made a covenant at the start
For a people meant to be
He shed His Blood, He died for us,
That we would be free
Now this liar, deceiver, rebellious one
A dilemma findeth him
He has no crown - He has no throne
He lost it all to Ha Shem.

Up to 1Corinthians speaking of the temple of God, the word temple [O.T. haykal] means sanctuary, a building. After that, in most cases, the Scriptures that speak of the temple of God is the word *naos or naio* which means 'to dwell*, [It is #3845 in Strong's Concordance] and the same word Jesus uses in John 2.19-21 *Jesus answered and said to them, Destroy this temple, and in three days I will raise it up... But He was speaking of the temple of His body.* .

So for the rest of the Bible that speaks of the temple, [except in few cases] it is pertaining to the lover of God, the believer, the redeemed of the Lord - the temple of the Holy Spirit [John 14.23], Who lives and abides in us.

Every Lover of God is His Habitation.

1Cor 3.16 *Know ye not that you are the temple of God.*

1Cor 6.19 *What? Know ye not that your body is the temple of the Holy Spirit who is in you, whom ye have of God, and ye are not your own. For ye are bought with a price; therefore, glorify God in your body and in your spirit, which is God's .*

This leaves us with our soul, heart and emotions. And what do these things mean? Your soul, heart and emotions express who you really are. This is where your Free Will comes into play. This is your character, personality, your desires, your decisions. This is where you either accept the truth of Who is God, and what Jesus did for you; or you reject it and live for yourself, giving place to the liar. It is your choice. When your mind is made up about any subject, you act out in this context. That's why your mind and hand are connected. You believe and you do [Revelation 13.16]. So, what are you going to do?

You Can Have the Liar or the Truth.

Galatians 1.6-9 *I marvel that you are turning away so soon from Him who called you in the grace of Christ, to a different gospel, which is not another; but there are some who trouble you and want to pervert the gospel of Christ. But even if we, or an angel from heaven, preach any other gospel to you than what we have preached to you, let him be accursed. As we have said before, so now I say again, if anyone preaches any other gospel to you than what you have received, let him be accursed. .*

Your heart, mind [conscience] and emotions are the driving force in your life to choose which way you will go. Yes indeed - we have a choice. That's the reason for the Cross. Jesus gives us this opportunity.

Will you allow the Spirit of God to lead you or not? One day the disciples asked, *What shall we do that we might work the works of God? Jesus answered, this is the work of God, that you believe on him whom he has sent.* If we truly believe this, then we will walk in Kingdom truth. Jesus walked in the perfect will of God. And this is the work God desires of us, that we put our faith in the One Who died for us and walk in the will of God. This is coming into maturity and allowing God to grow us up in Christ [John 6.28]. .

Our Mind and Our heart Agree with the Works of Our Hands and to Be a Witness to the World Of His Love and Salvation.

So, let this truth abide in you; what you have heard in the beginning; you are the temple of the living God and all you want to do is believe on Him with your whole heart, mind and soul. Is Jesus your First Love? Is He buried in your inner most being, that you will never forget Him; that all your life issues are dependent on His Word and His truth? So be it! Don't let it be said that, *you have left your first love* [Revelation 2].

Now, the devil knows we were created to be the temple of God, but he wants to get in on the glory. He led Adam to believe there was something better than the God he knew, and set the trap that ensnared. The devil wanted this amazing creation, covered with God's glory - to be his; to worship him in this beautiful garden with the glory he envied. Never did he think they would all be thrown out.

So now, what does he do? He takes over the mind and emotions of those stubborn rebellious ones and makes them *his* temple. Paul speaks of men who will lead people away from the true gospel, so satan works in people to propagate his lies. Now we can look to what God tells us in His Word. He wrote it to us so we would know the truth. [Please read 1 John and Ephesians].

The four gospels reveal Who Jesus is and what He came to do. They show us how-to live-in Christ, how to walk in the Kingdom of truth. John's gospel reveals the God of love and the Acts of the disciples has carried out the love Jesus has for His people. Paul's letters are the 'how to's and then John again. In God's love for His people, He shows us how to overcome evil and walk in truth. Now comes God's revelation of how He will deal with this evil one.

The Revelation of Jesus Christ is a continuation of the book of Acts and John's love letters all the way to the end of time. God wants us to know He loves us so much, and doesn't want us to be afraid of what's coming in the end. There has been Christ deniers in the world ever since Jesus showed us the real truth; but His truth will prevail. Actually, unbelief ran rampant in the Old Testament also.

The Book of Acts tells us how the disciples carried out the words Jesus spoke to them before He returned to His Father's side. They went to the Jew first, then to the Gentiles [Acts 1.8; Matthew chapter 10].

Acts Chapter 8 tells us that great persecution arose against the Jews who turned to Christ, and caused them to scatter to the uttermost parts of the earth. Remember pagan Rome ruled, which actually had control of most of Europe and across the Mediterranean Sea; all those countries that surrounded Israel. Christians went through terrible times of persecution and death, but would not deny their Messiah Who rose from the dead. They would not deny His Name.

1 John 4:1-2 *Beloved, do not believe every spirit, but test the spirits, whether they are of God; because many false prophets have gone out into the world. By this you know the Spirit of God: Every spirit that confesses that Jesus Christ has come in the flesh is of God.*

Now the Revelation of the end time is given to John. First revealed is the Majesty of our Lord God. Here, the Perfect Lamb of God, sacrificed for sin; dead, buried - and resurrected to live forever in a sanctified human body, *the Firstborn from the dead*. Now He who is alive forevermore, is searching for His bride throughout all His churches [Rev 1-3].

Seven Golden Lampstands - His Church –
Has the Attention of the One Who Died for Her.
Captain victorious - The First and The Last
There is no other God.
He stands in golden attire
With predestination,
His heart on fire
Eager to gather His saints to Himself
He calls to His valiant ones
These are ready to hear His voice
These are ready to rejoice
As they join with Him in one accord
Forever with their Lord.

Worthy is He Who shed His Blood, to redeem His creation, that we might worship Him only. Chapter five reveals the Lion of Judah opening the scrolls to release God's final will. And He only is worthy to take the scroll and begin to shake the world of its very foundation. His purpose...to set His people free from bondage, free to worship the One True God; to raise up a body of believers and lovers of God who would separate themselves from worldly things, to desire eternal life with their Savior,

Gone from Visitation to Habitation.

John 3.16-21 *For God loved the world so much that he gave his one and only Son, so that everyone who believes in him will not perish but have eternal life. God sent his*

Son into the world not to judge the world, but to save the world through him. .

Jesus Always Did the Will of the Father;
We Can Do No Less.

John 3.19 *There is no judgment against anyone who believes in him. But anyone who does not believe in him has already been judged for not believing in God's one and only Son. And the judgment is based on this fact. God's light came into the world, but people loved the darkness more than the light, for their actions were evil. All who do evil hate the light and refuse to go near it for fear their sins will be exposed. But those who do what is right come to the light so others can see that they are doing what God wants.* [Holy Bible, New Living Translation].

Our Father God has created within Himself
A place called home
It is an ever-expanding place
Of acceptance, warmth and love.
It was deliberately
Formed in the center of His Being,
Surrounded by His arms of love,
So that all His children would fit,
And be forever safe.

For Your Compassion and Mercy on Me! Thank You.
For Your Life That Flows Through Me and Your
Love That Is Established in My Heart, Never
to Leave Me nor Forsake Me, Thank You.

All Praise, Glory and Honor
To Our Most High God.

THE MAN OF SIN

[One who] *opposes and exalts himself above all that is called God, or that is worshiped, so that he, as God, sits in the temple of God, showing himself that he is God. .*
[2Thess 2.4 KJV] And just what temple is he sitting in?

Who Could That Possibly Be?
Man Was Created to Be a Temple.

He captures them in his web, *with all deceivableness of unrighteousness in them that perish, because they received not the love of the truth, that they might be saved. These false teachers are like dangerous hidden reefs lying in wait to shipwreck the immature* [3 John]. .
[Excerpts from the book on the Reformation by H. Grattan Guinness]. "All the kings of the West reverence him as God on earth. This man of sin sits in the temple of God, showing himself that he is God on the earth. His voice was as the voice of God. The people think of him as the one God who has power over all things in earth and in heaven. He is another God on earth. He speaks and governs as God, and the world bows down to believe and obey. They worship him. He wears robes more than kingly royalty, and a crown, for power on earth, heaven and hell where he claims to rule. He believes he holds the keys of the Kingdom; And he takes the name that Jesus gives only to the Most High God" [John 17.11].

[Don't know yet who he is...Read Revelation 17].

Who is this man of sin, how does he deceive us, and in what temple does he pretend to be God? First of all, man was created to be a temple...notwithstanding, the temple of God's Holy Spirit. But if we make other choices, well.....

2Corinthians 6.16 And *what agreement has the temple of God with idols? For you are the temple of the living God; as God has said, I will live in them and I will be their God and they shall be my people.* .

2Thessalonians 1.12 *That the name of the Lord be glorified in you, and you in Him, according to the grace of our God and the Lord Jesus Christ.* .

1Corinthians 11.18 *First of all, when you come together in the Church, I hear that there are divisions among you; and I partly believe it, for there must be heresies among you, that they who are approved may be made manifest among you.* [approved: shown to be a false prophet] *How* Does this Happen? Well - Read the Word and Compare!

2Peter 2 But *there were false prophets also among the people, even as there shall be false teachers among you, who secretly bring in false heresies, even denying the Lord.* .

From the Beginning, this 'Man of Sin' Was Characterized as 'One Who Is Against the Truth'.

[Genesis 3.5 & Isaiah 14.14; Both wanted to be their own god]. There are many who believe Jesus is *only* the 'son' of God, and not '*the* true God'; and in some Bibles He is called 'a god'. But He would be called the Son, so as to lead many of us sons to God the Father; because Jesus portrayed what the true sons of God would be. There is also a compromising of Scripture that waters down the whole truth and nothing but the truth, and very often will add their own doctrines, rules and regs, as did the Pharisees [Ephesians 5.6].

There is a contrast here. [Colossians 2.8] *Beware lest*

any man spoil you through philosophy and vain deceit, after the tradition of men, after the rudiments of the world and not after Christ. .

Please read the gospel of John - first chapter, in a legitimate Bible. There is also a deception in the notes of some Bibles. The Scripture is true, but in the notes, they add their own interpretation. Please beware and ask God's wisdom.

But who or what could be sitting in the temple of the unbeliever? Is it the personification of the liar, deceiver who would harness the mind, the hand?

2 Thess 2 *because they did not receive the love of the truth, that they might be saved. And for this reason, God will send them strong delusion, that they should believe the lie. .*

Romans 9.1-6 *I tell the truth in Christ, I am not lying, my conscience also bearing me witness in the Holy Spirit, that I have great sorrow and continual grief in my heart. For I could wish that I myself were accursed from Christ for my brethren, my countrymen according to the flesh, who are Israelites, to whom pertain the adoption, the glory, the covenants, the giving of the law, the service of God, and the promises; of whom are the fathers and from whom, according to the flesh, Christ came, who is over all, the eternally blessed God. Amen.*

Isaiah 9.6-8 *For unto us a Child is born, Unto us a Son is given; And the government will be upon His shoulder. And His name will be called Wonderful, Counselor, Mighty God, Everlasting Father, Prince of Peace. Of the increase of His government and peace There will be no end, Upon the throne of David and over His Kingdom, to order it and establish it with judgment and justice From that time forward, even forever. The zeal of the Lord of hosts will perform this. .*

So, Who Was This Child, This Son Who Was Given Who Is After All, the Mighty God, the Everlasting Father,

Prince of Peace? Of Course, It Is Jesus. But it is not that the Word of God has taken no effect. The Truth Is of No Effect on Those Who Refuse to Recognize Truth of the Word of God.

There are men [and women] even now who corrupt the Word of God and lead blind people down the road to destruction. Blind because they refuse the truth, wanting to continue in their own life style [John 9:39].

I have no doubt that there will be, even now is, a man, totally controlled by satan who will lead people; those who already deny the truth that Jesus is God, and by their own free will, deny their need for any salvation.

They will fall into further deception and death, and will fulfill their own destiny as revealed in God's Word. Some of them are pastors! This man is alive among us at this time, saying that a relationship with Jesus is not a good thing. If they continue in this trend, it is likely they will be deceived into agreeing with his mark, separating themselves forever from the presence of God. Please note: God does not send anyone to hell, they do it themselves by denying they need God.

And Jesus Will Say, *Be Gone I Never Knew You!*

This mark, this sign, which I will share about in the next chapters, has to do with a religious system that has been in the world ever since carnal man has insisted on his own way. This mark and seal is their mind and hand given over to serve and worship the man of sin, the works of a carnal selfish ego, self-satisfying their own flesh. *Because the carnal mind is enmity against God; for it is not subject to the law of God, nor indeed can be. So then, those who are in the flesh cannot please God.* Romans 8:7-8 .

They are sealed into this destruction unless they turn their heart to the real God and Savior. There are many cultures in the world that worship their own gods. I know in these last days God is bringing about a worldwide revival as the Holy Spirit reveals the One True God. Ask God to lead you in prayer for these people and nations to turn to Him before it is too late.

So, this antichrist spirit is alive in all the earth and will dwell in the temple of unbelief no matter what nation or person is involved in idolatry. He will make himself their god. The head [your mind] and the hand [your works] will be to exalt him. So, what is the mark of the beast? It is the seal of satan on the unbeliever; a person who chooses to live his own life apart from the One True God; having his own religious system that exalts the works of man.

Revelation 13.18 '666 - *the number of a man*'. The mark of [a carnal] man [Revelation 14.18], One who will approve of added doctrine that does not find sanction in the true Word of God.

Philippians 3:3 *For we are the circumcision, who worship God in the Spirit, rejoice in Christ Jesus, and have no confidence in the flesh. .*

Deuteronomy 4.2 You *shall not add to the word which I command you, nor take from it, that you may keep the commandments of the Lord your God. .*

Mark 7.13 *making the word of God of no effect through your tradition... and many such things ye do.*

Colossians 2.8 Beware *lest anyone cheat you through philosophy and empty deceit, with the tradition of men, and disregarding the teachings of Christ, our only Redeemer*

1Timothy 2.5 *One God and one mediator between God and men, the man, Christ Jesus. .*

We know that New Testament truth is a continuation of Old Testament truth. God has His eye on Israel. They belong to Him. But as Christians we are gathered into that vine of the Lord. The 12 tribes of Israel will have their inheritance but there is also a relationship through them towards us. *Christ has redeemed us from the curse of the law, having become a curse for us (for it is written, Cursed is everyone who hangs on a tree), that the blessing of Abraham might come upon the Gentiles in Christ Jesus, that we might receive the promise of the Spirit through faith.* [The mark is about who you worship].

Galatians 3.13-15 & Romans 11.17&24 Here explains what it means to be grafted into Israel's vine. .

Ephesians 2.11-22 *Therefore remember that you, once Gentiles in the flesh — who are called Uncircumcision by what is called the Circumcision made in the flesh by hands — that at that time you were without Christ, being aliens from the commonwealth of Israel and strangers from the covenants of promise, having no hope and without God in the world. But now in Christ Jesus you who once were far off have been brought near by the Blood of Christ. .*

For He Himself is our peace, who has made both one, and has broken down the middle wall of separation, having abolished in His flesh the enmity, that is, the law of commandments contained in ordinances, so as to create in Himself one new man from the two, thus making peace, For through Him we both have access by one Spirit to the Father. Now, therefore, you are no longer strangers and foreigners, but fellow citizens with the saints and members of the household of God, having been built on the foundation of the apostles and prophets, Jesus Christ Himself being the chief cornerstone.

So, Do You Get It? We Have Been Made Partakers of The Promises Made to Israel, Both to Become One New Man.

But have you done John 1.12...? Received Him?

As an example, we can see how the names of the tribes of Israel apply also to those born-again children of the Most High God that come from the Gentile race. Israeli family names always list beginning with the first born. Reuben was the eldest son of Jacob, then came Simeon, Levi, Judah, Dan, Naphtali, Gad, Asher, Issachar, Zebulun, Joseph, and Benjamin. Their names and the meaning of each is revealed in Genesis 29-30 and 35.18, when they were born.

But, Revelation 7.4 begins with Judah, and Manasseh was not a son of Jacob, one of the 12 tribes. Manasseh was the first-born son of Joseph, who was a son of Jacob. Simeon and Levi, 2nd and 3rd sons; see where they are! This list actually reveals all the born-again family of God. See how it reveals our inheritance. So, here is the body of Christ, the bride, marked, sealed and protected from the evil one. Here is the identity of the Sons of God, Jew and Gentile; our born-again journey revealed in the Word of God. The names below reflect our journey into knowing God. This is the New Man -

The Sons of God Joined Together to Come Before Our Lord in Holiness and Glory to Worship Him.

1. Judah - Praise
2. Reuben - Behold a son
3. Gad - a Great Company
4. Asher - Joy or Fulfillment of Joy
5. Naphtali - to Overcome
6. Manasseh - to Forget the Past
7. Simeon - the Lord Hears
8. Levi - to Be Joined
9. Issachar - the Price Is Paid
10. Zebulun - Dwelling Place
11. Joseph - Added to or Fruitful,
12. Benjamin - Son of My Right Hand.

Does This Describe Our Entrance into the Kingdom of God and the Inheritance of the Body of Christ?

Here is the fulfillment...ONE NEW MAN.

1.To praise God for our salvation, 2.Adopted as His

child, 3.into His family, 4.Filled with His joy, 5.Faith and grace to overcome the enemy, 6.To forget our past sins and regrets, 7.To listen for His voice, [And My Sheep Will Hear My Voice], 8. Be joined to Christ, 9. Because the price has been paid, 10.We are His dwelling place, 11.We develop the fruit of the Spirit in living for God [God Has Taken Away Our Reproach] 12.And we are the sons of His right hand.

Dan is missing, his name means judge. God has already judged us. But also, the tribe of Dan fell into idolatry; they cannot be included [1 Kings 12. 28-31].

Paul did not have a King James Bible. He preached truths that were established in the Old Testament; brought them more into light, grace and love, through the power of the Holy Spirit. God's Word is truth and nothing is to be added or taken away from what His Word is saying to us, to lead us into His salvation and eternity [Revelation 22.18-19; Deuteronomy 12.32, 4.2; Joshua 1.7-8; Proverbs 30.5-6].

Revelation 14.1-2 Then *I looked, and behold, a Lamb standing on Mount Zion, and with Him one hundred and forty-four thousand, having His Father's name written on their foreheads.* This 144,000 is not the Jews who will evangelize Israel. It is symbolic, a representation of the government of God; the body of Christ, the Bride, sealed to the Kingdom of His nature sealed in the mind of His people. 144,000, the image of completeness.

Every lover of God has been set free from the tyranny of our sin nature and it has no more dominion over us. The lordship of satan over us has been broken by the blood of Jesus, [that's what it means to 'bruise the head'] [Genesis 3.15]. We have been made free to worship God alone; to acknowledge Jesus as Lord and King, Redeemer of our body, soul and spirit as He lives in us and we live in Him; And So...

Have We Yet, Learned To Love?

Colossians 11.1-14 *Strengthened with all might, according to His glorious power, for all patience and longsuffering with joy; giving thanks to the Father who has qualified us to be partakers of the inheritance of the saints in the light. He has delivered us from the power of darkness and conveyed us into the Kingdom of the Son of His love, in whom we have redemption through His blood, the forgiveness of sins.*

Colossians 3.1-4 *If then you were raised with Christ, seek those things which are above, where Christ is, sitting at the right hand of God. Set your mind on things above, not on things on the earth. For you died, and your life is hidden with Christ in God. When Christ who is our life appears, then you also will appear with Him in glory. .*

Concordance: Sons of God Are Defined - Male and Female.

From Death to Life and Grace to Grace. God has made the way...He is the Way. Make Him the Lord of your life. He loves you so much He gave up His life for you; and why would He,

Because...

God created each of us
To fulfill His every dream
We each received a gifting
For more than we have seen
He's releasing His promise
We have waited so long
For His breath to enter our spirit
To impart His life and His song
He sings to our spirit
Our soul and our heart
For the joy that brings a dance
If you've never let yourself go
Why not give it a chance?
The life of God within you
Will complete His creation
And there will never be
A chance of separation
For He created each of us
To fulfill His every dream
And heart has never known
Nor lips have ever said
Those things we've never seen
But He has promised!

BABYLON

Concerning Genesis 6... The sons of God and the daughters of men. '*Took them wives*' considers that they lived together in marriage. Hebrews 1 tells us angels were created to be, *sent forth to minister for them who shall be heirs of salvation. He makes His angels spirits, and His ministers a flame of fire.* Angels were not created with the equipment to pro-create. But we do know that many angels fell from heaven in their rebellion and it was satan's plan to corrupt the race of man so that the Messiah would not come. [He is still corrupting our race but there is deliverance in the cross of Jesus].

Fallen Angels Are Not Called The 'Sons of God'.

So here we have a situation that people have different ideas. We know it is that some people are influenced or even possessed by these demonic spirits; and so, it is easy to surmise these 'sons of God', the offspring of Enosh, were seduced by the daughters of men [the offspring of Cain]. Remember Genesis 4.26. From Enosh, *then began men to call on the name of the Lord.* Were these the 'sons of God' that fell away? And can You Imagine a demon spirit Being a Husband? [Genesis 6.2].

We know this because of Israel's history [and our own] with women of those idolatrous nations; and it is certainly happening today with adultery and divorce. In their departure from God's commandments, we can see these men were taken over by these evil spirits just as man is convinced today that he can 'have his cake and eat it too'.

So, these men were taken over [possessed] by these spirits and their offspring were demonically possessed to be so evil that God had to destroy all on the earth except for Noah and his family. But since the evil one is spirit, naturally he and they did not die. They continued in Ham, eventually in Nimrod, and to this day. We can certainly see even today there are people demonically enslaved as to do terrible things to others. This satan even has control over nations.

Genesis 10.8-10 From Ham, the rebellious one, came Cush and he begot *Nimrod; he began to be a mighty one on the earth. He was a mighty hunter before the Lord; therefore, it is said, Like Nimrod the mighty hunter before the Lord. And the beginning of his Kingdom was Babel.* .

[Babylon, name means confusion] - *'before the Lord' basically* means 'against'. He would be god on the earth and build a tower and a city to flaunt himself that he was god and king; and made slaves of the people under him.

Genesis 11.8-9 tells us the Lord scattered all these people and they quit building the city; but Babylon was thriving in 2KIngs 17.30 and 20.12. Now would come Hezekiah king of Judah; he showed all the treasures of the Temple of God to the king of Babylon and v.17; it's not hard to guess that it was all looted and brought to Babylon. Finally, 24.10; through chapter 25, Nebuchadnezzar's army overran Jerusalem and v.9, they broke down the wall and burned down the temple [to retrieve the gold] and destroyed *every great man's house.*

2 Kings 23 Josiah was the only king of Israel to turn to the Lord with all his heart. His son learned nothing from his father and was quickly dethroned. The rest of 2Kings shows us that Babylon had charge of Jerusalem and built the Ishtar Gate. I did some digging and realized that even modern man values the idolatry of nations that God

destroyed so long ago. We dig up artifacts and put them on display to be admired. The spirit of Babylon was raised up with Nimrod and continued in despotic kings. Read the rest if you are interested [research further on the web].

King Nebuchadnezzar II reigned 604–562 BCE, the peak of the Neo-Babylonian Empire. He is known as the biblical conqueror of Jerusalem. He ordered the construction of the Ishtar gate and dedicated it to the Babylonian goddess Ishtar. Babylon is the most famous city from ancient Mesopotamia whose ruins [because it was dug up and moved so much] lie in modern-day Iraq 59 miles southwest of Baghdad. The name is thought to derive from bav-il or bav-ilim which, in the Akkadian language of the time, meant 'Gate of God' or 'Gate of the Gods' and Babylon means 'confusion'.

Re-construction of the Ishtar Gate and Processional Way was built at the Pergamon Museum in Berlin [Hitler wanted the demonic power of the goddess Ishtar]; out of material excavated and finished in the 1930s. It includes the inscription plaque. It stands 46 ft high and 100 ft wide. The excavation ran from 1902 to 1914, and, during that time, 45 ft of the foundation of the gate was uncovered. President Saddam's palace sat on a hill overlooking the great throne room of Nebuchadnezzar's palace. [Saddam believed he was the reincarnation of Nebuchadnezzar].

Note: This is about Hussein's old history but we can see what he was planning to take over.

The following is from more research on the web...

"Babylon has never been on the list of world heritage sites. Now more than ever Babylon needs the care, attention and advice that being a world heritage site would ensure it received, A separate report has been compiled by Polish archaeologists. A further report is being compiled by the Iraqis on the damage to Saddam Hussein's palace, built in a corner of the site, and which had already been looted before allied forces began camping out in the shell. The site had such symbolic importance to Saddam that he rebuilt many of the walls and gates, using bricks stamped with his name, many of which have been stolen.

[So, This Demonic Power Now Resides in Iraq].

An international effort will clearly be needed as the same contractors, were used to develop and maintain the site throughout. In a walk through the ancient city there is observed damage to...The Ishtar Gate, "Cherished monuments defaced and ancient inscribed fragments found in spoil heaps'.

Unbelievable! That any person or Company would re-establish a demonic stronghold in this day and age, as recorded in the Book of Revelation and reveals the anger of our God.

Revelation Chapter 17 tells the story [1-14].

Revelation 17.3-6 *So he carried me away in the Spirit into the wilderness. And I saw a woman sitting on a scarlet beast which was full of names of blasphemy, having seven heads and ten horns. The woman was arrayed in purple and scarlet, and adorned with gold and precious stones and pearls, having in her hand a golden cup full of abominations and the filthiness of her fornication. And on her forehead a name was written*

MYSTERY, BABYLON THE GREAT, THE MOTHER OF HARLOTS AND OF THE ABOMINATIONS OF THE EARTH.

I saw the woman, drunk with the blood of the saints and with the blood of the martyrs of Jesus. And when I saw her, I marveled with great amazement. .

I Do Believe These Verses Refer to Spiritual Babylon.

[Heads and horns are a metaphor for nations and governments that are under her command].

43

Revelation 17.14 *These will make war with the Lamb, and the Lamb will overcome them, for He is Lord of lords and King of kings; and those who are with Him are called, chosen, and faithful.* .

In Revelation prophecy, a woman is a metaphor for Church, a religious system. The woman in Revelation 12 reveals the Church of God, filled with the Holy Spirit and the woman in Chapter 17 is the apostate Church led by the antichrist spirit.

Revelation 18.2-8 *And I heard another voice from heaven saying, come out of her, my people, lest you share in her sins, and lest you receive of her plague ..* Whoever messes with God's plan will find themselves partners with this demonic spirit.

For her sins have reached to heaven, and God has remembered her iniquities. Render to her just as she rendered to you, and repay her double according to her works; in the cup which she has mixed, mix double for her. In the measure that she glorified herself and lived luxuriously, in the same measure give her torment and sorrow; for she says in her heart, 'I sit as queen, and am no widow, and will not see sorrow.' Therefore, her plagues will come in one day — death and mourning and famine. And she will be utterly burned with fire, for strong is the Lord God who judges her. .

Please know that Ishtar, Isis, Diana, Jezebel, Tammuz, Ashtoreth, Semiramis [the idol mother with child] and the 'Queen of Heaven' are all the same demonic spirit who goes after women - Jezebel and Molech... child sacrifice. 2Kings 23 [Josiah] *And he defiled Topheth, which is in the Valley of the Son of Hinnom, that no man might make his son or his daughter pass through the fire to Molech.* .

King Josiah cleansed the land of idolatry but after he died his son brought it all back; and we can see that the spirit of Molech is alive even now, today, in the abortion industry.

Jeremiah [44] prophesied to the Jews in Egypt... *Oh, do not do this abominable thing which I hate. You provoke me to wrath. Then all the men who knew that their wives had burned incense to other gods, with all the women who stood by, a great multitude, and all the people who dwelt in the land of Egypt, in Pathros, answered Jeremiah, saying As for the word that you have spoken to us in the name of the Lord, we will not listen to you!*

But we will certainly do whatever has gone out of our own mouth, to burn incense to the queen of heaven and pour out drink offerings to her, as we have done, we and our fathers, our kings and our princes, in the cities of Judah and in the streets of Jerusalem. For then we had plenty of food, were well-off, and saw no trouble. But since we stopped burning incense to the queen of heaven and pouring out drink offerings to her, we have lacked everything and have been consumed by the sword and by famine.

The women also said, and when we burned incense to the queen of heaven and poured out drink offerings to her, did we make cakes for her, to worship her, and pour out drink offerings to her without our husbands' permission? So, the Lord could no longer bear it, because of the evil of your doings and because of the abominations which you committed. Therefore, your land is a desolation [See Jeremiah 7.17-34]. .

Jeremiah 44.24-29 Moreover Jeremiah said to all the people and to all the women, Hear the word of the Lord, all Judah who are in the land of Egypt! Thus says the Lord of hosts, the God of Israel, saying 'You and your wives have spoken with your mouths and fulfilled with your hands, saying, We will surely keep our vows that we have made, to burn incense to the queen of heaven and pour out drink offerings to her. You will surely keep your vows and perform your vows! Therefore hear the word of the Lord, all Judah who dwell in the land of Egypt 'Behold, I have sworn by My great name,' says the Lord, 'that My name shall no more be named in the mouth of any man of Judah in all the land of Egypt, saying, The Lord God lives. .

Remember that from the tribe of Judah came David, a worshiper of the one true God [Judah/praise]. So, they have renounced their inheritance, the blessing of a worshiper of God for the idolatry of the queen of heaven. There are many today who give precedence to this queen of heaven who have a problem with the name of Jesus. *Yet a small number who escape the sword shall return from the land of Egypt to the land of Judah; and shall know whose words will stand, Mine or theirs. .*

As I said, worshiping this evil spirit brings her partner Molech into this movement to destroy women and their offspring. This spirit of Babylon is very much alive in the world today. And who is this 'queen of heaven' alive and well, dwelling in the hearts of too many souls for whom Jesus died? The spirit of deception fills their heart and mind to enfold them in the darkness of sheol. Be aware that if you turn to the only Redeemer, Jesus Christ, and inherit eternal life in the Kingdom of God, you will be safe.

But God! Revelation 17.1-2 *Then one of the seven angels who had the seven bowls came and talked with me, saying to me, Come, I will show you the judgment of the great harlot who sits on many waters, .*

Revelation 18.1-3 *After these things I saw another angel coming down from heaven, having great authority, and the earth was illuminated with his glory. And he cried mightily with a loud voice, saying, Babylon the great is fallen, is fallen, and has become a dwelling place of demons, a prison for every foul spirit, and a cage for every unclean and hated bird! For all the nations have drunk of the wine of the wrath of her fornication, the kings of the earth have committed fornication with her, and the merchants of the earth have become rich through the abundance of her luxury.* [This fornication is spiritual adultery].

Revelation 18.21-22 *Then a mighty angel took up a stone like a great millstone and threw it into the sea, saying, thus with violence the great city Babylon shall be thrown down, and shall not be found anymore.*

When we were created, there was formed in us a place waiting to be filled with God's Holy Spirit. We will be *brought out of darkness into His glorious light* [Ephesians 1.12-13]. But if we prefer darkness, the god of this world delights in moving in to keep us bound in his chains of evil. Only Jesus can free us from his deception.

Revelation 19.1-11 After *these things I heard a loud voice of a great multitude in heaven, saying, Alleluia! Salvation and glory and honor and power belong to the Lord our God! For true and righteous are His judgments, because He has judged the great harlot who corrupted the earth with her fornication; and He has avenged on her the blood of His servants shed by her...Then he said to me, Write 'Blessed are those who are called to the marriage supper of the Lamb!' And he said to me, these are the true sayings of God.* .

Matthew 11:28-30 *Come to Me, all you who labor and are heavy laden, and I will give you rest. Take My yoke upon you and learn from Me, for I am gentle and lowly in heart, and you will find rest for your souls.* .

For My yoke is easy and My burden is light.

From birth to death is the transition of life, so there are more changes to come, more than we can number. We just have to listen and understand what God is really saying to us in these days of so much confusion. God said,

"It's Time to Shatter Some Traditions".

THE SEAL

You have two witnesses [2 next chapters in this book] of this notorious Mark and Seal from the book of Revelation. I wrote them both at different times, and both have the same - and different references to make my point. There is no need to fear what our grievous enemy would do to try to entrap God's people. He's a liar and deceiver. With the foregoing knowledge you will be equipped to understand exactly how to protect yourself from his lies. And know this - he cannot force anyone to do anything. Herein are some things repeated, but it would be good to get this information doubled in your heart so that you know that you know - there is nothing to fear.

God has given His word to all His people that we should not be afraid of what will come in the end of time. He has given His assurance of our safety [Romans 8].

Joshua 1:8-9 *This Book of the Law shall not depart from your mouth, but you shall meditate in it day and night, that you may observe to do according to all that is written in it.*

For then you will make your way prosperous, and then you will have good success. Have I not commanded you? Be strong and of good courage; do not be afraid, nor be dismayed, for the Lord your God is with you wherever you go. .

God's promises of protection are forever.

There is no fear in God's perfect love [1 John 4.18]. The mystery of the Gentiles is...*Christ in you, the hope of glory* [Colossians 1.27]. *Nothing shall ever separate us from the love of God in Christ.* . [Read Romans 8]. I hope and pray that you will research every Scripture I have noted herein. First it must be understood that ....

2 Timothy 3.16 *All Scripture is given by inspiration of God, and is profitable for doctrine, for reproof, for correction, for instruction in righteousness, that the man of God may be complete, thoroughly equipped for every good work.*

2 Peter 1.20-21 *knowing this first, that no prophecy of Scripture is of any private interpretation, for prophecy never came by the will of man, but holy men of God spoke as they were moved by the Holy Spirit.*

John 5.39-40 *You search the Scriptures, for in them you think you have eternal life; and these are they which testify of Me. But you are not willing to come to Me that you may have life.* .

As You Read These Verses - Are You Willing?

If we are depending on the true Word of God, we will find a second or more witness to its truth. Every 'principle' Scripture in the Bible has its second or more witness. Remember Paul preached from the Old Testament. The witness of Scripture is woven throughout the Word so that we can be sure it is not just an arbitrary word of man. Yes, the Bible does have some words spoken by man. Many are an arrogant answer to the Truth they did not want to hear.

Our Bible - Scripture has been given to us that we might seek after the God Who created us and as a progressive revelation of who we are; how God sees us and just what are His plans for this creation and the world in which we

49

live, so He gives us understanding of what it's all about. We just have to search.

If you search for Me with all your heart you will find Me.

Deuteronomy 19.15-*16 By the mouth of two or three witnesses the matter shall be established.*

Matthew 18.16 *that by the mouth of two or three witnesses every word may be established*

2 Cor 13.*1 This will be the third time I am coming to you. By the mouth of two or three witnesses every word shall be established. .*

The Word Is a Witness to Itself.

Deuteronomy 31.26-27 Take *this Book of the Law, and put it beside* [within] *the ark of the covenant of the Lord your God, that it may be there as a witness against you;* The Word of God is a witness. Deuteronomy 32.26-28 & us; Rev 11; and Acts 1.8-9 *But you shall receive power when the Holy Spirit has come upon you; and you shall be witnesses to Me in Jerusalem, and in all Judea and Samaria, and to the end of the earth.*

1 John 5.6 *And it is the Spirit who bears witness, because the Spirit is truth. .*

Romans 9.1; Heb 2.4; 1John 5.6, 5.9-10, Rev 1.5,3.14.
The Two Living Witnesses Are
The Believer and The Word; the Old and New Testament.

God told me, 'We are Witnesses of His Love'.

End-time witnesses will not be delegated to Jerusalem only. Every believer and lover of God is to go into all the world and share this good news [next door neighbor, at your workplace, people you meet, places you go]. This happened in the first century and has been ever since. Praise God! Remember His martyrs! They would spread the good news no matter what.

Now, Truth Will Blast like a Fire
With the Words of Our Mouth.

The first three chapters of John's Revelation has Jesus coming to search for His Bride. In all the circumstances that we experience, how are we living for the Kingdom of God? Jesus came to show us where we need correction, how to be an overcomer, and what would be the reward for faithfulness.

John lived in the middle of the Roman Empire and was exiled to the Island of Patmos because of his testimony of the Messiah, but his faith exploded as John was shown the downfall of this ruthless kingdom that slaughtered Christians and fed them to the lions. We must remember that in the beginning we are told this is a book of prophecy. Images, allegories, parables that have a deeper meaning; understanding that Revelation is a book of the history of the world, changing as Jesus is bringing about His plan to pull down the world's kingdoms and fulfill the Kingdom of God. He began with the Roman dynasty Rev11.15.

Investigating world history from the first century, we would see that the Roman Empire ruled over vast territories as it did for nearly 800 years; but totally decimated by the fifth century AD. It is probable that in Revelation 4 when John was told he would see things which must be hereafter, that he would 'see' the demise of this world power.

With His first century language how would he describe what he saw, warfare beyond his capacity. Those horses represent commerce, economy, agriculture, an empire being decimated, and the pale horse is actually a green horse. Now we see that those who died for love of God are being comforted. Verse 12; an earthquake in prophecy is the upheaval of government powers as in v.13, 'the stars of heaven falling', are nothing but the Caesars who saw themselves as gods; but they all died.

So, let's see how far this research will take us as we journey through the Word to establish what God wants us to understand. Our Bible is a book of history. From the day of creation, there has been recorded the history of the world, but especially the history of man and what God has in mind for us. The Gospels reveal to us Who is Jesus and Revelation is only a continuance of the book of Acts and leading to His culmination. The books in between are instructions, preparing us for eternal life in Christ Jesus. More especially it is the history of God/Jesus as He relates to man at an intimate level; how we can know God.

And God Always Begins at the Beginning,
So, Here Is the Beginning.

It is crucial to our understanding that we begin at the beginning for what the 'mark' [Revelation 13] really stands for. So, we research the beginning of what it means; Israel's deliverance out of the darkness of slavery even before they have left Goshen. And it begins with the Blood. [Old Testament comparison]. God Does Not Want Us To Be Ignorant.

Exodus 12.12-13 *For I will pass through the land of Egypt on that night, and will strike all the firstborn in the land of Egypt, both man and beast; and against all the gods of Egypt I will execute judgment I am the Lord. Now the blood shall be a sign for you on the houses where you are. And when I see the blood, I will pass over you; and the plague shall not be on you to destroy you when I strike the land of Egypt.*
Exodus 12.14-*15 So this day shall be to you a memorial; and you shall keep it as a feast* [Passover] *to the Lord throughout your generations. You shall keep it as a feast by an everlasting ordinance.*

2 Chronicles 16.9 *For the eyes of the Lord run to and fro throughout the whole earth, to show Himself strong on behalf of those whose heart is loyal to Him. .*

And this Applies Also to His New Testament Believers.

Exodus 12.21-27 *Then Moses called for all the elders of Israel and said to them, pick out and take lambs for yourselves according to your families, and kill the Passover lamb. And you shall take a bunch of hyssop, dip it in the blood that is in the basin, and strike the lintel and the two doorposts with the blood that is in the basin. And none of you shall go out of the door of his house until morning.*

For the Lord will pass through to strike the Egyptians; and when He sees the blood on the lintel and on the two doorposts, the Lord will pass over the door and not allow the destroyer to come into your houses to strike you. It is the Passover sacrifice of the Lord, who passed over the houses of the children of Israel in Egypt when He struck the Egyptians and delivered our households. .

REMEMBER THIS DAY. This was a commandment to be physically observed just as the law was to be observed; that God's people would remember always, that it was the mighty hand of God Who brought them safely out of bondage to Egypt. So let's be clear about what God wants His people to remember. It was the Blood that set them apart; and because of that, they would be released from bondage to Egypt. The destroyer would not harm them.

The word says in Exodus 12.37 *about six hundred thousand men on foot, besides children*. But certainly, there were also women and 12.38, many others. How many would that make, as they set out into the desert for where, they knew not. Now, even as they were crossing this great expanse of wilderness, and before they came to the Red Sea, Moses was instructing them further on what they were to remember. It was crucial to their relationship with the God Who had just devastated a once powerful nation and its many gods.

Exodus 13.3-16 *And Moses said to the people Remember this day in which you went out of Egypt, out of the house of bondage; for by strength of hand the Lord brought you out of this place.* Verse 8 *And you shall tell your son in that day, saying, 'This is done because of what the Lord did for me when I came up from Egypt.'* It shall be as a sign to you on your hand and as a memorial between your eyes, *that the Lord's law may be in your mouth; for with a strong hand the Lord has brought you out of Egypt. You shall therefore keep this ordinance in its season from year to year.* Passover [See verse 16 reiterated] It *shall be as a sign on your hand and as frontlets between your eyes, for by strength of hand the Lord brought us out of Egypt.*

Please Read All These Passages
It Will Give You More Understanding.

Deuteronomy 6.3 *Therefore hear, O Israel, and be careful to observe it, that it may be well with you, and that you may multiply greatly as the Lord God of your fathers has promised you.* This has everything to do with what you think and do.

Deuteronomy 6.6-9 *And these words which I command you this day shall be in your heart; You shall teach them to your children, speaking of them when you sit in your house, when you walk by the way, when you lie down, and when you rise up.* You shall bind them as a sign on your hand, and they shall be as frontlets between your eyes. *You shall write them on the doorposts of your house and on your gates. For if you carefully keep all these commandments which I command you to do — to love the Lord your God, to walk in all His ways, to hold fast to Him.* . They were to know the God Who delivered them.

Deuteronomy 11.18 Therefore *you shall love the Lord your God, and keep His charge, His statutes, His judgments, and His commandments always. Therefore,*

54

you shall lay up these words of mine in your heart and in your soul, and bind them as a sign on your hand, and they shall be as frontlets between your eyes. Frontlets to go around the head, or bind; a fillet [for the forehead] a strip of any material used for binding. [Strong's Concordance and The American College Dictionary].

So, to make themselves remember, they have made these signs physical. You've seen what Jewish men wear when they go to the wall to pray. The box that is bound to their head [mind] contains the Word, the promises of God bound to their mind. It's an outward observance but written in their thoughts and memory so they don't forget, and their right hand bound all the way to their elbow...so they don't forget; He is their God and they will obey Him; but now it is by the Spirit we are sealed

Ezekiel 9.4 And *the Lord said to him, "Go through the midst of the city, through the midst of Jerusalem, and put a mark on the foreheads of the men who sigh and cry over all the abominations that are done within it. .*

And so, four times from Exodus to Deuteronomy [and so many other places] the instructions are given to remember what God has done for His people; to get their mind wrapped around the fact that now they are free after 430 years of bondage [Genesis 15.13], and belong to God; and the works of their hand shall be to obey His Word and to love the '*Lord thy God*', as they were given the law etched in stone. So, has this witness been given as truth? This nation was raised up to walk in the ways of God and to worship Him only.

They Have Been Sealed, Marked by God to Be His Own People; And They Are to Pass it down to All Generations.

As we can see, there is the witness of this commandment given several times to affirm what God has said. Please read the references. Israel has been marked and sealed by God to remember their deliverance from bondage to Babylon and slavery. This was a physical sign and seal that Israel would never forget down through the centuries even to this day [Psalm 119.93-94].

AND WHAT DID GOD DO FOR US? Colossians 1.13.

We Are Always to Remember What God Did for Us!

The seal of God the Christian bears is that they remember Jesus brought them out of the darkness of sin into His glorious light. It is the mind that remembers and the hand that is always ready to do God's will. [John 14.15 *If you love me*]. .

Revelation 13.16-18, mark *of the beast*...no!

The God of creation is jealously protective of those who belong to Him. The true Christian has already been marked and sealed by God. PLEASE BE SURE TO RESEARCH THESE SCRIPTURES FOR A PROOF WITNESS, Eph 4.30; Rev 9.4, 14.1; 2.13; 12.17; 15.2-3; 2Cor 1.22; John 3.33, 6.27; 2Tim 2.19; 1 John 1.3, 2.22-24, 4.13-19, 5.4-5; 2 John 1.9; Rev 15.2-3; 7.3; and please read all of 1John.

Ephesians 1.7-14 *In Him we have redemption through His blood, the forgiveness of sins, according to the riches of His grace which He made to abound toward us in all wisdom and prudence, having made known to us the mystery of His will, according to His good pleasure which He purposed in Himself, that in the dispensation of the fullness of the times He might gather together in one all things in Christ, both which are in heaven and which are on earth — in Him.*

In Him also we have obtained an inheritance, being predestined according to the purpose of Him who works all things according to the counsel of His will, that we who first trusted in Christ should be to the praise of His glory. In Him you also trusted, after you heard the word of truth, the gospel of your salvation; in whom also, having believed, you were sealed with the Holy Spirit of promise, who is the guarantee of our inheritance until the redemption of the purchased possession, to the praise of His glory. .

God Always Has His People Covered by His Love and Grace. And for What Purpose - That We Would Worship No Other.

So, do you understand what the seal or mark of God is for the true believers in Christ? It is the knowledge that Jesus shed His blood for our redemption. We know the lamb's blood for Israel was the shadow of the Blood Jesus shed for us. He did the same for us so that we are marked and sealed by our God as long as we confess -

'Jesus Is My Lord and My God, I Will Worship No Other'.

1 John 4.2. *By this you know the Spirit of God, every spirit that confesses that Jesus Christ is come in the flesh is of God.* This mark or seal on the forehead and hand has to do with what you think and what you do. So, who do you think about and Who do you obey? Where is your life going and Who has precedence in your life? Who do you worship? Now not a physical sign, but marked by the Spirit

Ephesians 1.13 Sealed *with the Holy Spirit of Promise.*

Colossians 1.9-14 *That you may be filled with the knowledge of His will in all wisdom and spiritual understanding; that you may walk worthy of the Lord, fully pleasing Him, being fruitful in every good work and increasing in the knowledge of God; strengthened with all might, according to His glorious power, for all patience and longsuffering with joy; giving thanks to the Father who has qualified us to be partakers of the inheritance of the saints in the light. He has delivered us from the power of darkness and conveyed us into the Kingdom of the Son of His love, in whom we have redemption through His blood, the forgiveness of sins.* .

Brought out of "Egypt' into His Kingdom.

Why are we sealed by God? So we would have the mind of Christ [1Corinthians 2.16] so that we would -

Luke 10.27 *Love the Lord your God with all your heart, with all your soul, with all your strength, and with all your mind*, [and do the 'works of God', John 6.29; Hebrews 13.21].

So That We Would Never Deny Him.

Just know in the bottom of your soul and spirit that...

He brought us out of the power of darkness and has translated us into the Kingdom of His dear Son, Jesus. .

Into Our Promised Land.

1 John 2.20-29 *But you have an anointing from the Holy One, and you know all things. I have not written to you because you do not know the truth, but because you know it, and that no lie is of the truth. Who is a liar but he who denies that Jesus is the Christ? He is antichrist who denies the Father and the Son. Whoever denies the Son does not have the Father either.* The spirit of antichrist lives in the heart of the unbeliever...

Therefore, let that abide in you which you heard from the beginning. If what you heard from the beginning abides in you, you also will abide in the Son and in the Father. And this is the promise that He has promised us — eternal life. These things I have written to you concerning those who try to deceive you. But the anointing which you have received from Him abides in you, and you do not need that anyone teach you; but as the same anointing teaches you concerning all things, and is true, and is not a lie, and just as it has taught you, you will abide in Him [John 1.12-13] .

58

Yes, We Are The Children of God *[2Cor 6.18]*.

V.28 And now, little children, abide in Him, that when He appears, we may have confidence and not be ashamed before Him at His coming. If you know that He is righteous, you know that everyone who practices righteousness is born of Him.

As believers we don't need that box on our forehead, we are sealed by the Holy Spirit of promise and we trust Him. The whole idea of being marked and sealed by God means that we worship Him alone.

Israel In The Desert Began To Know
The God Of Their Salvation.

We should never be afraid that we will bear the 'mark of the beast'. We are anointed of God and we know the truth. We know who we are and to Whom we belong. We have the mind of Christ and we are always mindful of the will of God for our lives. Yes, new born-again Christians are marked for God and He will always keep them safe.

Fire will burn paper, and wood - it'll burn your house down and fire burned San Francisco to the ground ... But it didn't burn those three boys that were thrown into the burning fiery furnace. Daniel 3.28 *He Delivered His servants who trusted in Him...That they might not serve nor worship any god, except their own God.* . Please read Colossians 2 all of it... and

Colossians 3.1-4 If *then you were raised with Christ, seek those things which are above, where Christ is, sitting at the right hand of God. Set your mind on things above, not on things on the earth. For you died, and your life is hidden with Christ in God. When Christ who is our life appears, then you also will appear with Him in glory.* .

To Worship Him Forever.

Ephesians 1:13-14 *In Him you also trusted, after you heard the word of truth, the gospel of your salvation; in whom also, having believed, you were sealed with the Holy Spirit of promise, 14 who is the guarantee of our inheritance until the redemption of the purchased possession, to the praise of His glory.* .

Israel in the desert learned the hard way Who it was they should worship. The seal on their mind and hand was to love God and serve Him only. And then He taught them to worship Him through the Tabernacle in the Wilderness. And for us also, we must learn to worship Him. As we receive the fulness of His love and grace, we develop in our heart and spirit true worship for the God *Who delivered us out of darkness into His Kingdom of light.*

We Will Never Deny Our God.

1 John 4:*1 Beloved, do not believe every spirit, but test the spirits, whether they are of God; because many false prophets have gone out into the world. 2 By this you know the Spirit of God: Every spirit that confesses that Jesus Christ has come in the flesh is of God,*

Philippians 3:3 *For we are the circumcision* [of the heart], *who worship* [only] *God in the Spirit, rejoice in Christ Jesus, and have no confidence in the flesh.*

To know You Lord
Is the hunger of my heart
To worship You in all I do
To feel Your love flowing through me
Like a river of the water of life
Coming from the throne of God
And from the Lamb
To be that tree of righteousness
Planted by Your river
To drink of Your living stream
To be all that You made me to be
Is the hunger of my heart.
Come into My throne room, child
Sit with me and drink of My love
Let My hand of grace overcome
The troubles and trials of life.
In your weakness
I shall strengthen you
In your failures, come to Me
And in time you will surrender
All of life that you could be.

THE MARK #2

So here we go again to re-affirm the witness of the Word. The Word of God from Genesis through Revelation is a continuous history of Who is God and who are the people He created for Himself. Seth [his name means substituted] was given in the place of Abel. Both were after the heart of God, The son of Seth was Enosh [name means mortal] and he began to proclaim the name of the Lord, but somewhere, sometime, again, mortal man decided he did not need God and became so wicked [Genesis 6.5] that God decided to begin again; and so He chose Noah to refresh His creation. But alas...

Anarchy Began All Over - Again.

But a promise is a promise [Gen 9.11] and so God continued on with His 'Plan A', [there never was a plan 'B']; the process to redeem His creation from all our blunders and creative idolatry. Our Sovereign God knew to make preparations before He created anything, and so here we have...

Rev 13.8 *The Lamb slain [in sacrifice] from the foundation of the World* [Ampl Bible]. Done in the Spirit realm then brought forth in the appointed time [Galatians 4.4] .

God waited to find the right man to begin the process, and so here we have another beginning; Abraham, a man who would choose to hear and obey no matter what the price. He thought it would cost his beloved son, BUT HE TRUSTED GOD! His generations were set apart to be separated unto God, to be His witness to the world that God is a good God and loves His creation. They would receive the blessings that were stored up in the Kingdom for His chosen.

There had to be a miracle for them to become true believers and so after four hundred years of slavery, of crying out for a Redeemer, they were set free. Not free to go their own way, but to be sealed and marked by God to be His own people, to know Who it was that set them free; free to serve the living God.

We have to understand that the Word of God is its own witness. Deuteronomy 31.26-27 Take *this Book of the Law, and put it in the side of* [within] *the ark of the covenant of the Lord your God, that it may be there as a witness against you.*

2 Corinthians 13.*1 By the mouth of two or three witnesses every word shall be established.* It has always been so. [Matthew 24.14; Acts 1.8;14.17] .

And because of this we can take any principle in the Word and look for a second or third witness to establish it. Be a Researcher, a Berean. An archeologist has been known to dig up dead things; but how about we dig up the life-giving resources of our living God.

So, Who Is this Lord God, and How Does He Relate to His People?

We must know that God doesn't just throw things at us. He leads us step by step and confirms His word that we will gain understanding of what He wants to do to lead us on His path of salvation.

Day by day, year by year God continued to show Himself to man; manifesting His holiness and revealing how we could know Him; know Him as our God. Now God has made the blood sacrifice as the only way we could come back into the relationship He has always wanted. First the substitute, the lamb sacrificed in the temple; then the reality, Jesus on the cross. Yes, God Himself has paid the penalty for our sin and has indeed become our Savior [Romans 5]. You can make Him your Savior today. Just ask.

We Owed a Debt We Could Not Pay
He Paid the Debt He Did Not Owe.

The children of God are sealed by the Holy Spirit and we choose to exalt *the Holy One of God, the Creator of all there is*, Yahvahshua, Jesus the Messiah. [Eph 1.13, 4.30; 2 Cor 1.22; 1Jn 4.2; Rev 7; Rev 13; Rev 22.4;].

As we go along here, we will understand what the mark or seal actually means, and it is all referenced in the Word of God. He does not want us to be ignorant. Our eternal life depends on what we understand. In our mind we know that we know, and with our hand we work the works that Jesus taught us. *Then they said to Him, what shall we do, that we may work the works of God? Jesus answered and said to them, this is the work of God, that you believe in Him whom He sent* [Jn 6.28-29]. And we have the mind of Christ [1Corinthians 2.16] .

Lovers of God - Don't Be Ashamed of Who You Are.

What we think and what we do is all to exalt His Majesty, our King Jesus; the sign on our forehead [our mindset] and the works of our hand is that we belong to Jesus

[Revelation 14.1 & 9-13: please read these].

John 14.15 *If you love Me, keep My commandments.* . We will never deny Him. We know that we know, we are sealed by His Holy Spirit, and He will never abandon us.

Is it trusting in the one true God, Creator of all there is; or do we believe in the liar who caters to our fleshly

64

desires as [we think] we have control of our own life? What might be the hour of temptation? Millions of Christians died in this hour because they would not deny their Lord or the Word of Truth.

For 1260 years, for the so-called 'middle ages', the martyrs of Christ have shed their blood, 50 million of them for centuries, tortured beyond description and burned at the stake. They would not deny Christ and the truth of His Word. They would not trust or believe manmade theology that could not be confirmed in the true Word of God. This is why we must study the Word. [We can find this world history in research on the computer]. And this scenario is happening again in so many countries. The newspapers and television are full of stories of Synagogues and Christian churches being burned. Christians in Arab nations have been and still are murdered because of who they are; and any Muslim that converts to Christianity will be murdered if they are found.

You See - the Mark or the Seal Is Referenced
To What We Believe and Who We Worship.

Again, I admonish you to please be sure. research these Scriptures for proof witness. Eph 4.30; Rev 9.4; 14.1; 2.13; 12.17; 15.2-3; 2Cor 1.22; John 3.33; 6.27; 2Tim 2.19; 1 John 1.3; 2.22-24; 4.13-19; 5.4-5; 2 Jn 1.9; 7.3. Rev 14.1 & 15.2-3 *Then I looked, and behold, a Lamb standing on Mount Zion, and with Him one hundred and forty-four thousand, having His Father's name written on their foreheads. Rev 15.2 And I saw something like a sea of glass mingled with fire, and those who have the victory over the beast, over his image and over his mark and over the number of his name, standing on the sea of glass, having harps of God. They sing the song of Moses, the servant of God, and the song of the Lamb* [songs of deliverance]. .

65

The number of man is six. Have you overcome your human nature, taken on the nature of God - holiness?

1 John 1.3-4 *That which we have seen and heard we declare to you, that you also may have fellowship with us; and truly our fellowship is with the Father and with His Son Jesus Christ. And these things we write to you that your joy may be full.* .

This mark is engraved in the forehead, and is the same root word for 'character', our 'nature'. Do you have the character of God - or the nature of the antichrist?

Which one do you have?
Who are you following after?
What is your nature?
Man was created in the image of God.
Whose qualities are you in union with?

Revelation 22.4 *And we shall see His face and His name shall be in our forehead.* [always knowing who we are in Christ. We have the mind of Christ]. So, the mark or seal represents our spiritual attitude, and the image of anything is the qualities it represents. The image of God is in the born-again ones representing His qualities - holiness, a forgiving spirit, love, kindness etc. So, Who do You Worship?

The above verses tell us Who believers in Christ worship. The mark or sign or seal on us is 'who do we worship'. The number of a man; 666, symbolic of our body, soul and [man's] spirit. But if we've given our life to Jesus, we have been transformed to be like Him. There are also rebellious ones who think they are in charge of their life. Ones who don't care who they hurt; they live for themselves, and give over to worship the evil one, whether they know it or not. They are caught in his trap, just as we once were; but we've been brought out of his darkness by the love and Blood of Jesus. God has not

66

assigned us for wrath; He has marked and sealed His people to Him, unto the day of redemption.

1Thes 1.10 and 5.9 - *Delivered from the wrath to come.*

Thank You Jesus for Loving Me So Much...

Ephesians 1.13-*14 In Him you also trusted, after you heard the word of truth, the gospel of your salvation; in whom also, having believed, you were sealed with the Holy Spirit of promise, who is the guarantee of our inheritance until the redemption of the purchased possession, to the praise of His glory. .*

Ephesians 2.18-22 *For through Him we both have access by one Spirit to the Father. Now, therefore, you are no longer strangers and foreigners, but fellow citizens with the saints and members of the household of God, having been built on the foundation of the apostles and prophets, Jesus Christ Himself being the chief cornerstone, in whom the whole building, being fitted together, grows into a holy temple in the Lord, in whom you also are being built together for a dwelling place of God in the Spirit. .*

Jew and Gentile - God's New Man.

We who are sealed with the mark of God will trust the Word of Truth, the gospel of our salvation, and believe that Jesus, God - has come in the flesh to die on the cross and bring us to the Father. ...*Christ Himself was an Israelite as far as His human nature is concerned, and He is God Who rules over everything, and is worthy of eternal praise* [Romans 9:5 New Living Translation].

For we are the temple of the living God, and we will never deny Him. In the hour of temptation, we are assured of one thing; we are sealed by the Holy Spirit and God shall never leave us nor forsake us, for we who belong to Him must never deny His name [Hebrews 13.5].

Research Strong's Concordance for meaning of mark/ seal - [Revelation 3.8,10,12]. The seal, the mark of God is to confess that Jesus is your Lord and Savior 1John 2.22 *Who is a liar but he that denies that Jesus is the Christ, he is antichrist that denies* [disavow, reject], *the Father and the Son.* And...

Acts 7.49-50 Heaven *is My throne, and earth is My footstool. What house will you build for Me says the Lord, or what is the place of My rest? Has My hand not made all these things?*

Isaiah 44.24 *Thus says the Lord, your Redeemer, And He who formed you from the womb I am the Lord, who makes all things... .*

Please Remember, God Himself has built our temple. Is He at rest in you? *That the power of Christ may rest upon me* [us]. 2 Corinthians 12.9.

His Hand Has Created Us.

1 Corinthians 6.17 *But he who is joined to the Lord is one spirit with Him.* He Made Us to Be His Temple.

1 Corinthians 6.19 *Or do you not know that your body is the temple of the Holy Spirit who is in you, whom you have from God, and you are not your own? For you were bought at a price; therefore, glorify God in your body and in your spirit, which are God's. .*

Evil will not give up easily and so he continues to darken the minds of men in a new scenario... the world of religion to capture 'the souls of men' [Rev 18.13] that were made to be slaves, fodder for this evil Kingdom.

Revelation 13.16-17 He *causes all, both small and great, rich and poor, free and slave, to receive a mark on their right hand or on their foreheads, and that no one may buy or sell except one who has the mark or the name of the beast, or the number of his name.* [one meaning of 'causes' is to require] PLEASE KNOW...

No one can force any one to take any mark. God has already marked and sealed his people to himself, because we love him. So, what is there to fear?

Psalm 23 *The Lord is my shepherd; I shall not want.*

He makes me to lie down in green pastures; He leads me beside the still waters. He restores my soul; He leads me in the paths of righteousness For His name's sake. Yea, though I walk through the valley of the shadow of death, I will fear no evil; For You are with me; Your rod and Your staff, they comfort me. You prepare a table before me in the presence of my enemies; You anoint my head with oil; My cup runs over. Surely goodness and mercy shall follow me All the days of my life; I will dwell in the house of the Lord forever. .

Ezekiel 9.4 *The Lord said to him, "Go through the midst of the city, through the midst of Jerusalem, and put a mark on the foreheads of the men who sigh and cry over all the abominations that are done within it.* .

Oh Yes, God Continues to Be Faithful to His People;

From the Beginning and Yes, Now and everlasting.

To reiterate... Ephesians 1.13, *being predestined according to the purpose of Him who works all things according to the counsel of His will...In Him you also trusted, after you heard the word of truth, the gospel of your salvation; in whom also, having believed, you were sealed with the Holy Spirit of promise, who is the guarantee of our inheritance until the redemption of the purchased possession, to the praise of His glory.* .

Acts 20.28 *Take heed to yourselves and to all the flock, among which the Holy Spirit has made you overseers, to shepherd the Church of God which He purchased with His own blood.* .

We Are His Purchased Possession. God Has Sealed

Us from the Day We Were Born Again. But on the Opposite End...

Revelation 14:11 *And the smoke of their torment ascends forever and ever; and they have no rest day or night, who worship the beast and his image, and whoever receives the mark of his name. .*

Revelation 13.16 The unbeliever is stamped and sealed with a badge of servitude to the 'beast'. The mark of the beast is the mindset to believe the lie that Jesus is not God and you can be satisfied with the things you desire for yourself. Your demands of life are satisfied in your flesh. This beast of our self-life [our sin nature] will believe anything that appeals to flesh. But the saints of God will never serve the antichrist. We are sealed and marked for God for the sake of security and safety. Isaiah 26.20; Jn 17.9-13; Revelation 14.1; 2Tim 2; John 6; John 3; Romans 4; 2Cor 1. To the pharisees He said...

John 8.23-24 *And He said to them, you are from beneath; I am from above. You are of this world; I am not of this world. Therefore, I said to you that you will die in your sins; for if you do not believe that I am He, you will die in your sins. .* But to a believer...

John 11.25-26 *Jesus said to her, I am the resurrection and the life. He who believes in Me, though he may die, he shall live. And whoever lives and believes in Me shall never die. Do you believe this? .*

So, Who Here Is the One We Worship? Every Day Is a Journey with Jesus - to Follow, to Learn, to Obey, to love, to Grow in Faith and Trust in God above All Things.

Ephesians 11.1-14 *In Him also we have obtained an inheritance, being predestined according to the purpose of Him who works all things according to the counsel of His will, that we who first trusted in Christ should be to the praise of His glory. In Him you also trusted, after you heard the word of truth, the gospel of your salvation; in whom also, having believed, you were sealed with the Holy*

Spirit of promise, who is the guarantee of our inheritance until the redemption of the purchased possession, to the praise of His glory. .

And We Worship Our Redeemer and Savior for His Love and Grace That Brings Us into His Presence.

Have you put all your faith and trust in the One Holy God of Israel with all His saints of the New Covenant? Do you trust Him to keep you safe in His arms no matter what happens? Would you give up your life to maintain this trust in Jesus, the One Who died for you?

Matthew 10. 28 *And fear not them who kill the body, but are not able to kill the soul. .*

2 Timothy 1.7 *For God has not given us a spirit of fear, but of power and of love and of a sound mind.*

If you belong to Jesus you have the promise of eternal life [1John 4.10-19]. Verse *10 In this is love, not that we loved God, but that He loved us and sent His Son to be the propitiation for our sins* - Jesus will set you free.

Please read the rest of the chapter.

God ask us ... 2 Timothy 2.24-26 *And a servant of the Lord must not quarrel but be gentle to all, able to teach, patient, in humility correcting those who are in opposition, if God perhaps will grant them repentance, so that they may know the truth, and that they may come to their senses and escape the snare of the devil, having been <u>taken captive by him to do his will</u> – .*

Revelation 7.2-3 Then *I saw another angel ascending from the east, having the seal of the living God. And he cried with a loud voice to the four angels to whom it was granted to harm the earth and the sea, saying, do not harm the earth, the sea, or the trees till we have sealed the servants of our God on their foreheads. .* [Perhaps these are ones who have been born-again in this time of trouble, to assure them of safety in the Lord]. But...

Revelation 9.4-6... *to torment only those men <u>who do</u>*

not have the seal of God on their foreheads. *They shall seek death and not find it* [Revelation 20.15].

But this is not the destiny of God's people, AND...

God Continues to Show Us to Whom We Belong.
The Martyrs of Christ Are Now Given Rest.

Revelation 14.1 *Then I looked, and behold, a Lamb standing on Mount Zion, and with Him one hundred and forty-four thousand, having His Father's name written on their foreheads. And I heard a voice from heaven, like the voice of many waters. These are they who follow the Lamb wherever He goes. They were redeemed from among men, the first fruits unto God and to the Lamb.* .

144,000 Is a Prophetic Number of the Government of God. Based on the number 12X12X12x12; It Symbolizes the Kingdom of God; All Faithful Saints and the Perfection of the Bride of Christ.

Did you know the number twelve is in the Bible, from Genesis to Revelation, at least 100 times?

[Numbers in the Bible have very significant meanings].
One- Signifies there is One God
Two- Witnesses
Three- Perfection, the Trinity
Four– Universality, 4 corners of the earth TPT
Five- Grace
Six- The nature of man
Seven- Divine perfection
Eight- New beginning
Nine- Blessing - fruit of the Spirit
Ten- Human government
Twelve - Divine government
Thirteen - Rebellion
Fourteen - Spiritual Perfection, Passover
Forty- Testing, trials

Fifty- Celebration, feasts, Jubilee
Seventy- Judgments, delegations
666 - Beastie - the number of man

The name 'antichrist' does not appear in the book of Revelation. It is quite possible that '666' refers to our body, soul and spirit, our human nature; this fallen nature that had us bound in sin. But Jesus took this to the cross to set us free to make our own choices. Now He says,

Matthew 11:29-30 *Come unto Me all ye who labor and are heavy laden and I will give you rest. Take My yoke upon you and learn from Me, for I am gentle and lowly in heart, and you will find rest for your souls. For My yoke is easy and My burden is light.* .

Sad to say not everyone is interested. These are ones who will live their life for their pleasure. These are ones who have no desire to live for, or even know God or Jesus. They already have the antichrist spirit. If the following is a repeat just get it again.

1 John 4:1-*5 Beloved, do not believe every spirit, but test the spirits, whether they are of God; because many false prophets have gone out into the world. By this you know the Spirit of God: Every spirit that confesses that Jesus Christ has come in the flesh is of God, and every spirit that does not confess that Jesus Christ has come in the flesh is not of God. And this is the spirit of the Antichrist, which you have heard was coming, and is now already in the world.* .

Has Been Since the Beginning.

Unbelievers already carry the spirit of antichrist, for they have no desire to change their lifestyle.

Verse 4 You *are of God, little children, and have overcome them, because He who is in you is greater than he who is in the world. They are of the world. Therefore, they speak as of the world, and the world hears them. .*

Next is The Passion Translation by Dr Brian Simmons.

Proverbs 1.7 *How then does a man gain the essence of wisdom? We cross the threshold of true knowledge when we live in complete awe and adoration of God.* [Broadstreet Press]

Certainly, we know there are many millions of believers who follow their Savior and love their Father God. Now we know that God has sealed His people with His mark and seal; that is to know Jesus and serve Him only. The antichrist spirit also has a mark and seal that testifies to the denial of the real Jesus. We must understand that the God Who loves His creation would not leave us to our own imaginations. He revealed to us Who He is [John 10.14] and gave us a Bible to know how we can live for Him and satisfy His concerns that we may inherit eternal life. So, we know He would not leave us in the dark as pertains to confronting any antichrist. Our life depends on what we know and how to be an overcomer. Jesus died to make this possible, AND...

Jesus Is the Way, the Truth and the Life.
Follow Him in all you do.

1John 2.22-27 *Who is a liar but he who denies that Jesus is the Christ? He is antichrist who denies the Father and the Son. Whoever denies the Son does not have the Father either; he who acknowledges the Son has the Father also. Therefore, let that abide in you which you heard from the beginning. If what you heard from the beginning abides in you, you also will abide in the Son and in the Father. And this is the* promise *that He has* promised *us — eternal life. These things I have written to you concerning those who try to deceive you. But the anointing which you have received from Him abides in*

you, and you do not need that anyone teach you; but as
the same anointing teaches you concerning all things, and
is true, and is not a lie, and just as it has taught you, you
will abide in Him.

[To deny Him means to contradict, disavow, reject and refuse to (John 1.12) receive Him as your God and Savior. Please read the letter John wrote and in 1.4; *That your joy may be full.* Our mind is sealed with 1 Corinthians 2.16 the *mind of Christ* [and], 1John 2.20 You *have an unction from the Holy One and you know all things. .*

We cannot add any of our imaginations to the truth of the Word, nor can we remove any truth from it. Colossians 2.8 Beware *lest anyone cheat you through philosophy and empty deceit, according to the tradition of men, according to the basic principles of the world, and not according to Christ. For in Him dwells all the fullness of the Godhead bodily; and you are complete in Him, who is the head of all principality and power.*

1 John 4.15-19 *Whoever confesses that Jesus is the Son of God, God abides in him, and he in God. And we have known and believed the love that God has for us. God is love, and he who abides in love abides in God, and God in him. Love has been perfected among us in this that we may have boldness in the day of judgment; because as He is, so are we in this world. There is no fear in love; but perfect love casts out fear, because fear involves torment. But he who fears has not been made perfect in love. We love Him because He first loved us. .*

Remember the hour of temptation. Don't save your body and lose your soul [Matthew 10.28] Don't fear for your children. God has His arms around them; they belong to the Lord. So, God has sealed all His people. We Must be Aware the Seal, the Mark of Antichrist - Is to Deny the Reality of Who is Jesus, That He is Our Only True Lord and God.

This Mark Has to Do with Who You Worship. Why Are We Sealed by God? To Have the Mind of Christ,

So That We Would Know the God of Our Salvation.

Revelation 14.11, *They have no rest day or night, who worship the beast and his image, and whosoever receives the mark of his name. The son of perdition, who opposes and exalts himself above all that is called God or that is worshiped, so that he sits as God in the temple of God, showing himself that he is God* [2 Thessalonians 2]. . Please read the context.

What Is the Image? Those Things Approved Of.

The Works of God OR the Works of Our Sin Nature.

An idol is the image of the demon behind it.

The antichrist spirit, the rejection of the Spirit of God, lives in the heart of the unbeliever. It is a spirit of self-worship; 'I am the god of my life; this is my body; no one can tell me what to do'. This attitude is prevalent in our society today.

Man was created to be a temple; albeit the temple of God. If the saints are the true temple of God, then whoever worships the beast are *his* temple. Revelation 9.4, *Hurt...only those men who have <u>not</u> the seal of God in their forehead*. When do we receive the seal of God? When we receive and believe the gospel of our salvation. Remember Ephesians 1.13 *After we heard the word of truth, the gospel of our salvation, in whom also <u>after we believed</u>, we were sealed with that Holy Spirit of promise.*

We Are Sealed and Marked by God.

Revelation 14.12-14 *Here is the patience of the saints, that they keep the faith of Jesus.*

Revelation 3.8, *You have not denied my name.*

1 John 4 In *this is love, not that we loved God, but that*

He loved us and sent His Son to be the propitiation for our sins. God abides in us, and His love has been perfected in us. By this we know that we abide in Him, and He in us, because He has given us of His Spirit.

1 John 4.19 *We love Him because He first loved us.*

1 John 5 *Whoever believes that Jesus is the Christ is born of God, for this is the love of God, that we keep His commandments. And His commandments are not burdensome. For whatever is born of God overcomes the world.*

And this Is the Victory That Has Overcome the World — Our Faith. Who Is He Who Overcomes the World, But He Who Believes That Jesus Is the Son of God.

Revelation 13.14 *Then I heard a voice from heaven saying to me, write 'Blessed are the dead who die in the Lord from now on. Yes, says the Spirit, that they may rest from their labors, and their works follow them.* So, we are confessing that Jesus only is the true God according to the Word of Truth. *Whoever denies the Son, the same has not the Father* [1John]. Remember...

Malachi 31 And *the Lord, whom you seek, Will suddenly come to His temple, Even the Messenger of the covenant.* Jesus had every right to establish His New Covenant in our hearts. He loves us so much.

Hebrews 10.15-16 *But the Holy Spirit also witnesses to us; This is the covenant that I will make with them after those days, says the Lord I will put My laws into their hearts, and in their minds, I will write them.*

[See Jeremiah 31.31-34; Isaiah 61.8; Heb 8.7-13].

This New Covenant prophesied here, was established in Jesus, The Messenger of the New Covenant.

He testifies to the New Covenant, the New Testament.

Hebrews 8.7 *For if that first covenant had been without defect, there would have been no room for another one, or an attempt to institute another one.* [Amplified Bible].

1 John 5.6-7 *And it is the Spirit who bears witness, because the Spirit is truth.* .

Acts 1.8 *And you shall be witnesses unto me... .*

The Word and the Spirit witness - The Old and the New Testament come together to witness the same God, the same Word; a continuation of the truth of the gospel of 'Who is Jesus and who we are in Him'. This is the gospel of the Kingdom of God. The sealing of God's people was first passed to Abraham through circumcision as he believed and trusted in the God he came to walk with. He was chosen to be *the Father of nations*; sealed forever in the Kingdom of God. Circumcision was the first sign of the seal of God. In the flesh, natural; it was a physical sign of blood, now the circumcision is in the heart, [spiritual].

Genesis 26.4-5 *All the nations of the earth shall be blessed; because Abraham obeyed My voice and kept My charge, My commandments, My statutes, and My laws.* .

So now God brings us back to the beginning. All the precepts and concepts of the Kingdom of God have a beginning somewhere in the Word, to give us a proper foundation [Hebrews 6.1-3]. God wants us to understand. He doesn't have mindless robots in His Kingdom. God teaches us with so much mercy and grace what is the Kingdom of God so that we may participate fully in our inheritance.

To understand the origin and the meaning of God's sealing, mark or sign, we can go back to The Old Testament. Remember that Scripture is verified in the mouth of two witnesses; Old and New Testament.

It is an amazing discovery and revelation [to me] that these signs were given as a physical reminder of the Passover that Israel had just celebrated the night before, their exodus from Egypt. Because of the blood on their doorposts, the angel of death passed over the slaves of Goshen. And even as they were crossing the desert headed for the Red Sea, Moses is telling them that they must have a reminder *every year* of the supernatural deliverance from Egypt's bondage; to keep this service [Passover] in this month. What month? the month they were delivered; to remember that, *with a strong hand the Lord has brought you out of Egypt*. This was to be their testimony

And They Were to Remember Always.

Here I will only reference the Scripture I quoted in the last chapter. If you need to, please go back and refresh your memory. SO...

This was not just a fleeting speech by Moses. It was a proclamation heralded throughout their journey to remember, never forget, because God knew there would be in the future, a counterfeit sign and seal. So, as His people were delivered from slavery and walking in freedom towards the Red Sea, Moses was teaching them about this faithful God Who would always be with them and protect them from any enemy to come against them as long as they were faithful. He wanted them to always remember and pass down to their children how they were delivered from darkness into His light. It was to be a spiritual sign that they were sealed unto God.

In the Old Testament, Laws and Covenants Were Manifested Physically; the New Testament by the Spirit Because God's Laws Are Written in Our Heart.

The first verses in Scripture that designated *A sign to be in your hand and on your forehead*, is in Exodus 12.13-14. But first came chapter 12. Blood on the door.

The Blood Is Always the First Sign.
By the power of The Blood of the Lamb
They and We Also Were Redeemed.

Exodus 13.8-16 This was the seal and a mark on their forehead and their hand to remember to Whom they belonged. To know Him and to obey Him. The seal on their [and our] head and hand. 'To know and to do'.

Deuteronomy 6.6-10 and 11.18-20, and the other verses to please remember all these verses from my previous chapter because these are a sufficient witness that God has marked His people with signs; to mark them to as to remember their deliverance out of Babylon, as it were, the feast of Passover; to remember God's sovereign hand of protection under the blood.

And that we must remember our deliverance out of darkness into His glorious light; Colossians 1.13, And we must teach this to our children. Our 'Passover' is salvation by the Blood of Jesus. He died on the feast of Passover to confirm again that He is our salvation and deliverance from the darkness of our soul. He delivered Israel and us Gentiles into the Kingdom of His dear Son, Jesus our Messiah.

We Are Marked and Sealed unto God.
Our Mind and Our Hand - to Know Him and to Do
According to the Word of God.

Nehemiah 1.9 *keep My commandments and do them.*
John 6.29 Jesus *answered and said to them, This is the work of God, that you believe in Him whom He sent.*
The verses in red in your Bible, are Kingdom principles.
John 14.*15 If you love Me, keep My commandments.*

So, this Is the Work of Our Hands,
Revealed in the New Testament.

Now they Have Been Sealed, Marked by God To Be His Own People; To Pass it down to All Generations. And God made sure that it was passed down to our generation.

1 John Tells Us Where Our Mind Should Be. All These Verses Will Assure Us of Who We Are in Christ.

Hope You Will Read Them. This Is Our Witness -
The Love That Binds Us to Our Faithful God.

So now, what are we to remember? Bound to our mind and hand; Colossians 1.12-14 Giving *thanks to the Father who has qualified us to be partakers of the inheritance of the saints in the light. He has delivered us from the power of darkness and conveyed us into the Kingdom of the Son of His love, in whom we have redemption through His Blood, the forgiveness of sins.*

The Exodus Blood Covered Them First -
Now the New Covenant Blood of Jesus Covers Us.
They Were Given a Law but Couldn't Keep it -
So Now this Law Is Written in Our Heart.

I pray you will read these verses and know that God loves us so much He has turned the world upside down to reveal Who He is and what is our inheritance in Him.

1 John 1.3 *Our fellowship is with the Father and His Son.*

1 John 1.9 *If we confess our sins, He is faithful and just to forgive us our sins and to cleanse us from all unrighteousness. But you have an anointing from the Holy One, and you know all things. Who is a liar but he who denies that Jesus is the Christ? He is antichrist who denies the Father and the Son. Whoever denies the Son does not have the Father either; he who acknowledges the Son has the Father also.* . [The pharisees would not].

1John 3.1 *Therefore the world does not know us, because it did not know Him.* [Too many do not want to know, they want to do their own thing, be their own god]. But... 1 John 4.13 *And we have known and believed the love that God has for us. God is love, and he who abides in love abides in God, and God in him.* .

Remember His Law Is Written in Our Heart.

The Mark, the Seal, and the Sign Have to Do With Your Spiritual Belief System. Who Will You Worship?

Therefore, you shall lay up these words of mine in your heart and in your soul. . Remember these words?

Beloved, We Are Now Children of God; And His Love for Us Is to Realize We Do Belong. Well, this means that [especially] the words in 1 John are bound in your heart, your soul and your mind; your thought life by agreeing with it so that you know for sure... The letter the Apostle John wrote to all believers in Jesus Christ is mind renewing and these verses are pertinent to our salvation and where we stand in God's Kingdom. Please read them again and take them to heart. It is the only door into the Kingdom of God and a defense against the influence of the antichrist [Ephesians 1].

John 3.16 *For God so loved the world...* And 1 John chapter 2.22-27; Chapter 3.1-3, 19-21; Chapter 4.1-2, 10-21; Chapter 5.1-5, 9-12, 20.

We should read all of this wonderful letter, but especially do so on these verses. Bring them into your heart, buried in your soul so that you live by them. In the end you will know that nothing can take you out of your Father's hand. You know your soul is the seat of your emotions, your conscience, your character, personality, it's who you are; which is why God saves our soul, then comes our body resurrection.

Genesis 2.7 *And the Lord God formed man of the dust of the ground, and breathed into his nostrils the breath of life; and man became a living soul. .*

> And on the Day of Pentecost, the Holy Spirit
> Breathed once again on His Holy Ones,
> And the Life of God Again Entered Man.

1 John 4.17-20 *Love has been perfected among us in this that we may have boldness in the day of judgment;*

because as He is, so are we in this world. There is no fear in love; but perfect love casts out fear, because fear involves torment. But he who fears has not been made perfect in love. We love Him because He first loved us. .

1 John 5.1 *Whoever believes that Jesus is the Christ is born of God, and everyone who loves Him who begot also loves him who is begotten of Him. By this we know that we love the children of God, when we love God and keep His commandments. For this is the love of God, that we keep His commandments. And His commandments are not burdensome; and* Hebrews 8.6-13, *I will put my laws into their mind and write them in their heart.* .

Remember Romans 4, *this was written for us also if we believe on Him who raised up Jesus from the dead.*

Romans 4.11 *And he* [Abraham] *received the sign of circumcision, a seal of the righteousness of the faith which he had while still uncircumcised, that he might be the father of all those who believe, though they are uncircumcised, that righteousness might be imputed to them also.* .

His righteousness is appointed to us in our faith.

1John 5.4 *For whatever is born of God overcomes the world. And this is the victory that has overcome the world, our faith. Who is he who overcomes the world, but he who believes that Jesus is the Son of God?*

Verse *13 These things I have written to you who believe in the name of the Son of God, that you may know that you have eternal life, and that you may continue to believe in the name of the Son of God.*

Verse 18 *but he who has been born of God keeps himself, and the wicked one does not touch him.* .

But now satan tries to mimic God's love for His people, pretending he cares about the people who have denied Jesus. He gives them fame and fortune, when all the time he hates God's creation and even God Himself.

Revelation 14.9 *If any man worships the beast and*

his image and receives his mark on his forehead or on his hand, the same shall drink of the wine of the wrath of God, tormented with fire and brimstone. .

So, the Mark is the sign of worship, whether it be for God or for the beast. And 'beast' is just another word for who's in authority, who has the power. And what about image, An image of anything is the qualities it represents; the nature, character, personality, motives, what you believe. The antichrist is driven by rebellion to the truth; so are unbelievers. The lovers of God have the mind of Christ. We are one Spirit [1Cor 6.17] and will never deny Him. *Proverbs 4.23 So, above all guard the affections of your heart, for they affect all that you are. TPT Bible.* Man was created in God's image. Those who love God are a copy of His holiness. The image of the beast is to copy his rebellion towards God, to believe his lies, and these verses tell it like it is...

Romans 8.5-8 *For those who live according to the flesh set their minds on the things of the flesh, for to be carnally minded is death, Because the carnal mind is enmity against God; for it is not subject to the law of God, nor indeed can be.* [These people are the temple of the antichrist spirit]. *So then, those who are in the flesh cannot please God...* [v.19] *But you are not in the flesh but in the Spirit, if indeed the Spirit of God dwells in you. .*

This Revelation 13. 16-17, is about the mark of the beast for those of whom will agree with what the world stands for. They are already marked, 'to do my own thing and no one can tell me what to do'! BUT God has already marked and sealed His people because we do love Him.

John 14.15-17 *If you love Me, keep My commandments. And I will pray the Father, and He will give you another Helper, that He may abide with you forever; the Spirit of truth.* So, for Us Believers Now, What Is Meant by These Signs? That we Belong to the Kingdom of God!

1 John 4.18 *There is no fear in love, but* [His] *perfect*

love casts out fear... God's love for us was proven at the cross. *We love Him because He first loved us. .*

We may walk with the Lord for many years, but will we always remember that God snatched us out of 'Egypt', out of bondage to the spirit of darkness. Has He not translated us into the Kingdom of His dear Son? And we are...

Colossians 2. *buried with Him in baptism, in which you also were raised with Him through faith in the working of God, who raised Him from the dead. And you, being dead in your trespasses and the uncircumcision of your flesh, He has made alive together with Him, having forgiven you all trespasses.*

Have You Thanked Him - Every Day?

Deuteronomy 6.12-15 *Lest you forget the Lord who brought you out of the land of Egypt, from the house of bondage. You shall fear the Lord your God and serve Him, and shall take oaths in His name. You shall not go after other gods, the gods of the peoples who are all around you, for the Lord your God is a jealous God among you, lest the anger of the Lord your God be aroused against you and destroy you from the face of the earth.*

Today there are many gods worshiped on the earth. So many different religions that don't honor the true God. Am I being too harsh? *Our God changes not*! Matthew 22.37-40 Jesus *said to him, you shall love the Lord your God with all your heart, with all your soul, and with all your mind. This is the first and great commandment. And the second is like it. You shall love your neighbor as yourself. On these two commandments hang all the Law and the Prophets. .*

Yes, this applies even now to all of God's people. We know there are many cults in the world, manmade ways to reach 'god' or to be god! This 'new age' religion has many people deceived. Just because they use the name of Jesus, it may not be God's true only Son, Who is

God Himself [Romans 9.5]. Some believe Jesus is only 'a god'; others believe He is really Michael the Archangel, and some believe that God Himself was once a man and worked His way to Godhood and so can they.

Their insecurity makes them believe anything others may say, and a deceitful heart causes them to believe the liar. But the One True God is just a whisper away. When I met Jesus I said, "I want to know You, I want to know Who You are. And for 48 years, He has been so gracious to me. He has become my Father, I am His daughter, delivered out of darkness into His light.

I Give All glory to the Most High God. If You've Never Read or Understood the Chapter of Romans 8, God Will Help

You to See How it Applies to the Born-again Christian,

Deuteronomy 7.6-9 *For you are a holy people to the Lord your God; the Lord your God has chosen you to be a people for Himself, a special treasure above all the peoples on the face of the earth. The Lord did not set His love on you nor choose you because you were more in number than any other people, for you were the least of all peoples;* .

[We are His 'are nots' 1 Corinthians 1.26-28].

Malachi 3.16-17 *Then those who feared the Lord spoke to one another, And the Lord listened and heard them; So a book of remembrance was written before Him For those who fear the Lord And who meditate on His name. They shall be Mine, says the Lord of hosts, in the day that I make them My jewels. And I will spare them as a man spares his own son who serves him.*

John 17.16 *We are not of this world,* [just like Jesus]

Daniel 9.4 [This is part of the character of our God] *Therefore know that the Lord your God, He is God, the faithful God...O Lord, great and awesome God, who keeps His covenant and mercy with those who love Him, and with those who keep His commandments... who keeps covenant and mercy for a thousand generations with those who love Him and keep His commandments. .*

Romans 4 tells us from where we came. Abraham the father of all who walk by faith; right standing with God handed down to all who believe, and affirmed by the Blood of Jesus, Savior, Lord and King. So, for what purpose were the signs on the head and hand... Please read the whole passages in the verses in Exodus and Deuteronomy that I have referred to. It was for them to remember their deliverance from slavery and through the Red Sea; and their hand bound with remembering to do the law which at that time was legitimate.

Now we are bound to His New Covenant; His Word, His law is written in our hearts by the Holy Spirit Who was given to us, [Very Important - Acts 15.19-29].

They teach their children of how God delivered them from slavery in Egypt. One of their feast days always commemorates that day. It's called Passover because of the blood on the door, they were passed over - passed from slavery to freedom and they were marked; sealed into the Kingdom of God to worship Him alone. And remember Hebrews 10.16-18. He is the offering.

Jesus Died on Passover to Set Us All Free.
This Applies to Us As New Covenant Believers.

God seals us to remember our deliverance out of slavery to sin; out of darkness and into His glorious light. God had sealed us to Himself when we are born-again [Eph 1.3-23 & Col 1]. And to what do we put our hand? The works of His Kingdom. And Romans 12 tells us to, R*enew your mind* so you will know. *Our mind is stayed on Christ* [Isaiah 26], the work of our hands and our walk in His path. We are marked, sealed by the Kingdom of God and He will never let us go because we will always remember that glorious day when Jesus filled us with

His love as He forgave our sin and brought us into His Kingdom. Please remember...

He has delivered us from the power of darkness.

And remember Jeremiah 31.31,24.7; Isaiah 61.8; Ezekiel 36.26-27; Heb 8.6-13, 9.14 & 10.16. All these Scriptures verify that there was to be a new covenant established in the Blood of Jesus. And now as Malachi 3.1 proclaims, *Behold, I send My messenger, and he will prepare the way before Me. And the Lord, whom you seek, Will suddenly come to His temple, Even the Messenger of the covenant, In whom you delight. Behold, He is coming," Says the Lord of hosts.*

Jesus is the One Who came to us; Daniel 9.27 *Confirmed the covenant with many for one week...* NOW VERIFIED...

Luke 22.20 *Likewise He also took the cup after supper, saying, This cup is the new covenant in My blood, which is shed for you.* .

We Are Covered by His New Covenant and Yes, He Has Delivered Us from Bondage Just as He Delivered Israel.

1Corinthians 2.16 We *have the mind of Christ* to know what is our calling in His Kingdom; and the works of our hand. Remember

Genesis 3.15. The heel represents the foundation and walk in relationship with God, and satan has been trying to destroy that very foundation of Christianity as we know historically, how the apostles and disciples of the first Church, and for more than 1200 years, they were murdered; and this still is happening in other countries. He's still trying to stamp out Christianity. But at the cross, Jesus bruised satan's head – He broke the authority and power he's had over us as we stand in the power and authority of Jesus

Luke 10.18-20 *And He said to them, I saw Satan fall like lightning from heaven. Behold, I give you authority to trample on serpents and scorpions, and over all the power of the enemy, and nothing shall by any means hurt you. Nevertheless, do not rejoice in this, that the spirits are subject to you, but rather rejoice because your names are written in heaven.* .

Now we know satan's head [his authority over us] is crushed every time, [Rom 16.20] soon to be finally totally crushed under our feet forever. Praise Jesus. And God's people stand with Him on Mt Zion, Rev 14.1, *Having his Father's name written in their foreheads.*

And We Who Believe and Trust in Our Savior Jesus,
    Will Live Eternally, Face to Face with Our God.

The whole Bible is God's testimony of how, one step at a time, he brought His people out of the world and into His glorious Kingdom to rule and reign with Him forever. How can we not be thankful and praise His Holy Name?

So, who is this 'man of sin', and what is his seal or mark that will send anyone to a Christless hell for eternity? Please know that God doesn't send anyone to hell. It is man's own free will - to not accept His glorious salvation. They have no desire to know Jesus.

1 John 2.22-27 *Who is a liar but he that denies that Jesus is the Christ? He is antichrist, that denies the Father and Son. Whatever you have heard in the beginning is no lie and the anointing which you have received, you have no need that any man teach you.* .

God's truth is in His Word. Remember, *If any man take away or add to the words of this book, God shall add to him the plagues that are written, and take away his part from the tree of life and out of the holy city.* .

[Revelation 22.19; Deuteronomy 4.2].

No Rebels Will Enter the Kingdom of God.

It is likely that this man of sin lives on the earth at this moment and for the spirit of antichrist to come into total control, he will try to break down the world system as we know it. Money, food and the system of law will break down, so he may assume a place of great leadership to bring peace out of the panic of the 'great tribulation' many people will experience. If we don't have our foundation built on the Kingdom of God, we will fall for his deception. These days there is a counterfeit new age corruption that is gathering together all religions whether true or false, into a one world religion. Don't be deceived. The gods of this world are getting together to call true Christians to be 'haters' if we don't join them. Our true God will cause us to know the truth.

John 8.31-32 *Then Jesus said to those Jews who believed Him, If you abide in My word, you are My disciples indeed. And you shall know the truth, and the truth shall make you free.*

Revelation 21.7-8 *He who overcomes shall inherit all things, and I will be his God and he shall be My son.* .

The mark of the antichrist is on those who live for themselves; Verse 8, *the cowardly, unbelieving, abominable, murderers, sexually immoral, sorcerers, idolaters, all liars shall have their part in the lake which burns with fire and brimstone, which is the second death.* .

Matthew 7.24 *Therefore whoever hears these sayings of Mine, and does them, I will liken him to a wise man who built his house on the rock and the rain descended, the floods came, and the winds blew and beat on that house; and it did not fall, for it was founded on the rock. But everyone who hears these sayings of Mine, and does not do them, will be like a foolish man who built his house on the sand and the rain descended, the floods came, and the winds blew and beat on that house; and it fell. And great was its fall.* Don't Be the Foolish Man.

Ephesians 2.19-22 *therefore, you are no longer strangers and foreigners, but fellow citizens with the saints and members of the household of God, having been built on the foundation of the apostles and prophets, Jesus Christ Himself being the chief corner stone, in whom the whole building, being fitted together, grows into a holy temple in the Lord, in whom you also are being built together for a dwelling place of God in the Spirit. .*

This next excerpt is taken from the Spirit Filled Life Bible, the New King James version, Thomas Nelson publishers, General Editor Jack W. Hayford, Litt.D. copyright 1991. Notes on page 2001.

"#666... Six in Biblical numerology is the number of man, just short of perfection, whereas seven is the number of perfection. So, 666 may refer to the quintessential humanist who will probably go along with the lies. The forehead represents our will, our volition, while the hand represents our activities. The Bible warns us that if we have the mark of the beast, we will then share the terrible fate of the beast. No one should fear 'accidentally' taking the mark of the beast. To do so involves 'worshiping' the beast [Rev 13.15], and the decision will be clear enough that it will be a life-and-death matter. However, we should still be sensitive today, for if we regard the forehead as the center of the will; the hand symbolic of what we do, it seems that the mark is more than some technological device. What we are really talking about here is 'who gets our allegiance'. In a real respect, the spirit of antichrist is active already".

John 2.18]. Will we give to the spirit of the world, our minds and our work? If our allegiance is to God, we will not serve the antichrist spirit, and we will not take his mark, meaning that we will not worship him. Who is this beast, this antichrist and this man of sin and what is his image; see Rev chapter 17...?

We Will Not Worship This Beast!

Refusing the mark of the beast has everything to do with the One to Whom we pledge our allegiance, and our relationship with Jesus. On the other hand, it is a religious spirit that demands we adhere to, *their philosophy and vain deceit, after the traditions of men, after the rudiments of the world and not after Christ* [Colossians 2.8].

For a true born-again Christian, It's Just Not Gonna Happen! <u>We must never cower </u>to this false prophet; this liar who assumes he has power over God's people. He has none!

Romans 9.5 If we say that we have no sin, we make him a liar and the truth is not in us. Who is a liar but he that denies that Yahshua has come in the flesh, and that, *He is God.* Any that denies Him, has the spirit of antichrist.

After All Is Said and Done, We Realize That the Mark, the Seal and the Sign Are All about Who We Will Worship. Is Jesus Our Lord and King or Will We Bow Before Satan? Do We Want the Seal of Antichrist and the Lake of Fire? Or Heaven's Seal of Love for Eternity.

Here are some verses to be kept in context about worshiping the beast and his image. Remember the image means the works of anything. Everything has an image...Its nature and character; what does it do, what does it stand for? That's the image. Very often there will be a statue as in Daniel 3.15, but not always. Revelation 13.4,12,15; 14. 9,11; 16.2; 10.20 speaks of the beast and his image.

In Jeremiah 44, Israel was in Egypt and worshiped the queen of heaven. This is not a new one. People are still giving her place in their heart as she overrides Jesus. Revelation 17 reveals who she is and she proclaims:

Revelation 18:7 for *she says in her heart, 'I sit as queen, and am no widow, and will not see sorrow".* No, she won't, she has many lovers. But then there is judgment day...

92

Worship God and receive eternal life. Worship the beast and it will be eternal damnation.

Please read 1 John, especially 2.22-27. Whoever will receive Him has this promise;

John 1.12 *But as many as received Him, to them He gave the right to become children of God, to those who believe in His name who were born, not of blood, nor of the will of the flesh, nor of the will of man, but of God.* .

We can *know that we know Him,* because we have His anointing. Remember this also,

Colossians 2.8 Beware *of traditions.* And here's another -

Isaiah 26.20-27.1 *Come, my people, enter your chambers, and shut your doors behind you; Hide yourself, as it were, for a little moment, Until the indignation is past. For behold, the Lord comes out of His place to punish the inhabitants of the earth for their iniquity; The earth will also disclose her blood, and will no more cover her slain* [Matthew 25.31] .

So, Where Do We Hide?

Psalm 32.7 *You are my hiding place; You shall preserve me from trouble; You shall surround me with songs of deliverance.* .

Psalm 119.114 *You are my hiding place and my shield; I hope in Your word.* Did You Get That?

Psalm 46.1-2 *God is our refuge and strength, A very present help in trouble. Therefore, we will not fear.* .

And from The Passion Translation by Brian Simmons

Psalm 46.1-2 *God, you're such a powerful place to hide, a proven help in time of trouble; more than enough and always available whenever I need you.*

Vs 7 The mighty Lord of Angel-Armies is on our side. Be silent and stop your striving. TPT Bible SO.....

2 Timothy 2.11-12 *This is a faithful saying for if we died with Him, we shall also live with Him. If we endure, we shall also reign with Him.* .

93

Colossians 1.27 *To them God willed to make known what are the riches of the glory of this mystery among the Gentiles* <u>*which is Christ in you,*</u> *the hope of glory.* This hope is not for the rapture, it is Christ in you.

Revelation 22.1-5 And *he showed me a pure river of water of life, clear as crystal, proceeding from the throne of God and of the Lamb. In the middle of its street, and on either side of the river, was the tree of life, which bore twelve fruits, each tree yielding its fruit every month. The leaves of the tree were for the healing of the nations. And there shall be no more curse, but the throne of God and of the Lamb shall be in it, and His servants shall serve Him. They shall see His face,* and *His name shall be on their foreheads. There shall be no night there. They need no lamp nor light of the sun, for the Lord God gives them light. And they shall reign forever and ever.* .

Here are some Scriptures I left out this second time Exodus 12.13-14, 8-16,19; Colossians 1.13-14; Deuteronomy 6.6-10,11.18-20; Numbers 15.40; I John 3.1-2, 4.13 Please forgive my repetition.

Tidbits or Pages...

I'm learning to live by the pages of God
To walk in trust and faith
To go each day to the Word and prayer
And surrender to His love and grace
No tidbits will do - I need it all
Cause I'm called to radical love
A tenacious life in Christ it is
In Him I live and move
To give all that I am and all I can be
To walk in His glorious way
The desire of my life, The desire of my heart
I surrender all that is me
I'm learning to live by the power of God
To walk in trust and faith
To go each day to the Word and prayer
And surrender to His love and grace.

Please read Deuteronomy 4.30-35.
    '*Take Him a nation from the midst of another nation*'.
And Now... He took the New Man Creation out of the midst of the nation of the world for His glorious purpose. I pray you will understand what saith the Word of God. Please read it for yourself.
        Oh, Hallelujah, Our God Reigns.

    I'm No Longer a Slave to Sin, God Opened the Door to His Kingdom and Invited Me In. Oh, What Joy to Know We Belong to the Family of God and He Will Never Abandon Us.

95

DANIEL CHAPTER 9

This Revelation was written in the symbolic language of the prophets; a book of prophecy and metaphors, signs, allegories, analogies. The credibility of the Bible stands or falls on prophetic accuracy.

I hope you will read this with patience. I tried to contain some of this but there is so much evidence, it was very hard. I tried to keep things in order and if I repeated, it was so that the paragraph would refer to the correct issue. All too often a verse or even in context can be misinterpreted because someone says they have 'insight'. But if it can't be compared with other proof text, or even by known history, then it must be further researched or scrapped.

In prophecy there is a divine time line; events i.e. 'moeds'; God's precise timing for Kingdom events. Daniel was given massive visions of world events. It was revealed to Daniel that the 70 years of Babylonian captivity was now finished. It's interesting that at the time of this restoration of Israel, he was given a deeper revelation of another restoration, and the coming of the Messiah. If you have never considered these verses, well,

Daniel 9.23-27 are the verses that are central to the greatest controversy in the Christian Church.

Verse 10.1 says Daniel understood there was a time appointed for all these prophecies. For some he saw the fulfillment of in his lifetime. For other prophecies it would be centuries and incur major nations.

Galatians 4.4 In *the fulness of time*.... And Mark 1.15, *The time is fulfilled*... What time is this that God is speaking of to Daniel? It is a precise Kingdom time line when Jesus would arrive on earth and bring His Kingdom with Him.

This chapter is a part of the research I've done over a period of more than 30 years. There is much more but I had to stop somewhere. I am aware that some people have certain conclusions about this subject, so I hope you will pray your way thru all this and see what more God has to say. It may be hard to accept some things I've said here - but if it is true, God will help you break thru some questions you may have concerning my conclusions, and which are also based on many other's research which confirmed so much of what I had already concluded. If I am wrong, I beseech God to correct me.

Remember Ephesians 4.11-16. As I said before, I greatly desired to know God and to know His truth. Because I had been reading the Word and was trying to understand what it was really saying; some time in 1974 I began to question what was being taught about this subject of a rapture and I prayed, 'God please show me where I'm wrong and show me Your truth'.

In researching Scripture, it was a slow process of many years, and some things came from many other resources to confirm what I thought the Bible was saying; and there was so much witness to me because of the church I was raised in. When I was a little girl, I had a great desire to be an archeologist, dig, dig, dig. God told me He put that desire in me and He made me an archeologist in His Word. Dig, dig, dig.

Please read Ephesians 1.17-19; 3.14-21.

See Revelation 13 and 17. Horns means power and the 'beast' is one in authority. So much is revealed in Scripture if only there was research into it. There is a dynasty, empire if you will, that fits this description very well. Remember a woman in prophecy is a church. We don't need to fear what is coming. Trust in God.

So, here is what I have concluded after much research, about this most, yes, controversial subject of all; Daniel 9.24-27, the most pivotal Scripture in the Bible concerning the first coming of the Lord Jesus into our world and what He would accomplish. We must depend on the absolute correct interpretation of these verses just as much as the rest of the Word of God, because it had been set up to define the ministry of Jesus in the earth hundreds of years before He came to our world. We must be careful of how we understand the Word.

We Know How Some People Deliberately Misuse The Words of Jesus, Even to Deny His Virgin Birth And His Resurrection - and Pervert Other Passages.

Daniel 9.22 *And he* [Gabriel] *informed me, and talked with me, and said, "O Daniel, I have now come forth to give you skill to understand. .*

And Daniel 10.1 *The third year of Cyrus king of Persia a message was revealed to Daniel, whose name was called Belteshazzar. The message was true, but the appointed time was long; and he understood the message, and had understanding of the vision.* So, He understood what it meant even though it would not be fulfilled for many centuries. So get out your Bible and follow along.

In verse 24, All 70 weeks are determined for Daniel's people - not for the world - only his people, Israel, and - upon his [Daniel's] holy city - Jerusalem. Verse 23 *Therefore understand the matter, and consider the vision*

Now verses 24... *70 weeks are determined...*
to finish the transgression...
to make an end to sin...
reconciliation for iniquity....
to bring everlasting righteousness...
to seal up the vision and prophecy...
and to anoint the most Holy.

Question...What vision and prophecy had to be sealed? SEAL to close up, to make an end [to the prophecy of Daniel 9.23-27]. It seems to me that God meant for this prophetic Scripture to remain 'sealed', not to be divided into different times, especially the last verse. I take this to mean that all these verses would be fulfilled in its proper time. The understanding of the prophetic day for a year helps to give understanding. See Genesis 29.26-28. *Fulfill her week and we will give you this also for the service which you will serve with me yet seven other years.*1 week = 7 years; and Ezekiel 4.4-6, *I have appointed you each day for a year.*

The Jews understood this prophetic principle.

Daniel 9: *Seventy weeks are determined upon your people and upon your holy city. From the going forth of the commandment to restore and build Jerusalem* (the city), *unto the Messiah, the Prince, there shall be seven weeks,* [49 years] - *The street shall be built again, and the wall even in troublous times.* This is understanding that King Cyrus allowed the Jews to return to Jerusalem to rebuild their temple in the fifth century BC. Amid horrible persecution, they finished it; then Nehemiah came and restored the wall around the city. At this time, he also rebuilt the city. The city alone took 49 years. *This is exactly when the timeline would begin.*

Ezra and Nehemiah will attest to this. After the wall was restored, Nehemiah went back to Babylon. Then after some time the king gave him permission to return and rebuild the city. It took [Seven weeks], 49 years for Nehemiah to rebuild the city as he and Ezra also restored the law and priesthood. The temple was already finished.

In the New Scofield's Reference Bible page 913, note 1 - [quote] "The entire prophecy is concerned primarily with Daniel's 'people' and their 'holy city' - i.e. Israel and Jerusalem". And yet in note 7 he declares that the 'final' week will be separated for the Church age and then comes the future 'prince - antichrist'. How Can We Have It Both Ways?

The prophecy tells us that when the command to Nehemiah went forth to build the city, [not the temple, verse 25], to Messiah would be 7 weeks and 62 weeks; 69 prophetic weeks or 483 days/years, and then another week to make seventy. *70 weeks are determined for your [Daniel's] people.* I reiterate... this prophecy was only for Jerusalem, so, why was the time in weeks broken up like this? Because they were defined for 3 different purposes.

In 538 BC Cyrus decreed to rebuild the temple. 300 years before he was born, he was named to do this [Isaiah 44.28]. Then in 457 BC Artaxerxes [Esther's son, Xerxes was her king] gave permission for Nehemiah to go back to Jerusalem and rebuild the wall; then after spending some time back in Babylon, He came again to rebuild the city of Jerusalem. So we count from that edict, 483 years until Messiah shows up at the River Jordan in 27 AD. The 49 years of building the city was pointed out so that we would know this is where the time line would begin.

Nehemiah 6.15 *Now the city was large and spacious, but the people in it were few, and the houses were not rebuilt.* [people were not bringing the tithes to the warehouse and so the priests had to leave the city to plant and grow their own food. Nehemiah fixed that! It was more appropriate for the priests to live in the city.

Nehemiah 7:4 *The city was large and spacious, but the people in it were few, and the houses were not rebuilt.*

From the time they began to rebuild the city it took 7 weeks, '49 years' and then plus 62 weeks, 483 years brings us to AD 27. Jesus appeared and was baptized in the Jordan.

He was 30 years old, the age when a man would enter the office of the priesthood. Jesus was actually born before 4 BC. Historians say that king Herod died in

4 BC. So, Jesus had to be born before Herod died. *The time is fulfilled, the Kingdom of God is at hand.* Galatians 4.4 *When the fulness of time had come..., God sent forth His Son.* Now, what time had to be fulfilled? Daniel's 69 weeks.

So, the time in weeks was broken up like this, because they were defined for 3 different purposes. The last week [verse 27] was lived out as Jesus chose His 12 disciples and taught them Kingdom principles for 3½ years and reminded them of the promise of Jeremiah 31.31-34.

The 70th Week Was the Time of Jesus' Ministry. Daniel 9.27 He fulfilled vs 24 and the Spirit anointed the 120 at Pentecost.

Please read it all. This new covenant would override keeping the law of do's and don'ts because first...

Malachi 3:1 And *the Lord, whom you seek, Will suddenly come to His temple, Even the Messenger of the covenant, In whom you delight. Behold, He is coming, saith the Lord of hosts. . So* Who came to bring the new covenant - of course it was Jesus. None of God's people will welcome the man of sin. [but the pharisees didn't receive Jesus either].

Jeremiah 31:31-33 *But this is the covenant that I will make with the house of Israel after those days, says the Lord:* [after the law of Moses was fulfilled]*, I will put My law in their minds, and write it on their hearts;* and see Jeremiah 24.7 and Isaiah 61.8*.; and Hebrews 8.8.* Who made this promise? God. After what days? When the disciples shared the good news and people were saved and baptized in the Holy Spirit. Remember the three thousand [Acts 3.41]. Anointing came with Power.

Then in the midst of the week, because He was crucified, the sacrifice of the lamb in the temple ceased being of any value. The final Lamb shed the Blood of redemption not just for Israel, but for the whole world. It became an abomination for the priests to continue, and an insult to the Father Who had just sacrificed His beloved Son.

Daniel 9:27 *He* [Jesus] *shall confirm the covenant with many for one week* [He preached the principles of this New Covenant to thousands of people], *But in the middle of the week He shall bring an end to sacrifice and offering* [in the temple - when He became the final sacrifice], *and for the overspreading* [to cover the whole issue] *of abominations he shall make it desolate* [ruined], *even until the consummation* [in the end Titus destroyed the temple], *and that determined* [prophesied beforehand] *shall be poured upon the desolate* [to devastate, to make destitute, destroy the meaning of]. From Moses to Christ - the law - It was finished.

But some have taken this verse 27 and broke it in half to substantiate their theory of a 'rapture'; that before the last 3½ years, Christians would be taken off the earth so they don't get caught in the great tribulation. A very nice deception to keep believers from learning to trust God explicitly; that no matter what happens in their life, God is still in charge. See my chapter on the 'rapture'. The Word of Truth. [See 1 Thess 1.10; 5.9].

Jesus Is Not Coming Back for A Wimpy Fearful Bride.

Revelation 19 His *wife has made herself ready*...ready to rule with Him! Ready to sit at His right hand and judge the nations, especially to smash satan under our feet.

So to continue for Daniel 9; In 538 BC, Cyrus decreed for the Jews to go back to Jerusalem and rebuild their temple. They quit after two years because the harassment from neighboring people who were not Jews, was too powerful. Those people did not want the Jews to come back and rebuild their temple, so after 2 years, only the foundation was completed. Many years passed between the time Cyrus gave permission and the temple was finished. God sent Haggai to get them moving. They started again and finished in 515 BC. Several kings passed thru in the meantime. Some kings stopped the work and some kings let it continue.

In my book, The Temple of God Restored, I wrote about the history of the second temple finished in 515 BC. As compared to how God builds our temple,

1Cor 3.16 *Know ye not that you are the temple of God.*

Nehemiah came and rebuilt the wall and gates in 52 days, then had to return to Babylon. After some time, he was allowed to go back to rebuild the city. This is where the time line begins. It took him 7 weeks, 49 years to rebuild the city. From the time he started we count another 69 weeks, 483 years till Messiah. [See verse 25].

From the time Artaxerxes gave permission for Nehemiah in 457 BC to go back and rebuild the city we count 69 weeks, a year for a day; 7 times 69= 483 years until Messiah. Jesus was born in 4BC, [before king Herod died] and was about 30 years old in 27 AD when He shows up at the River Jordan to be baptized.

Now there is one more week, 7 years which comes to the 490 years fulfilled. During this last week [Daniel 9. 27], it says, 'in the midst', in the middle of the week [after 3½ years of teaching His disciples what the Kingdom of God was all about; read the gospels] he is cut off, sacrificed on the cross.

TO FINISH THE TRANSGRESSION. What Adam did.

1 Corinthians 15.45 *Thus it is written, The first man Adam became a living being (an individual personality);* [But he brought death to all of mankind] *to the last Adam (Christ) became a life-giving Spirit [restoring the dead to life].* Amplified Bible

The Broken Law Must Be Justified.
Adam Brought Death, Jesus Brought Life.

103

Galatians 2:16 *knowing that a man is not justified by the works of the law but by faith in Jesus Christ, even we have believed in Christ Jesus, that we might be justified by faith in Christ and not by the works of the law; for by the works of the law no flesh shall be justified. .*

TO MAKE AN END TO SINS

2 Corinthians 5.21 *For He made Him who knew no sin to be sin for us, that we might become the righteousness of God in Him.*

RECONCILIATION FOR INIQUITY

Ephesians 2.16 *and that He might reconcile them both* [Jew and Gentile] *to God in one body through the cross,*

TO BRING EVERLASTING RIGHTEOUSNESS

1 Peter 2.24 *Who Himself bore our sins in His own body on the tree, that we, having died to sins, might live for righteousness.*

TO SEAL UP THE VISION AND PROPHECY

John 19.28 *So when Jesus had received the sour wine, He said, "It is finished!" And bowing His head, He gave up His spirit. .*

AND TO ANOINT THE MOST HOLY

[Not to anoint Jesus, He was already the anointed Son of God].

Acts 2.1-4. On the feast of Pentecost, God's Holy Spirit breathed His life on the 120; anointed His most holy people.

1 Peter 1.15-16 *but as He who called you is holy, you also be holy in all your conduct, because it is written, "Be holy, for I am holy." .* He has made us His holy people

Luke 22. 20.. At the Last Supper Jesus declared;

And in like manner, He took the cup after supper, saying, This cup is the new testament or covenant [ratified] *in My blood, which is shed (poured out) for you. This is My blood of the New Testament/covenant* [Amplified Bible]. This is the covenant Jesus is confirming from Daniel 9.27&Jer 31.31.

I hope you will read these verses and ones following for they show the fulfillment of this prophecy.

Malachi 3.1, *I will send my messenger to prepare the way...the messenger of the* [new] *covenant.* In verse 27, *And He,* [only Jesus], *shall confirm the covenant. .*

I shared about this in the last chapter.

This was not the covenant God made with Abraham, the old covenant of circumcision or for a son, or for the land. The covenant of laws that Moses taught Israel in the desert; this would pass away. Now is the new covenant prophesied in Jeremiah 31.31 and several other places, *Behold the days come, says the Lord, that I will make a new covenant with the house of Israel and with the house of Judah. I will write my laws on their heart.* Jeremiah 32.40 *I will make an everlasting covenant; v.39 I will give them one heart;* Isaiah 61.8 I *will make an everlasting covenant. .*

These are all future promises made centuries after He fulfilled the first covenant with Abraham to bring his people into the promised land. See also Hebrews 10.9-10; *He took away the first* [the law of Moses] *to establish the second.* and Ezekiel 36.26; 37.21-28. a covenant of peace, an everlasting covenant. No one makes covenant with Israel except their Messiah, as He did in the past. And this covenant is passed down to born again Gentiles through our faith in Jesus.

After the death of Jesus, there remained yet another 3½ years to complete the 70th week/years. This new covenant had to be confirmed with the Jews and everyone else who accepted salvation through the blood of Jesus. This covenant must be confirmed for one week. For 3½ years, Jesus taught His disciples what the Kingdom was all about - hence we have the four gospels as their witness. After His resurrection -

105

Matthew 28.19 *Go ye therefore and teach all nations.*
The next 3½ years were not to be separated from this week, this 7-year prophecy. It is still only pertaining to Israel, Daniel's people and his holy city. We continue to count a day for a year. 69 weeks plus the last 1 week we have the 70 weeks from Dan 9.24. *70 weeks are determined upon thy people.* This is an exclusive application concerning the Jewish nation only, specifically the city of Jerusalem. This prophecy was fulfilled in its time; it does not concern the whole world in the last days of tribulation. See what happened after Jesus was 'cut off', crucified, and for the last 3½ years...

The Next 3½ Years Were Fulfilled Beginning in Acts 1.8; Not Delegated to the End of Time.

Only Jesus could do this. *But you shall receive power when the Holy Spirit has come upon you; and you shall be witnesses to Me in Jerusalem, and in all Judea and Samaria, and* [then] *to the end of the earth.* [Amplified Bible]

Now the day of Pentecost - once again, God breathed on His people and flames of Spirit fire anointed the 120. In Acts 2.5 God sent Jews from every nation to witness His first outpouring of the revelation of the New Covenant. They didn't know that's why they were there! 3000 were saved and then went home! Now to finish this last 3½ years, Acts 1.8 the disciples would witness first in Jerusalem, in all Judea; then on to Samaria and to the uttermost parts of the earth. But when did those last 3½ years come to a close? Perhaps the disciples were not aware, but God was. Chapter 8 discloses the plan. It is most enlightening to read the book of Acts to see how God led the first world revival to share His plan of redemption and the new covenant; and it all began as those last 3½ years witnessing to the Jews in Jerusalem were finished and the disciples went to the world.

They Had the Word and They Had the Anointing.

The Two Witnesses; the Believer and the Word -
To Go to the Jew first, then into All the World.
This New Covenant Is Explained in Paul's Letters.

This was to fulfill this last 3½ years of Daniel's prophecy first, before going to the Gentiles. When Jesus said it was finished, I do believe He was referring to Daniel's prophecy; to take on the sin nature of man, to satisfy the law of sin and death. It was to bring about the New Covenant. He knew His disciples would be faithful so that the last 3½ weeks/days/years, would be fulfilled and this prophecy would be sealed, finished. SO NOW....

Acts 8.1-4 *At that time a great persecution arose against the church which was at Jerusalem; and they were all scattered throughout the regions of Judea and Samaria, except the Apostles... As for Saul, he made havoc of the church, entering every house, and dragging off men and women, committing them to prison. Therefore, those who were scattered went everywhere preaching the word. Then Philip went down to the city of Samaria and preached Christ to them.* [Just as they were told]. Peter and John went to Samaria also but verse 25, they returned to Jerusalem. The last 3½ years of verse 27 were finished, *He confirmed the covenant with many for one week.* Daniel's prophecy was totally fulfilled [verse 27] by 37 AD.

Now Saul was to have a 'moment' to challenge his fury at this religion that was 'blaspheming' his God and his law. He would not have it! But God had His own plans for this arrogant 'in charge' man. In this 'moment', God exploded all of Saul's plans to annihilate this new religion, and threw him down off his high horse. Now blinded in his own little Kingdom, God brought him into the Kingdom of light. Ananias, His name means 'grace of God', was sent to Saul. He received his sight by grace, and God made him to be Paul [which means 'little'], Paul, anointed with

God's grace wrote with God's mercy and grace to those who would inherit the Kingdom.

Galatians 29 *And when James, Cephas, and John, who seemed to be pillars, perceived the grace that had been given to me, they gave me* [Paul] *and Barnabas the right hand of fellowship, that we should go to the Gentiles and they to the circumcised.* .

Now to the Jews Paul spoke,

Acts 13.46 It *was necessary that the word of God should first have been spoken to you, but seeing you put it from you, and judge yourselves unworthy of everlasting life, lo, we turn to the gentiles.* .

Romans 1.*16 I am not ashamed of the gospel...the power of God...to the Jew first, and also to the Greek.* .

Acts 12.2 Herod killed James and imprisoned Peter but he escaped. The Bible only mentions the deaths of two Apostles, James who was put to death by Herod Agrippa I in 44 AD and Judas Iscariot who committed suicide shortly after the death of Christ. The details of the deaths of three of the Apostles (John, the Beloved, Bartholomew and Simon the Canaanite) are not known at all, either by tradition or early historians. The deaths of the other seven Apostles are known by tradition or the writings of early Christian historians. According to traditions and the Bible, eight of the Apostles died as Martyrs. At least two of the Apostles, Peter and Andrew were crucified.

Peter was crucified upside down. Some believe he died in Rome. They say Peter and Paul both died in Rome, but Paul was in Rome, in prison for several years. In all his writings, he never mentioned Peter was there. It would have been so disrespectful for him not to mention a fellow Apostle in the same city, as he named so many others. The Romans in Jerusalem were fond of crucifixion and so was the martyrdom of Peter. Most of the Apostles went to other countries. Here are possibilities.

Andrew went to Greece; Matthew to Ethiopia; Thomas

went to India; Jude (Thaddeus) according to tradition Jude taught in Armenia, Syria and Persia where he was martyred. Tradition tells us he was buried in Kara Kalisa in what is now Iran. John was exiled in Patmos after he was boiled in oil. Obviously, it didn't kill him for God had other plans for His apostle of love; the magnificent vision of the end time purposes of our Creator Who has every right to bring about the final judgment of His people. He has made every resource available. The last 3½ years were fulfilled beginning in Acts 1.8 to bring His creation into relationship with Himself, but so sad to say too many want to do their own thing. But to His believers He says...

Romans 1.29-*13 Let love be without hypocrisy. Abhor what is evil. Cling to what is good. Be kindly affectionate to one another with brotherly love, in honor giving preference to one another; not lagging in diligence, fervent in spirit, serving the Lord; rejoicing in hope, patient in tribulation, continuing steadfastly in prayer...* .

To continue with the sacrifice of blood on the altar in the temple for the sins of Israel even for one more week, after Jesus was crucified for the sin of the world and forever; was an affront to the Father Who had just sacrificed His precious Son. So, in AD 70 came the end, the consummation, the destruction of the temple. *For the overspreading of abominations* [temple sacrifice] *he shall make it desolate*. The ritual sacrifice of the lamb on Passover would no longer have meaning. The sacrifice in the temple was made of no value [desolate, it became idolatry to continue] because of the blood of Jesus - *even until the* consummation of all things, [the end] *poured out on the desolate,* the Jews. *He shall cause the sacrifice* [in the temple] *and oblation* [tributes, donations] *to cease.*

In AD70, *the people of the prince*, Titus totally destroyed this second temple that Zerubbabel built in the 5th century [read about this in the book of Ezra]. There would be no more sacrifice of the lamb on the altar. The

Jews went into exile in 70AD and were blinded to the truth of their Messiah for 2000 years. But in this century, God has brought them back to their land and their Messiah is being revealed. Now. As much as I believe Daniel's prophecy has been fulfilled; there is sometimes a duel fulfilment in the Old Testament and the New. So, as Matthew 24 speaks of the abomination of desolation, a distressful time just before Jesus comes back

Many will say here or there He is, but He will only 'appear in the sky' with His angels and loud trumpet to gather His Elect.

1 Thessalonians 4:16-17 *For the Lord Himself will descend from heaven with a shout, with the voice of an archangel, and with the trumpet of God. And the dead in Christ will rise first. <u>Then we who are alive and remain</u> shall be caught up together with them in the clouds to meet the Lord in the air.*

Oh yes, and there may be an antichrist standing in the temple. Just keep your eyes and heart on the real God.

Just remember Who it is that we worship.

Some things were never meant to be
We make mistakes in the course of our life
We sometimes pursue a forbidden path
Not knowing the trouble out-of-sight
We try and try to make it work
Blinded by self-satisfaction
We ride along on stress and fear
And never take any action
We live a life of loneliness
As though it will be alright
But in the final course of life
It dissolves into the night.
So Lord Jesus, I give to You
The life You have given me
For the plans and purpose
You already have
Cause that's what I was meant to be.

He's Coming Back To
Redeem His World.
Oh Yes, Come Lord Jesus.

TWO PRINCES

As I said before, there is a prophecy in the Old Testament, in the most controversial Scripture in the whole Bible. It is a prophecy revealed to Daniel, that told the precise time of the Lord's ministry on the earth. Sadly, the ones who possessed all the books of the Old Testament did not, or would not recognize the coming of Israel's Redeemer. For centuries Israel prayed for a Messiah, but where He was revealed in their Scriptures, they would not believe. This prophecy revealed the time He would come, what He would do, and when He would leave. All this in Daniel 9.23-10.1... of which I shared in the previous chapter.

And I want to point out that Jesus brought the truth of this Scripture to His disciples on the road to Emmaus, as I'm sure these two would pass on to the other disciples what Jesus shared.

Luke 24.25-28 *Then He said to them, O foolish ones, and slow of heart to believe in all that the prophets have spoken! Ought not the Christ to have suffered these things and to enter into His glory? And beginning at Moses and all the Prophets, He expounded to them in <u>all the Scriptures the things concerning Himself</u>. And the disciples' eyes were opened.* That's why later on, they would understand Acts 1.8 to know about the close of the last week. .

So, we can all go along with the crowd who will put their faith in the words of other people, or we can seek for the truth from God's Word and His Holy Spirit.

John 5.39-*40 You search the Scriptures, for in them you think you have eternal life; and these are they which testify of Me. But you are not willing to come to Me that you may have life.* .

2 Timothy 3.16 *All Scripture is given by inspiration of God, and is profitable for doctrine, for reproof, for correction, for instruction in righteousness, that the man of God may be complete, thoroughly equipped for every good work.*

James 1.5-8 *If any of you lacks wisdom, let him ask of God, who gives to all liberally and without reproach, and it will be given to him. But let him ask in faith, with no doubting, for he who doubts is like a wave of the sea driven and tossed by the wind. Or let not that man suppose that he will receive anything from the Lord; he is a double-minded man, unstable in all his ways.* .

It behooves us all to search the Scripture for God to reveal His wisdom and understanding. No, I am *not* infallible. God has given me the incentive to search until I find. I am never satisfied to just read the Word. I have to know what it means. I was reading Psalm 19 and saw verse 13, *Keep me back from presumptions sins.* The Lord reminded me of Job, how they all thought they 'knew' the Lord; but what did God have to say.

Job 40:1-*2 Moreover the Lord answered Job, and said:*

"Shall the one who contends with the Almighty correct Him? He who rebukes God, let him answer it. They presumed to know God, the Lord of the universe.

They Were All Brought to the Carpet!

We should make sure to rely on God's wisdom and not our own imaginations.

John 8.31-32 Then *Jesus said to those Jews who believed Him, If you abide in My word, you are My disciples indeed. And you shall know the truth, and the truth shall make you free.* I am not ashamed of the gospel and the truth it conveys to all who will explore it for the truth that makes us free. There are many resources to research - Dictionary, Strong's Concordance, other Bible translations are used along with God's wisdom; and the writings of men and women of God who have listened and researched.

And God's Holy Spirit Who Lives in Us, Will Always Prove What Is True and Reliable; to Confirm Our Conclusions.

Scripture always proves itself by 2 or 3 witnesses.

Daniel 9.23-10.1 The prophecy revealed to Daniel, he understood that it was true, but the time appointed was long into the future. *But he had understanding of the vision.* And we know that God gives us understanding of His Word in these end times. He does not keep His people in the dark, and I assure you that I'm not the only one who now understands what this is revealing. I expect my readers to evaluate these things by the Holy Spirit, and also understand what God is telling us. I will highlight what I understand it is saying.

Please Forgive My Repetition.

Daniel 9.24 *Seventy weeks are determined upon thy people and thy holy city.* This prophecy is for Israel and Jerusalem, not for the whole world. This in a nutshell It tells us exactly when the Messiah will come and what He will do. Finish the transgression, [remember He said...*It is Finished* (The law)]; make an end of sin, reconciliation for iniquity, bring in everlasting righteousness, seal up the vision and prophecy, and anoint the most holy.

These verses are the foretaste of the prophecy - exactly what will happen and when. To repeat these verses again would be redundant. So. Just this one.

V.9.25 *Know therefore and understand, that from the going forth of the command to restore and build Jerusalem Until Messiah the Prince, there shall be seven weeks. The street shall be built again, and the wall, Even in troublesome times.*

And now separating the 49 years of building the city, there is three score and 2 weeks. From the time the city of Jerusalem began to be built, it would be all together 483 years to Messiah the Prince. At this precise fulfilment of time, Jesus arrived at the river Jordan to be baptized by John [Galatians 4.4; Matthew 3]. Through His baptism, Jesus so identified with sinners for the first time - *To Fulfill all Righteousness.*

This prophecy is for [please note] Daniel's people and their holy city, Jerusalem. Verse 24, Who shed His blood for our sins, said it was finished, and made us righteous in the eyes of God? Only Jesus. We are now reconciled to our heavenly Father. All this was done to bring an end - to what, let's find out. *And to anoint the most holy...* well Jesus was already anointed. So, who are the most holy? It is God's people. First the 120 in the upper room - then?

In Verse 25 Messiah Is Called the Prince.

Now There Is a Second Prince.

Vs 26 *And the people of the [other] prince who will come will destroy the city and the sanctuary.* [Amplified Bible]

Titus's father was a Roman General stationed in Turkey, north of Israel. He was planning on stopping the Jewish rebellion in Jerusalem but the Roman Caesar had just died and he was recalled to Rome. He charged his son Titus to fulfill His plans. So, from Turkey, 'prince' Titus descended on Jerusalem and Daniel 9:26, And *the people of the prince who is to come shall destroy the city and the sanctuary. The end of it shall be with a flood, and till the end of the war desolations are determined.* .

In 70 AD Titus and his army of Muslims and other men in Turkey's regiments, declared war on Jerusalem. They came down like a flood and the city was totally destroyed. The desolations were determined *for the overspreading of their abominations*. Because of Israel's unbelief, the consequence would be - *that determined would be poured out on the desolate* [see Jeremiah 7.34].

They continued in the same ritual of the sacrificial lamb as though Jesus, the Lamb of God, had never existed; had never made the ultimate sacrifice for them. So, this tabernacle built in the 5th century was torn apart stone by stone. I'm sure the Roman soldiers who were already in Jerusalem, also took part in this. The people were either slaughtered or taken into slavery. The determined consummation was poured out on the desolate. Dragged into slavery with only the clothes on their back; for 2000 Years they scattered all over the earth.

For Their Unbelief They Became Desolate of God.

Verse 26 And *the people of the prince that shall come shall destroy the city and the sanctuary, the end of it shall be with a flood, and till the end of the war desolations are determined*.

It has to be Titus who destroyed Jerusalem in 70AD. He did not make a covenant with Israel. He destroyed the city, the temple, and murdered thousands of Jews and sent the rest of Israel into exile.

There Are Only 2 Princes Mentioned in this Prophecy, The Messiah Jesus - and Titus.

Vs 25 - Messiah the Prince - Vs 26- Titus the prince

Titus came down like a flood. He destroyed the city and the sanctuary and sent Israel into exile.

So, let's break this down. Malachi 3.1 *the messenger of the covenant whom you delight in.* Believing that this is speaking of a future antichrist 'prince' who will make a covenant with Israel, will deny the truth of God's Word. If this is the prince who makes covenant with Israel and sits in the temple,

When Will He Come Down Like A Flood And Destroy The City And The People As It Plainly Reads?

Now for the 70th week; remember it is 7 years; for 3½ years, Jesus taught His disciples what the Kingdom was all about. Only God makes covenant with people. And what covenant did Jesus confirm? Well again, it was the New Covenant He had already revealed in Isaiah 61.8; Jer 31.31; Ezek 36.26; Heb 8.6-13. *'I will write my laws on your heart'*. So, this was a prophecy given in the Old Testament in so many places, so that it could be confirmed as many other prophecies in the Word of God have been. And it was fulfilled by Messiah the Prince.

The Law of Moses Was Fulfilled by Jesus Walking in Obedience to the Letter of the Law, Then Brought to Its Fulfillment by His Blood Shed on the Cross. It's very probable that Adam was taught he was to worship God alone; but his eyes were distracted by the premise – he could be like God. He forgot he was already created in the image of God.

Here is the prophecy of the new covenant that Jesus brought and confirmed from the foregoing Scriptures.

Hebrews 8 *Behold, the days are coming, says the Lord, when I will make a new covenant with the house of Israel and with the house of Judah — not according to the covenant that I made with their fathers in the day that I took them by the hand to lead them out of the land of Egypt, My covenant which they broke, though I was a husband to them, says the Lord. But this is the covenant that I will make with the house of Israel after those days, says the Lord I will put My law in their minds, and write it on their hearts; and I will be their God, and they shall be My people.* So plainly is this written in Jeremiah 31.31.

No more shall every man teach his neighbor, and every man his brother, saying, 'Know the Lord,' for they all shall know Me, from the least of them to the greatest

117

of them, says the Lord. For I will forgive their iniquity, and their sin I will remember no more. .

After we are born-again, God's love wraps around us and His new covenant of life takes the place of all the old laws and rituals we've been trying to obey; which only brought death. It's the covenant we believers are now covered by. He has indeed written His laws in our hearts and mind so that we are free to obey Him.

God's covenants were made between He and mankind; but carnal man is incapable of keeping covenant with God. As He did with Adam and Abraham [Gen 15.7-21]; He again makes covenant with man through the blood; always the blood of the innocent. Our flesh is incapable of keeping covenant with God; it's only by His grace and mercy. And the New Covenant was established by the Blood of the Lamb of God, His flesh for ours, as we died with Him. Our sin nature was brought to death on the cross with Jesus.

We must know that satan does not make covenant with anyone. He subtly deceives and creeps in unawares, until his victim is overtaken by his lies. A man who would be possessed by satan would know nothing of what covenant means. The Law of Moses was given to prove to man that we could not keep it as Israel's failures time after time proved. Gentiles are no different. Too many of us break even the law of the land we live in, so God gives us a mandate.

John 14.15-18 *If you love Me, keep My commandments. And I will pray the Father, and He will give you another Helper, that He may abide with you forever — the Spirit of truth, whom the world cannot receive, because it neither sees Him nor knows Him; but you know Him, dwells with you and will be in you. I will not leave you orphans; I will come to you. .*

My dear Jesus, we are so not worthy of the trust you have in us. But for your mercies and grace we can trust in You and Your Holy Spirit to help us in our infirmities. Thank You God.

The law of Moses was commandments we must 'keep and do' in our flesh. Jesus set us free to walk in grace because His Holy Spirit has taken residence in our life that we would freely obey God because of His love. Now Daniel Verses 26-27; The 'prince' who some believe will sit in the temple at the last days, is not included in this Scripture. Verse 27 reveals the 70th week, the ministry of Jesus for 3½ years, then the final 3½ years.

Verse 25 <u>Messiah the Prince</u> Who died for our sin and established the New Covenant.

<u>Verse 26 Titus the prince</u>, who destroyed the temple and the city in AD 70.

Daniel 9.26 *And the people of the [other] prince who will come will destroy the city and the sanctuary* [Ampl Bible] Yes, Titus's father was a Roman General; and sent his son to crack down on those rebellious Jews. He destroyed the city and the temple. The sacrifice ceased and Indeed, the temple and the people were made desolate, evicted.

Matthew 24 *I say to you, not one stone shall be left here upon another, that shall not be thrown down.* .

Now as far as some people believe the prince of verse 26 is the antichrist...well, if it is, he's not going to destroy the temple, he will sit in it and declare he is god.

Daniel 9.27- [Messiah the prince] *He shall confirm the covenant with many for one week.* As I have shown, it is Jesus Who confirmed the New Covenant previously prophesied in the Scriptures I mentioned.

I am aware that end time preachers refer this Scripture to the antichrist who will confirm covenant with Israel. I do believe that prophecy can be twofold; having different time frames. God can do anything He wants to fulfill His purposes; but I also believe this particular prophecy; the 70th week/7 years was appropriated and finished in the first century with the disciples of Jesus.

119

Jesus taught His disciples for 3½ years then confirmed it all by the Spirit on the day of Pentecost. In the midst of the last week, He died on the cross - the last sacrifice for sin; so that the temple sacrifice and oblation [a sacrificial offering] was to cease. But they continued anyway. This ritual had become idolatry. It was an abomination to the Father Who had just sacrificed His Son for the sin of the world. But they didn't receive Jesus or acknowledge His sacrifice. So, He made it desolate [of no value] *even until the consummation* [the end] *and that time determined shall be poured out on the desolate*. The end came in AD 70. The end of their sacrifice, the end of their temple, and the end of their life as they knew it. They were indeed desolate!

So, what happened when Jesus died on the cross? He was the Only Begotten Son of the Father; came into our world to be The Lamb of God chosen before the foundation of the world [Revelation 13.8]. He made an end to our sin nature and reconciled His people to Himself through forgiveness and

2 Corinthians 5.21 For *He made Him who knew no sin to be sin for us, that we might become the righteousness of God in Him.*

In the midst of the week He shall cause the sacrifice and oblation [the tributes] to cease. Jesus had just been sacrificed as the perfect Lamb of God. There would be no more need for the sacrifice of the lamb in the temple but we know the priests never acknowledged what Jesus had done; they continued as usual. So the temple sacrifice was made desolate...of no value whatsoever.

Daniel 9.24 To seal up the vision and *prophecy and to anoint the most holy*. This vision was contained in itself. This last week would not be split in half and fulfilled at the time of the end so that the last 3½ years of this prophecy has to wait, to include this rapture theory. And to *anoint the most holy* does not mean Jesus. He was already the

Anointed Most Holy Son of God. The 'most holy' in this verse was the 120 in the upper room who were anointed with God's Holy Spirit on the day of Pentecost. So, they came together and prayed; and on that day, God's Holy Spirit came in the rushing wind, as Father once again breathed His Spirit on His creation; and so, His most holy people were anointed. Remember God said....

1Peter 1.16 You *be holy for I am holy*

So now we are left with the second part of the week, 3½ years. Jesus was not yet done with His instructions to His disciples. We see in Acts Chapter one; Jesus is giving His final instructions before He goes back to His Father, and we know He was with them for 40 days teaching them, *and* [Acts 1.3] *speaking of the things pertaining to the Kingdom of God.* He most certainly would remind them of Daniel 9, so pertinent that His mission would be completed.

[More than 500 people saw Him after He was resurrected]. *Wait for the promise of the Father, and you shall be baptized with the Holy Spirit.... you shall receive power after the Holy Spirit is come upon you; and you shall be witnesses unto me in both Jerusalem and in all Judea, and in Samaria and unto the uttermost part of the earth. .*

So, on the day of Pentecost, they were endued with this Holy Spirit power. Now the disciples went all over Jerusalem and Judea proclaiming the good news of salvation. For 3½ years they understood what they were to do according to what Jesus had told them and thousands were saved, healed and delivered. They even prophesied to the rulers, the elders and scribes, even the high priest, which brought on persecution, but they did not quit. Steven, so bold with the truth, was God's first New Covenant martyr; and Jesus stood up from His throne to welcome him home.

Persecution became a way of life for them, but they

had a mandate and would not be quiet. They continued to do what they were told and gladly suffered at the hands of the pharisees and high priest. But now, there came more direct and 'great persecution' from one who would murder them as he caught them in their homes [Chapter 8] Saul. Well, God had His perfect timing because according to historians this was AD34, [from 27AD to 34AD-7 years]; the second 3½ years are now fulfilled. Here is where the disciples were scattered abroad [v.4] and Philip went down to Samaria, just as Jesus had told them. Peter and John joined him that the new believers might receive the Holy Spirit. Then they went to the Ethiopian and the Centurion.

The greatest of persecutors became the greatest of evangelists, and wrote most of the New Testament, as God endowed him with love and grace for God's people. He brought the gospel from Turkey to Rome and places in between. And so, the most important prophecy in the Word of God, the one that revealed God's timing for our salvation is brought to a close, total fulfilment. There is no 3½ years left to dangle at the time of the end for God's people to hope they will escape God's plan. We are to be filled with God's Holy Spirit and power; we are overcomers. If we can't learn to trust God in these days, fear will have a party in your imagination when things get really tough.

Herein is our love made perfect, that we may have boldness in the day of judgment, because as He is. So, are we in this world? There is no fear in love, but [His] perfect love casts out fear, because fear has punishment. He that fears has not been made perfect . [1 John 4.17-18].

If the book of Revelation causes anxiety and fear in your heart, it is because the devil is at work to make you believe his lies. Please do a study on trusting God and give all your fears to the Lord Who died for you so that you would have His peace.

James 4.6-10 But *He gives more grace. Therefore, He says God resists the proud, but gives grace to the humble. Therefore, submit yourself to God. Resist the devil and he will flee from you. Draw near to God and He will draw near to you... Humble yourselves in the sight of the Lord, and He will lift you up.* .

In Christ I Will Always Be, What Joy Is This Has Filled My Soul, To Be Complete in Christ. Until That Day And Forever More, He Is My Heart - My Life.

Jesus did not come to confirm Moses' law, He came to establish a New Covenant with His people as was prophesied in Daniel 9.27; in Jer 31.31; in Isaiah 61.8 and confirmed in Heb 8. Yes, the old has passed away.

Luke 19.43-44 *For days will come upon you when your enemies will build an embankment around you, surround you and close you in on every side, and level you, and your children within you, to the ground; and they will not leave in you one stone upon another, because you did not know the time of your visitation* . [Jesus warned them - prophecy for AD 70].

Daniel 9.27 The abomination was 'continuing the blood sacrifice of animals' when Jesus was the 'final sacrifice'. *He shall cause the sacrifice and the oblation to cease.* Because they decided He was of no value to them, they continued to sacrifice the lamb and so Israel was made desolate, *the consummation* [the end] *was poured out on the desolate*; their sacrifice was now of no value for their sin. What an insult to our holy God Who had just sacrificed His Beloved Son.

As a result, Jerusalem and their temple were destroyed in AD 70, and Israel was exiled for 2000 years. But there were many of whom did come to know Him as their Messiah, and after He was resurrected, He poured out His

Spirit and confirmed His New Covenant in their hearts as they spread the Good News.

Acts 2.46-47 *So continuing daily with one accord in the temple, and breaking bread from house to house, they ate their food with gladness and simplicity of heart, praising God and having favor with all the people. And the Lord added to the Church daily those who were being saved. .*

Three thousand the first day - *WoW!*

I do believe, and it is confirmed by Scripture, that Daniel 9.23-27 was a prophecy declared wholly to Daniel's people and the holy city, Jerusalem. Check it out, see for yourself. It concerns exactly when the Messiah would come, when He would die and how this last week would be finished. Vs 27, After 3½ years, Jesus died; 3½ years left. See Acts 1.8 as the disciples were told what to do. First minister in Judea to the Jews, then [8.1-5] Persecution arose; they were scattered and Philip went to Samaria, but chapter 9, it escalated; Saul *breathing out threatenings and slaughter against the disciples of the Lord,* made things even worse for them.

This was a sign to them that they were to go to the Gentiles. Romans 2.10-11 *To the Jew first and also to the Greek. For there is no partiality with God.* So, the last 3½ years were fulfilled, they were dispersed to the world of the Gentiles. This last week was perfectly fulfilled by Jesus and the disciples in AD 1. Philip went to Samaria, preached Christ and many miracles happened. Peter and John saw to it they were baptized With the Holy Spirit.

Philip then went to the Ethiopian eunuch and Peter went to The Gentile Cornelius. Chapter 11 tells us they went to Antioch. Now this great prosecutor Saul has an explosive moment with the Lord of these Christians, and becomes Paul, the great apostle, evangelist and writer.

His letters make up the majority of the New Testament. Have you read them? Now would be a good time. If I seemed to repeat again and again; it was on purpose. Please pray about these things that God will reveal to you His end-time plan for those who love Him.

There's no condemnation
To those in Christ
He's set us free from sin
When He came, He brought His Kingdom,
Now He invites us to come in.
There's treasures and blessings
We know nothing about
Mysteries, secrets, darkness and light
And He calls us to search them out
We live in Christ, He lives in us
Such joy we have never known
But revelation comes to us
From the seeds we have sown.

So You Would Know the Truth
And the Truth
Will Make You Free.

WHAT'S THIS ABOUT
A RAPTURE?

Such controversy goes on in the body of Christ about being snatched away before the heat of the end time battle. Before the 19th century no one, Apostles, Prophets, Teachers, Evangelists, and Pastors - none ever taught on this subject. Paul could have, should have. He had many opportunities, but not a word that we would be snatched off the earth by a secret appearing of Jesus. Too many Scriptures are taken out of context and out of the timing of what God has planned.

Where did it come from? That's a very long story. Suffice it to say that a librarian, S.R. Maitland [1792-1866] keeper of the manuscripts in the Library of the Church of England, discovered this futurist view of Daniel 9.27 as written by Jesuit Francisco Ribera from Spain in the 16th Century, and Maitland published it just for the sake of interest; ['Oh, look what I found!'] It was concerning the last week of this verse, in that the last 3½ years were delegated to the end of the age. Ribera split the time line of a prophecy that was actually fulfilled in the first century by the disciples of Jesus. Read on.

Ribera's and Maitland's errors were magnified by soon coming preachers and teachers who obviously did not pray about this and study the Word on it for themselves. And we have a teenager who claimed she had a dream of people flying through the air. It would be best to just show in the Word of God, why I do not believe in it. I do not demean their Christianity, only that they should have used James 1.5 and 2Tim 3.16-17.

Prove All Things by the Word of God.

God never leaves us to our own imagination. What craziness sprouts from our own desires for our destiny. If we would depend on the Word of God and Holy Spirit interpretation, we would know the truth and the truth will make us free. Please read on and see for yourself.

2 Timothy 1.6-8 *Therefore I remind you to stir up the gift of God* [the anointing] *which is in you, For God has not given us a spirit of fear, but of power* and of love and of *a sound mind.* .

2 Timothy 1.12 I *am not ashamed, for I know whom I have believed and am persuaded that He is able to keep what I have committed to Him until that Day. Therefore, do not be ashamed of the testimony of our Lord.* .

Revelation 19.10 *Worship God, for the testimony of Jesus is the spirit of prophecy.* This is the Word of God Who has promised that we are truly, *delivered safely into His Kingdom.*

This doctrine of the pre-trib rapture very effectively is preventing believers from preparing themselves for 'end time tribulation'. Now will be the time to strengthen our trust in our God, and the armor of God [Ephesians 6] for protection against the lies of the devil, and to know where we stand in God.

Do You Know Him - And Is He Your Lord?
And Does He Know You?

If people believe God will take them from the earth before the 'great tribulation', which is exactly satan's plan to deceive God's people; will we have the ability to stand in the power of the Lord, trusting in Him in this hour of trial and deception; or will fear cause many to deny Him? Pastor John Paul Jackson expressed his belief in a dynamic sermon; 'If we escape tribulation, what will God say to those who went through the holocaust, and Christians who died in the communist China revolution'.

Not many people know that there was a great falling away from Christ in China because they believed that God would take them out before the communists came after them and many were killed, so they denied they knew Him. And in Russia, many Christians fell away when communism took over. Or in the middle ages when 50 million Christians were murdered for their faith? Where was the rapture in all of this?

Does satan's lies still have power and authority over God's redeemed ones? I recorded in the last chapters just what the mark of the beast meant. It refers to who you will worship and who will you obey.

Colossians 1. 12-14 *Giving thanks to the Father who has qualified us to be partakers of the inheritance of the saints in the light. He has delivered us from the power of darkness and conveyed us into the Kingdom of the Son of His love, in whom we have redemption through His blood, the forgiveness of sins.*

In tribulation we have 'pressure, affliction, anguish, [the fear of – see 1John 4.18, God's perfect love will cast out the fear of persecution and being murdered'. What about these things? Our soul can be tormented by issues that have wounded us in the past; so many fears that taunt us. Does the prince of this world have anything in you? [John 14.30] Ask God - He is happy to show you those things that prevent you from fully trusting in the God Who loves you so much that He died for you. Please study the hundreds of verses in the Word that will teach us to trust in God; and think about these 2 points

#1 - What general would remove his troops before the battle and #2 - Romans 16.18-20 ...*and by smooth words and flattering speech deceive the hearts of the simple. For your obedience has become known to all. Therefore, I am glad on your behalf; but I want you to be wise in what is good, and simple concerning evil. And the God of peace will crush Satan under your feet shortly.* . [While we are on the earth].

Please Read Ephesians 6.10-18 Put on the Armor,
Walk in the Truth of the Word.

2 Corinthians 10.3-6 For though we walk in the flesh, we do not war according to the flesh. For the weapons of our warfare are not carnal but mighty in God for pulling down strongholds, casting down arguments and every high thing that exalts itself against the knowledge of God, bringing every thought into captivity to the obedience of Christ, and being ready to punish all disobedience when your obedience is fulfilled.

The knowledge of God is the Bible, and satan loves the counterfeit. When will we have the privilege to crush satan under our feet and watch his demise before our very eyes? When do we get to use the weapons God gave us to their full extent? Whenever we're ready!

Isaiah 54.16-*17 Behold, I have created the blacksmith Who blows the coals in the fire, Who brings forth an instrument for his work; And I have created the spoiler to destroy. No weapon formed against you shall prosper, and every tongue which rises against you in judgment You shall condemn. This is the heritage of the servants of the Lord, and their righteousness is from Me, Says the Lord.* .

Do you have the spoiler anointing?

God has brought His people forth to be His spoiler [the waster, to destroy, utterly perish] the works of the devil. This is our inheritance, to totally destroy the one who has caused us so much trouble, and watch him thrown into the lake of fire. OH YES!

We must know that God has given His Word to reveal to us the weapons of our warfare. It's all there if we would study it and research deep, not only read 'our daily bread'. If you seek me you will find me, if you search with all your heart. And the truth will make you free. So, are you searching in the Word of God for truth that will make you free [of fear] of what may come in the future?

Now is the time to allow God to search us and see if there be any place in us for satan to get a foothold, buried in us, especially fears. God will give the wisdom and knowledge to understand. We need to repent and do 2Corinthians 10.3-6 so that satan has no hold on us through the fear of the unknown.

1 John 3.19-*23 And by this we know that we are of the truth, and shall assure our hearts before Him. For if our heart condemns us, God is greater than our heart, and knows all things. Beloved, if our heart does not condemn us, we have confidence toward God. And whatever we ask we receive from Him, because we keep His commandments and do those things that are pleasing in His sight. And this is His commandment that we should believe on the name of His Son Jesus Christ and love one another, as He gave us commandment. .*

I don't believe the mark or the seal is a pellet in our hand or 666 between our eyes. I shared in a previous chapter; the Mark-the Seal, where it comes from, [Israel in the desert] and that this pertains to our spiritual life. Do we trust in God and live for Him or is our life based on the standards of the world and live for ourselves? If

Jesus is the center of our life than anything the antichrist has to offer will not entice us to follow him or for him to have a hold on us.

See Revelation 19.20 They had the mark and worshiped his image. [The image of anything is the works attached]. Read the chapters on the mark again. It is the Word of God. Please be sure you have a tight grip on your Savior, Jesus Christ... *and from whom, according to the flesh, Christ came, who is over all, the eternally blessed God. Amen.*

Yes - Jesus Has Always Been God! [John 1]

1 John 5.4-5 *For whatever is born of God overcomes the world. And this is the victory that has overcome the world — our faith. Who is he who overcomes the world, but he who believes that Jesus is the Son of God?* .

1 John 5.20 *We know that the Son of God has come and has given us an understanding, that we may know Him who is true; and we are in Him who is true, in His Son Jesus Christ. This is the true God and eternal life.* .

1 John 4.17-18 *Love has been perfected among us in this that we may have boldness in the day of judgment; because as He is, so are we in this world.* .

1 John 1.2-4 *That which we have seen and heard we declare to you, that you also may have fellowship with us; and truly our fellowship is with the Father and His Son Jesus Christ. And these things we write to you that your joy may be full.*

1 John 3.1-3 *Behold what manner of love the Father has bestowed on us, that we should be called children of God! Therefore, the world does not know us, because it did not know Him. Beloved, now we are children of God; and it has not yet been revealed what we shall be, but we know that when He is revealed, we shall be like Him, for we shall see Him as He is. And everyone who has this hope in Him purifies himself, just as He is pure.* .

1 John 2.27 *But the anointing which you have received*

from Him abides in you, and you do not need that anyone teach you; but as the same anointing teaches you concerning all things, and is true, and is not a lie, and just as it has taught you, you will abide in Him. .

1 John 4.2 *By this you know the Spirit of God, every spirit that confesses that Jesus Christ has come in the flesh is of God.*

1 John 4.10 *In this is love, not that we loved God, but that He loved us and sent His Son to be the propitiation for our sins.*

1 John 4.15 *Whoever confesses that Jesus is the Son of God, God abides in him, and he in God. And we have known and believed the love that God has for us. God is love, and he who abides in love abides in God, and God in him.*

Matthew 24.23-25 *Then if anyone says to you, 'Look, here is the Christ!' or 'There!' do not believe it. For false christs and false prophets will rise and show great signs and wonders <u>to deceive, if possible, even the elect</u>. See, I have told you beforehand...* [all .]

How Can We Be Deceived If We're Not Here?

John 8.44 [For the unbelievers] ... *You are of your father the devil, and the desires of your father you want to do. He was a murderer from the beginning, and does not stand in the truth, because there is no truth in him. When he speaks a lie, he speaks from his own resources, he is a liar, the father of it.*

An unbeliever is already deceived by the master of deception, and just as the believer is the temple of God, the unbeliever is taken over by the enemy of their soul, to do his works. He lives in their temple.

John 14.23 *Jesus answered and said to him, if anyone loves Me, he will keep My word; and My Father will love* him, and We will come to him and make Our home with him.

John 14.15-19 If you love Me, keep My commandments. And I will pray the Father, and He will give you another Helper, that He may abide with you forever — the Spirit of truth, whom the world cannot receive, because it neither sees Him nor knows Him; but you know Him, for He dwells with you and will be in you. I will not leave you orphans; I will come to you.

Ephesians 2.2-3 *according to the prince of the power of the air, the spirit who now works in the sons of disobedience, among whom also we all once conducted ourselves in the lusts of our flesh, fulfilling the desires of the flesh and of the mind, and were by nature children of wrath, just as the others.. .* The unbeliever is already the temple of the antichrist spirit.

The only way to be saved from his cunning lies is to give your heart and soul to Jesus Who died for your salvation. Remember Jesus, *in whom we have redemption through His blood, the forgiveness of sins. .*

Colossians 2.6-11 *As you therefore have received Christ Jesus the Lord, so walk in Him, rooted and built up in Him and established in the faith, as you have been taught, abounding in it with thanksgiving. Beware lest anyone cheat you through philosophy and empty deceit, according to the tradition of men, according to the basic principles of the world, and not according to Christ. For in Him dwells all the fullness of the Godhead bodily; and you are complete in Him, who is the head of all principality and power. .*

Hebrews 13:5-6 *For He Himself has said, "I will never leave you nor forsake you". So, we may boldly say: "The Lord is my helper; I will not fear. What can man do to me?"* Read Mark 8.34-38; Luke 12.29-32. If we will not deny Him, *It is Father's good pleasure to give us the Kingdom.* Remember, *Greater is He that is in us than he that is in the world.* We must know that God has a hard grip on us that He will never let us go [Romans 8]. So let Him deal with all your fears, and trust Him.

1 Corinthians 6.17 *But he who is joined to the Lord is one spirit with Him.* What more can He do for us? Be Surprised! We are saved by faith because of God's grace. Divine redemption is actually the living experience with One Who has been raised from the dead; Jesus Himself, by the power of the Holy Spirit, is alive in each lover of God. It's relationship!

1 John 2.20-27 But you have an anointing from the Holy One, and you know all things. I have not written to you because you do not know the truth, but because you know it, and that no lie is of the truth. Let Truth Abide in You.

Therefore, let that abide in you which you heard from the beginning. If what you heard from the beginning abides in you, you also will abide in the Son and in the Father. And this is the promise that He has promised us — eternal life. These things I have written to you concerning those who try to deceive you.

Ephesians 1.13-14 We are already sealed by the Holy Spirit. All this has to do with Who it is that we worship. Oh yes, and - Revelation 2.29 *And of those who keep the words of this book. Worship God.* .

It is possible Jesus will return at the time of the Feast of Tabernacles, but we know not when. This is the only Jewish feast that has not been fulfilled by Jesus.

See the meaning of this in the chapter on Tabernacles.

The Feast of Tabernacles is the presence of our Lord and Savior. We are hidden in Christ.

Colossians 3.1-4 *If then you were raised with Christ, seek those things which are above, where Christ is, sitting at the right hand of God. Set your mind on things above, not on things on the earth. For you died, and your life is hidden with Christ in God. When Christ who is our life appears, then you also will appear with Him in glory.* John 14.16-18,21,23, 27;16.33;17.26. The Feast of Tabernacles is the only feast that Jesus did not fulfill in His time on the earth because this feast represents His presence with us, never again to leave.

Will He Return to Fulfill the Feast of Tabernacles?

Remember what you already read in the chapter 'The Mark, the Seal'. Atheism-there is no God. An Agnostic -is there really a God? *A double minded man is unstable in all his ways* [James 1], and easily deceived.

Revelation 13.18 Understand '666', *It is the number of a man.* Six is the number of a carnal man, so body, soul, and [man's] spirit is of a carnal nature; 666.

BUT 1 John 5.11-13 *And this is the testimony that God has given us eternal life, and this life is in His Son. He who has the Son has life; he who does not have the Son of God does not have life. These things I have written to you who believe in the name of the Son of God, that you may know that you have eternal life, and - That you may continue to believe in the name of the Son of God.*

It All Boils down to One Thing. Do You Believe the Word of God - or Not. Adam Did Not!

Not enough said Adam, I want to explore
Not what I have with You Lord,
I want much more
There's other ways and things to do
On the other side of the gate
To taste and see the wrong and right
And where should I put my faith
I'll try this, and I'll try that,
And then I will decide
But OH! If I could just turn back
I know now, I gave up my life.

As Adam betrayed his position in the Spirit realm, God's Holy Spirit left, they were no longer covered by the glory and they were naked. Now they would hide in fear of the presence of the Lord. He had face to face with his Creator; they were covered with the glory of God. He was shown the mysteries of the universe, and Adam made a decision that would rob them of all this. If they only would have repented instead of putting the blame on someone else. and so, he became worldly, carnal, to do as he pleased, to live by his self-will. After he disobeyed God, it was too late to turn back, and so, they lost their identity in God. But God must have forgiven them, He covered them with blood and skins of a lamb

Ephesians 1.7-14 *In Him we have redemption through His Blood, the forgiveness of sins, according to the riches of His grace which He made to abound toward us in all wisdom and prudence, having made known to us the mystery of His will, according to His good pleasure which He purposed in Himself, that in the dispensation of the fullness of the times He might gather together in one all things in Christ, both which are in heaven and which are on earth — in Him. .*

Please Make Him Enough for You.

In Him also we have obtained an inheritance, being predestined according to the purpose of Him who works all things according to the counsel of His will, that we who first trusted in Christ should be to the praise of His glory. In Him you also trusted, after you heard the word of truth, the gospel of your salvation; in whom also, having believed, you were sealed with the Holy Spirit of promise, who is the guarantee of our inheritance until the redemption of the purchased possession, to the praise of His glory. .

So, What Is Our Inheritance, Who Are We - And to Whom Do We Belong? We Are Bought with a Price - The Greatest Price of All in the Universe - The Precious Blood of our Creator God.

John 17.9-20 *I pray for them. I do not pray for the world but for those whom You have given Me, for they are Yours. And all Mine are Yours, and Yours are Mine, and I am glorified in them. Holy Father, keep through Your name those whom You have given Me, that they may be one as We are. I do not pray that You should take them out of the world, but that You should keep them from the evil one. They are not of the world, just as I am not of the world. Sanctify them by Your truth. Your word is truth.* .

John 17:20-23 *I do not pray for these alone, but also for those who will believe in Me through their word; that they all may be one, as You, Father, are in Me, and I in You; that they also may be one in Us, that the world may believe that You sent Me. And the glory which You gave Me I have given them, that they may be one just as We are one: I in them, and You in Me; that they may be made perfect in one, and that the world may know that You have sent Me, and have loved them as You have loved Me.* .

Please read the whole parable of the wheat and the tares [Matthew 13].

Here Is the Most Important Part.

Matthew 13.24 *Another parable He put forth to them, saying the Kingdom of heaven is like a man who sowed good seed in his field; but while men slept, his enemy came and sowed tares among the wheat and went his way. But when the grain had sprouted and produced a crop, then the tares also appeared. So, the servants of the owner came and said to him, 'Sir, did you not sow good seed in your field? How then does it have tares?' He said to them, 'An enemy has done this'.*

The servants said to him, 'Do you want us then to go and gather them up?' But he said, 'No, lest while you gather up the tares you also uproot the wheat with them. Let both grow together <u>until the harvest,</u> and at the time of harvest I will say to the reapers, <u>First gather together the tares and bind them in bundles to burn them, but gather the wheat into my barn.</u>

But the disciples did not understand; [James 1.5].

Matthew 13.36-43 *Explain to us the parable of the tares of the field. He answered and said to them He who sows the good seed is the Son of Man. The field is the world, the good seeds are the sons of the Kingdom, the tares are the sons of the wicked one. The enemy who sowed them is the devil, <u>the harvest is the end of the age,</u> and<u> the reapers are the angels.</u>*

<u>FIRST</u> *the tares are gathered and burned in the fire,* <u>THEN </u>*the righteous will shine forth as the sun in the Kingdom of their Father. <u>so, it will be at the end of this age</u>. <u>He who has ears to hear, let him hear!</u>* .

AND TO PLEASE UNDERSTAND James 1.4-8 Tares look like wheat but there is a poisonous black seed in the tares, and you can see the difference at harvest time.

Matthew 13.49-51 *So it will be at the end of the age. The angels will come forth, separate the wicked from among the just, and cast them into the furnace of fire. There will be wailing and gnashing of teeth. Jesus said to them, Have you understood all these things?*

<u>FIRST,</u> *they will gather out of His Kingdom all things that offend, and those who practice lawlessness, and will cast them into the furnace of fire.*

Luke 17.23 *And they will say to you, 'Look here!' or 'Look there!' Do not go after them or follow them. For as the lightning that flashes out of one part under heaven shines to the other part under heaven, so also the Son of Man will be in His day.* .

There Is No Secret to This.

So, satan has a secret weapon that could deceive even the elect. Jesus said so! Notice who was taken and who was left. The deceiver turns this around and says the elect will be taken.

Luke 17.25-30 *And as it was in the days of Noah, so it will be also in the days of the Son of Man They ate, they drank, they married wives, they were given in marriage, until the day that Noah entered the ark, and the flood came and destroyed them all. Likewise, as it was also in the days of Lot They ate, they drank, they bought, they sold, they planted, they built; but on the day that Lot went out of Sodom it rained fire and brimstone from heaven and destroyed them all.*

Days of Noah? Who was left on the earth? Lot was saved from the fate of Sodom. Who is taken and who is left? *So, will it be in the day when the Son of Man is revealed.* .

Matthew 24.39-41 FIRST *One will be taken - the other one is left here.* THEN *the righteous will shine forth as the sun in the Kingdom of their Father.*

So, The Lovers of God, the Elect, Are Still Here
On the Earth at the Coming of Our King.

2 Peter 2.5-6 *He did not spare the ancient world, but saved Noah, one of eight people, a preacher of righteousness, bringing in the flood on the world of the ungodly;*

Luke 17.33-34 *Whoever seeks to save his life will lose it, and whoever loses his life will preserve it. I tell you, in that night there will be two people in one bed the one will be taken and the other will be left* [New International Version 1996 by Zondervan].

The Message Bible says, *Two men will be in the same boat fishing, one taken the other left* [Eugene H. Peterson, NAVPRESS 1993].

The Amplified Bible 2015 edition says, *There will be two sleeping in one bed, the one - the non-believer will be taken away in judgment, and the other, the believer will be left.* And, *two women will be grinding together, the one will be taken and the other left. Two men will be in the field the one will be taken and the other left ...* [left on the earth]. Who Was the 'taken away' in Noah and Lot's Parable; and who was left?

I think it's clear about those taken were destroyed and who was left, kept safe. Here is a very famous Scripture...

1 Corinthians 15.51-*54 Behold, I tell you a mystery We shall not all sleep, but we shall all be changed — in a moment, in the twinkling of an eye,* <u>at the last trumpet</u>. *For the trumpet will sound, and the dead will be raised incorruptible, and we shall be changed. For this corruptible must put on incorruption, and this mortal must put on immortality. So, when this corruptible has put on incorruption, and this mortal has put on immortality, then shall be brought to pass the saying that is written "Death is swallowed up in victory.*

The last trumpet is in Revelation 11.15, so believers are still here even after much disaster has fallen on the earth; but God's people will be protected as Israel was in Goshen.

Romans 5:*9 Much more then, having now been justified by His blood, we shall be saved from wrath through Him.*

Yes, We Will Be Changed in God's Timing, but Where Does it Say Here That We Are Raised in a Rapture or That We Will Be Taken to Heaven for this to Happen?

I pray you will read the following Scripture very carefully - Paul is talking about the resurrection not a pre-trib rapture. Trust God, He has everything in His control.

1 Thessalonians 4.13-18 *But I do not want you to be*

ignorant, brethren, concerning those who have fallen asleep, lest you sorrow as others who have no hope. For if we believe that Jesus died and rose again, even so God will bring with Him those who sleep in Jesus. For this we say to you by the word of the Lord, <u>that we who are alive and remain until the coming of the Lord</u> will by no means precede those who are asleep. For the Lord Himself will descend from heaven with a shout, with the voice of an archangel, and with the trumpet of God. And the dead in Christ will rise first. Then we who are alive and remain shall be caught up together with them in the clouds to meet the Lord in the air. And thus, we shall always be with the Lord. Therefore comfort one another with these words.

Please Note, Jesus Is Coming Back with a Bang!
No Tiptoeing in to Sneak Away a Scared Bride.

The 'apostasy' falling away has happened many times in the past, and today, in some countries, many Churches are closing and Christians are walking away from the faith they once knew. *When He comes will He find any faith at all?* He will not look for faith in the unbelievers if the Christians are raptured. But no, we are here victorious over the enemy of our soul and praising the coming of our Redeemer. And He's not coming alone. He will bring His victorious ones.

For this we say to you by the word of the Lord, that <u>we</u> who are alive and remain until the coming of the Lord will *by no means precede those who are asleep.* The dead in Christ will rise first before anything happens with us.

Will this Happen at 'A Rapture'?

For the Lord Himself will descend from heaven with a shout, with the voice of an archangel, and with the trumpet of God.

This is not by any means a silent arrival of the Lord to snatch away anybody. And this magnificent 'Day of The Lord' arrives when He comes for His bride, His Elect; still here and waiting for our Bridegroom. *And thus we shall always be with the Lord. Therefore comfort one another with these words.*

And that song, 'I'll fly away' is for 'when I die'

Luke 18.8 *Nevertheless, when the Son of Man comes, will He Really Find Faith on the Earth?"*

If the saints are raptured out, will Jesus look for faith in the unbelievers? and this one - it is good to read it all, not take one verse out of context.

2 Thessalonians 2.1-12 *Now, brethren, concerning the coming of our Lord Jesus Christ and our gathering together to Him, we ask you, not to be soon shaken in mind or troubled, either by spirit or by word or by letter, as if from us, as though the day of Christ had come. Let no one deceive you by any means; <u>for that Day will not come unless the falling away comes first, and the man of sin is revealed,</u> the son of perdition, who opposes and exalts himself above all that is called God or that is worshiped, so that he sits as God in the temple of God, showing himself that he is God.*

Jesus Also Called Judas 'The Son of 'Perdition.'
It Means to Destroy Fully, Eternal Damnation.

Do you not remember that when I was still with you, I told you these things? And now you know what is restraining, that he may be revealed in his own time. For the mystery of lawlessness is already at work; only He who now restrains will do so until He is taken out of the way. And then the lawless one will be revealed, whom the Lord will consume with the breath of His mouth and destroy with the brightness of His coming. The coming of the lawless one is according to the working of Satan, with all power, signs, and lying wonders, and with all unrighteous deception among those who perish, because they did not receive the love of the truth, that they might be saved. And for this reason, God will send them strong delusion, that they should believe the lie, that they all may be condemned who did not believe the truth but had pleasure in unrighteousness. [Amplified version].

The falling away is 2 Timothy 4.1-5 Convince, rebuke, exhort, with all longsuffering and teaching. *For the time will come when they will not endure sound doctrine, but according to their own desires, because they have itching ears, they will heap up for themselves teachers; and they will turn their ears away from the truth, and be turned aside to fables, but you be watchful in all things.*

This Antichrist Will Be Glad to Gather in All Those Who Don't Care to Live for the Truth.

Remember 2 Timothy 4.10 &14 *For Demas has forsaken me, having loved this present world*, and, *Alexander the coppersmith did me much harm. May the Lord repay him according to his works. You also must beware of him, for he has greatly resisted our words.*

These days I am hearing about pastors are walking away and many churches are closing. I wonder if any had faith even the size of a mustard seed? We Should Follow No Man Nor Give Any Man Authority over Our Life. Remember Those 2 Cults that allowed a man to rule their lives and these 'pastors' convinced hundreds of them to commit suicide. Give yourself only to Jesus. He will lead you into life everlasting.

The one who is taken out of the way is not the Holy Spirit; otherwise who can be saved and Who will comfort and lead us in these troubled times? [John 15.27] Paul was speaking of the Roman Empire, [a totally satanic empire] that ruled half the world with an iron fist; but if he had said that was the antichrist, then more persecution would come down on them. The evil Roman Empire ruled by the Caesars, was evident as in the days of Paul; but 'taken out of the way'; I believe God caused this demise. This empire was totally decimated by the 5th century.

You can go on the web to 'the Fall of the Roman Empire'. You will find 'the man of sin' in Revelation chapter 17&18 and see 13.4, *And they worshiped the dragon* [Roman Empire] *who gave power to the beast*.

The beast is revealed in Revelation 17.4. A woman in Revelation prophecy is depicted as a church. None of these Scriptures speak of being taken up in a rapture.

Proverbs 3.5-8 *Trust in the Lord with all your heart, and lean not on your own understanding; In all your ways acknowledge Him, And He shall direct your paths. Do not be wise in your own eyes; Fear the Lord and depart from evil. It will be health to your flesh, And strength to your bones.* Here's another one

Luke 18.7-8 *And shall God not avenge His own elect who cry out day and night to Him, though He bears long with them? I tell you that He will avenge them speedily.* <u>*Nevertheless, when the Son of Man comes, will He really find faith on the earth?*</u> If all the Christians are raptured before He comes back the second time, why would Jesus look for faith among the unbelievers?

Remember Egypt and the plagues that never touched Goshen. Egypt was decimated, fields, cattle and army; yet Israel also walked away free with the riches and raiment of these 'masters' that made them slaves.

God's provision for these dark days; a Kingdom-wide fulfillment of the Feast of Tabernacles, personal fulfillment of Tabernacles; like rivers of living water; Christ manifested in us - *the hope of glory.*

John 7.37-39 *On the last day, that great day of the feast,* [of Tabernacles], *Jesus stood and cried out, saying, If anyone thirsts, let him come to Me and drink. He who believes in Me, as the Scripture has said, out of his heart will flow rivers of living water.* God intends to dwell in His people to the extent that they not only can stand in Him throughout every difficulty but finally...

Romans 16.20 *And the God of peace will soon crush satan under your feet.* We must be on the earth for this to happen. I point out to you chapter 13 of Mark. I pray you will read the whole chapter. Look at verse 20....

And unless the Lord had shortened those days, no flesh would be saved; but for the elect's sake, whom He chose, He shortened the days. Then if anyone says to you, 'Look, here is the Christ!' or, 'Look, He is there!' do not believe it. For false christs and false prophets will rise and show signs and wonders to deceive, if possible, even the elect. But take heed; see, I have told you all things beforehand.

Oh my - the ELECT, that's us lovers of God, still here. We that have this revelation will be at peace; and when will this happen? This is at the end when He comes back. False christs and prophets have been here for centuries and are still greatly deceiving people. But God has given us His Spirit to discern between the good and the ugly. Always trust God to lead you in truth and grace.

Malachi 3.17-18 *They shall be Mine says the Lord of hosts, On the day that I make them My jewels. And I will spare them as a man spares his own son who serves him. Then you shall again discern Between the righteous and the wicked, between one who serves God And one who does not serve Him.*

145

Scripture I have noted...1 Thessalonians 1:9-10

To serve the living and true God, and to wait for His Son from heaven, whom He raised from the dead, even Jesus <u>who delivers us from the wrath to come</u>.

Any Partial Scripture I Note, I Adjure You to Seek the Context.

Remember, Israel was never touched by the plagues of Egypt. Spend your life learning day after day that you can totally rely and trust in Jesus to keep you in His heart.

Hebrews 5.*14 But solid food belongs to those who are of full age, that is, those who by reason of use have their senses exercised to discern both good and evil.* Also see Matthew 16.3 and Luke 12.54-56

If we are going through difficult testings in these days, it is to call attention to the sins of the flesh and purge them from our personality, to crucify 'king self'; so that Jesus may sit on the throne of our life. The more we allow this, the more authority we have over the accuser. The strong man has been bound and spoiled [Mt 12.29]. We can cooperate with the Holy Spirit as He cleanses us from sin and self-seeking. We must learn to rest and abide in God through our Messiah. Trust Him.

John 6.53-58 Then *Jesus said to them, most assuredly, I say to you, unless you eat the flesh of the Son of Man and drink His Blood, you have no life in you. Whoever eats My flesh and drinks My Blood has eternal life, and I will raise him up at the last day. For My flesh is food indeed, and My Blood is drink indeed. He who eats My flesh and drinks My Blood abides in Me, and I in him. As the living Father sent Me, and I live because of the Father, so he who feeds on Me will live because of Me. This is the bread which came down from heaven — not as your fathers ate the manna, and are dead. He who eats this bread will live forever.* Then He explains.

John 6.*63 it is the spirit who gives life; the flesh profits nothing. The words that I speak to you are spirit, and they are life.*

Eating Him Means Intimacy with Him.
A Relationship That Restores Us Back to
The Image of God.

Psalm 91.14-16 *Because he has set his love upon Me, therefore I will deliver him; I will set him on high, because he has known My name. He shall call upon Me, and I will answer him; I will be with him in trouble; I will deliver him and honor him. With long life I will satisfy him, and show him My salvation.* John 10.27-28 *My sheep hear My voice, and I know them, and they follow Me. And I give them eternal life, and they shall never perish*; He keeps track of all His sheep.

John 14.27 *Peace I leave with you, My peace I give to you; not as the world gives do, I give to you. Let not your heart be troubled, neither let it be afraid.* Jesus said this just before He went to the cross.

Following Jesus means that sometimes we will stumble, or not be sure of what to do, we might have fear that we have lost our way. But as Joyce Meyer says, 'If you get lost Jesus will come and find you'. *He knows all them who belong to Him* [John 10.14; Galatians 4.9; Psalm 23 'My Shepherd'.

So, What Do We Have in all this? It Is Intimacy.

To know as we are known; To devour into our body, soul and spirit - the Life of Jesus.

Or will Jesus say to you, *be gone I never knew you.*

Lamentations 3.18-*26 And I said, My strength and my hope have perished from the Lord. Remember my affliction and roaming, the wormwood and the gall. My soul still remembers and sinks within me.* [Our memories help us to understand what we have to deal with. Jesus has given us power over this enemy], But...

This I recall to my mind; Therefore, I have hope. Through the Lord's mercies we are not consumed, Because His compassions fail not. They are new every morning; Great is Your faithfulness. The Lord is my portion, says my soul, Therefore I hope in Him! The Lord is good to those who wait for Him, To the soul who seeks Him. It is good that one should hope and wait quietly for the salvation of the Lord.

Colossians 1.27 *To them God willed to make known what are the riches of the glory of this mystery among the Gentiles which is Christ in you, the hope of glory.*

This is what happens when we are born again. Jesus comes to live in us, to dwell in our innermost being.

This Is a Beautiful Revelation Concerning His Body,

His Temple, The Dwelling Place of God,

Jew and Gentile, One New Man.

Some people have used this verse, *'the hope of glory'*, to refer to being raptured from the earth. This interpretation is not possible in the context of what it is really saying. The glory of God in the saints is the hope we will be strengthened in the dark days of the tribulation just as we are in these days of living for God and going through tough times, and *His glory shall be seen upon us* [Isaiah 60].

Isaiah 26.20-21 *Come, my people, enter your chambers, and shut your doors behind you; Hide yourself, as it were, for a little moment, Until the indignation is past. For behold, the Lord comes out of His place to punish the inhabitants of the earth for their iniquity; The earth will also disclose her blood, And will no more cover her slain.*

There is not one Scripture in the Bible that says we

will be raptured out of the world before the 'great tribulation'. If you want to quote 1 Corinthians 15.51-52, please see when the 'last trump' is sounded; Revelation Chapter 11. There's a lot going on before this. And if you will read 1Corinthians 15, these verses are talking about our mortal body being changed to immortal. That we would have a body like Jesus. Paul would have ample time to add, 'and we will at this time, be snatched out of the world'. But he didn't! And besides this - there is another trumpet blast after the seventh because Jesus is still on His throne in Revelation 11.15-16.

But when He comes back...

1 Thessalonians 4.16. *The trump of God...*

There is also no word in the Bible that says the tribulation will last for seven years. From what Scripture did anyone get that? From the last week of Daniel 9 prophecy? To authenticate their reason for the rapture before the last 3½ years. You can't take a verse out of context to mean what you want it to say. Daniel's prophecy was for his city [vs 24] declaring the first coming of the Lord; and vs 27, Jesus confirmed the covenant from Jeremiah 31.31 and finished it as in Acts 1.8 and chapter 8 [Saul].

See Hebrews 12.24; 13.20;8.6,8; Romans 11.26-27.

Please read the next verses very carefully and notice when it is we will join the Lord's presence. Repeating for emphasis and not taken out of context!

1 Thessalonians 4.13-*5.11 For this we say to you by the word of the Lord, that we who are alive and remain until the coming of the Lord will by no means precede those who are asleep. And thus, we shall always be with the Lord.* Please read all of these verses.

Like a Thief in the Night Means We Will Not Know
the Hour or the Day He Will Come, Just like the Parable
of the Virgins. Will You Be Ready and
Always Be Filled with the Spirit of God?

Revelation 11.3 This Scripture tells us God's people will be here on the earth in the last days, but hidden in Christ no matter what happens. Read Ephesians...know who we are, hidden IN HIM and sealed with a promise.

John 14.*23 Jesus answered and said to him, If anyone*

loves Me, he will keep My word; and My Father will love him, and We will come to him and make Our home with him. Yes, it is *Christ in you, the hope of glory.*

It is obvious that we must learn to trust in God - to put all our life into His hands. It is the only thing we can do. And after all is said and done - the words of Jesus spell true ...

If you love me, keep my commandments.

It's not good enough to say 'I love Jesus', then go about your own business. God will help us every time.

Philippians 2.12-16. Working out your salvation means to cooperate with God for the changes He arranges.

T'is Grace Has Kept Me Safe Thus Far
And Grace Will Bring Me Home.

This following excerpt is taken from Tabernacles and the Coming of the Lord, By Pastor Robert B. Thompson, Trumpet Ministries, Escondido, California...

The Churches know that the nightmare of the great tribulation is coming, but the doctrine of the pre-tribulation rapture very effectively is preventing the believers from preparing themselves [which is precisely what satan has planned]. The Christians are asleep spiritually because of the doctrine of pre-tribulation rapture. It is our opinion that this doctrine is unscriptural and has caused and is causing untold harm to the ability of the Lord's people to stand in the hour of testing. God has provided something for us which is infinitely better than pre-tribulation rapture; infinitely better than being forced to flee from the battle because satan has more power than we do. God has made a way for us to triumph in the last days, not by fleeing from the conflict, but conquering every adversity through means of His superior wisdom and power [Compare 1John 4.4].

Greater is He that is within us
than He who is in the world!

Joel speaks of the hour when the Son of Man is revealed. *The sun and the moon shall be darkened, and the stars shall withdraw their shining*

[sic] THE LORD ALSO SHALL ROAR OUT OF ZION, AND UTTER HIS VOICE FROM JERUSALEM; AND THE HEAVENS AND THE EARTH SHALL SHAKE; BUT THE LORD WILL BE THE HOPE OF HIS PEOPLE, AND THE STRENGTH OF THE CHILDREN OF ISRAEL [Joel 3.16].

Please know there are many Pastors and evangelists who do not propagate the rapture theory; and there is never any mention of a secret coming of Jesus in all the passages that speak of His Second Coming. [You Will Find Scriptural Proof as You Keep Reading].

Philippians 3:1

Finally, my brethren, rejoice in the Lord.
For me to write the same things
to you is not tedious, but for you it is safe.
For the Joy of the Lord
Is My strength.

WHAT'S IT ALL ABOUT

So, let's examine why the last seven years of this prophecy was split in half. For centuries, the Bible was written in Latin and denied to the populace. A monk named Martin Luther changed that and it began to be published in the vernacular. People were anxious to know what the final days would bring; and so, they poured over the book of Revelation. They wanted to know who was the antichrist and they discovered Chapter 17& 18. Now there arose two Jesuit priests concerned with what it was revealing.

Some of the following was taken from archives on the internet. As you will read in this paper, I copied from the web that I inserted here. There is information from the internet concerning this church and you will read about these 2 priests. The Jesuit Order was founded by a priest named Ignatius Loyola, in the 14th Century. Loyola was known to have mystical, occultic visions...Also known as 'the Black Pope'.

THE JESUIT Luis de ALCAZAR [1554-1613] wrote a paper on which he claimed the apocalypse was fulfilled in the destruction of Jerusalem by Titus, and the emperor Nero was the antichrist. It was to relieve this Roman church from the stigma of being called the Harlot church.

The Jesuit Francisco RIBERA in 1585, published an Apocalyptic Commentary on the issues of Babylon and the antichrist. The result was a twisting and maligning of prophetic truth. It's amazing how many were aware of Daniel's prophecy concerning the coming of the Messiah.

[My guess is that satan was very aware of it and he had to protect his masterpiece, the church, which has bound many billions of people to idolatry and so many other blasphemous lies. [I know, my family for generations, was one of them]. So now we look at Daniel 9.27.

This Ribera took the last part of the 7 years, [3½ years] and ripped it out of its rightful place in Jewish history, only to apply it to a future antichrist. So, in Ribera's 500-page commentary He deliberated to set aside the Protestant teachings that the papacy is the antichrist. He assigns the first chapters of Revelation to the first century to protect the pope and his regime.

The rest he restricted to a literal 3½ years at the end of time. The Jewish temple_would be built by a single individual, abolish the Christian religion, deny Christ, pretend to be God and conquer the world [1 John 2.22].

The Encyclopedia Britannica states, "Under the stress of the Protestant attack there arose new methods on the papal side. Ribera is identified as the founder of the Futurist school of interpretation. The futurist school of interpretation was created for only one reason... to counter the Protestant Reformation. Ribera's 500-page commentary is still housed in the library in Oxford, England.

S.R. Maitland, librarian and keeper of manuscripts at Lambeth Palace London, the massive library of the church of England, discovered this futurist view of Revelation by Ribera - and he published it just for the sake of interest, in 1826. He wrote tracts and published papers on it. Proverbs 18.13. *He who answers a matter before he hears it,* [or understands it] *is a folly and a shame unto him.*

Solomon Stoddard, grandfather of Jonathan Edwards wrote...

"WE ARE NOT SENT TO THE PULPIT
TO SHOW OUR WIT AND ELOQUENCE"

The Reconstructionists did a job on this. John Darby of the Plymouth Brethren picked up on this. [For more research John Darby]; and the stealing away of the army of warriors God is anointing to stomp satan under their feet [Romans 16.20]. The doctrine of a secret rapture was first conceived by John Nelson Darby of the Plymouth Brethren in 1827. Darby, known as the father of dispensationalism, invented the doctrine claiming there were not one, but two second comings.

Miss McDonald was a member of his church [No, Margaret McDonald did not come up with this rapture idea all by herself]. This teaching was immediately challenged as unbiblical by other members of the Brethren. Samuel P. Tregelles, a noted biblical scholar, rejected Darby's new interpretation as *the height of speculative nonsense*.

So tenuous was Darby's rapture theory that he had lingering doubts about it as late as 1843, and possibly 1845. Another member of the Plymouth Brethren, B.W. Newton, disputed Darby's new doctrine claiming such a conclusion was only possible if one declared certain passages to be renounced as not properly ours.

Sandeen writes, this is precisely what Darby was prepared to do. Too traditional to admit that biblical authors might have contradicted each other, and too rationalist to admit that the prophetic maze defied penetration, Darby attempted a resolution of his exegetical dilemma by distinguishing between Scripture intended for the Church and Scripture intended for Israel. Darby's difficulty was solved by assuming that the Gospels were addressed partly to Jews and partly to Christians. Thus, the doctrine of the separation of Israel and the Church, the foundation of dispensationalism, was born out of Darby's attempt to justify his newly fabricated rapture theory with the Bible. Dispensationalists believed justification for carving up the Scriptures came from 2 Timothy 2.15 (KJV) *rightly dividing the word of truth.* Subsequent dispensationalists divided the Scriptures in terms of categories of people Jew, Gentile, and Christian. Chafer taught that the only Scriptures addressed specifically to Christians were the gospel of John, Acts, and the Epistles!

Pettengill taught that the Great Commission was for the Jews only. Scofield taught that the Lord's prayer was a Jewish prayer and ought not be recited by Christians. Along with much of the New Testament, the Old Testament was described as not for today. Ryrie dismissed the validity of the Old Testament commands to non-Jews because the law was never given to Gentiles and is expressly done away for the Christian. Christians were even mocked as legalists for believing in the Ten Commandments! As other critics have observed, this segmentation of the Bible makes dispensationalism a Christianized version of cultural relativism [portioning things as they see fit].

Snowden and others traced the rise of modern premillennialism to a variety of religious splinter groups the Plymouth Brethren (developed dispensationalism), the Millerites (became the Adventists), There are Mormons, Jehovah's Witnesses, and Pentecostals. Dispensational premillennialism was marketed the same way as the cultic groups.

2 Timothy 4. *For the time will come when they will not endure sound doctrine, but according to their own desires, because they have itching ears, they will heap up for themselves teachers; and they will turn their ears away from the truth, and be turned aside to fables.*

Always Confess Jesus as Your Lord, God and Master and You Will Be Safe No Matter What Happens.

QUESTION: Where in the Bible Does it Say the great Tribulation Will Last for Seven Years? It Doesn't. Those people mentioned in this chapter, ripped Daniel 9.27 right out of the prophecy, saw that it was the last 7 years, etc, etc, etc. Jesus Has All the Answers. Can We Go to Him and His Word? for Truth?

155

What do we know? Is Jesus our Lord?
Do we read a few verses or do we study the Word?
Is it all a big puzzle -I don't understand?
Didn't you know James One Has a word for wisdom
You can know, yes you can, God
will help you Every time
If you confess 'Jesus is mine'!

2 PETER CHAPTER 3
AMPLIFIED BIBLE

1 BELOVED, I am now writing you this second letter. In [both of] them I have stirred up your unsullied (sincere) mind by way of remembrance,

2 That you should recall the predictions of the holy (consecrated, dedicated) prophets and the commandment of the Lord and Savior [given] through your Apostles (His special messengers).

9 The Lord does not delay and is not tardy or slow about what He promises, according to some people's conception of slowness, but He is long-suffering (extraordinarily patient) toward you, not desiring that any should perish, but that all should turn to repentance.

10 But the day of the Lord will come like a thief, and then the heavens will vanish (pass away) with a thunderous crash, and the [material] elements [of the universe] will be dissolved with fire, and the earth and the works that are upon it will be burned up.

So, do you believe the Elect will be safe in the hands of the God Who saved every last one of us?

11 Since all these things are thus in the process of being dissolved, what kind of person ought [each of] you to be [in the meanwhile] in consecrated and holy behavior and devout and godly qualities,

12 While you wait and earnestly long for (expect and hasten) the coming of the day of God by reason of which the flaming heavens will be dissolved, and the [material] elements [of the universe] will flare and melt with fire? [Isaiah 34.4 is quoted here.]

13 But we look for new heavens and a new earth according to His promise, in which righteousness (uprightness, freedom from sin, and right standing with God) is to abide. [Isaiah 65.17; 66.22.]

14 So, beloved, since you are expecting these things, be eager to be found by Him [at His coming] without spot or blemish and at peace [in serene confidence, free from fears and agitating passions and moral conflicts].

17 Let me warn you therefore, beloved, that knowing these things beforehand, you should be on your guard, lest you be carried away by the error of lawless and wicked [persons and] fall from your own [present] firm condition [your own steadfastness of mind].

18 But grow in grace (undeserved favor, spiritual strength) and recognition and knowledge and understanding of our Lord and Savior Jesus Christ (the Messiah). To Him [be] glory (honor, majesty, and splendor) both now and to the day of eternity. Amen (so be it)!

I quoted this chapter because it seems to me that Peter was preparing God's people for when Jesus comes back, not for a rapture but for the 'Day of the Lord', when He will bring all things to a close. See Verses 11&12;

Lovers of God Will Take Refuge in Him, as We Have in Our Spirit Filled Life Learned to Trust Jesus with All Our Heart and Soul. He Will Never Leave Us. Take Refuge in Him from the coming judgment; His covering and protection. Thank God we have the Written Word and the Living Word to lead us and guide into all truth. I don't trust anyone who speaks before they hear the whole matter; to research the Scriptures. Some people's faith has been destroyed because of Scripture taken out of context.

When I see You in Your glory
When I see You face to face
And I humbly bow before You
So captured by Your grace
Then my eyes will be opened
My heart enraptured by Your love
Will I ever be able to breathe again
There in Your presence
Now I humbly bow before you
So captured by Your grace
And unto You my Lord I sing
In audience with my King.

Thank You Jesus That
We Will Know the Truth -
And the Truth Will Make Us Free.

SCRIPTURES ON HIS COMING

Isaiah 8.20 To *the law and to the testimony! If they do not speak according to this word, it is because there is no light in them.* So how often do we pick and choose what verses will verify what we believe; even if out of context. The following Scriptures tell us that the only separation between the holy and profane peoples of the earth happens on the Day of the Lord when He returns to reconcile His creation. I pray that my readers will understand the revelation of what the Word of God is revealing. This is what will really happen when Jesus comes back as He promised, The Day of The Lord.

Read 2 Peter 3.10-14 *again.*

Romans 11.8-19 *For the wrath of God is revealed from heaven against all ungodliness and unrighteousness of men, who suppress the truth in unrighteousness.*

1 Thessalonians 1:10 [But we] *wait for His Son from heaven, whom He raised from the dead, even Jesus who delivers us from the wrath to come.*

1 Thessalonians 5:9 *For God did not appoint us to wrath, but to obtain salvation through our Lord Jesus Christ,*

1 Thessalonians 5.1-7 *But concerning the times and the seasons, brethren, you have no need that I should write to you. For you yourselves know perfectly that the day of the Lord so comes as a thief in the night. For when they say,*

160

Peace and safety! then sudden destruction comes upon them, as labor pains upon a pregnant woman. And they shall not escape. But you, brethren, are not in darkness, so that this Day should overtake you as a thief. You are all sons of light and sons of the day. We are not of the night nor of darkness. Therefore, let us not sleep, as others do, but let us watch and be sober.

This Would Have Been a Perfect Time for Paul to Tell Us We Would Be Raptured out Before this 'Day of the Lord'.

So, on the Day of the Lord, Jesus comes as a thief in the night because we know not the day nor the hour; but here we have the sons of darkness and the sons of light both experiencing this 'Day of the Lord' at the same time. The saints of God will be the only ones experiencing *'peace and safety'*.

In the parable of the virgins, those five who had no oil and did not know where to find it; they came back 'empty handed' and Jesus says, 'I know you not'. Obviously, they did not have a relationship with Jesus, because they would have had oil which is the filling of the Holy Spirit.

Paul speaks much of the day the Lord will return. He's speaking to Christians. Such an anointing of revelation had he, that certainly, if we would be raptured out before that Day of the Lord, he would have joyously shared this great news concerning the times and seasons. This day of darkness would not overtake us cause we would be 'outta here'. Paul would have been very clear about this as he was with other doctrine. *But you yourselves know perfectly well.* He was preparing them because many of them believed Jesus would come back in their lifetime. But now - this pertains to us.

Obviously, the Saints Will Be on the Earth - on the Day of the Lord. We Do Not Know When, but We Are Expecting Him,

And Will Have His Perfect Peace.

Isaiah 26.20-27.1 *Come, my people, enter your chambers, and shut your doors behind you; Hide yourself, as it were, for a little moment, Until the indignation is past. For behold, the Lord comes out of His place To punish the inhabitants of the earth for their iniquity; The earth will also disclose her blood, And will no more cover her slain.*

And Where Do We Hide Ourselves?

Colossians 3.2-4 *Set your mind on things above, not on things on the earth. For you died, and your life is hidden with Christ in God. When Christ who is our life appears, then you also will appear with Him in glory.*

1 Thessalonians 4.15-16 *For this we say to you by the word of the Lord, that we who are <u>alive and remain until the coming of the Lord </u>will by no means precede those who are asleep. For the Lord Himself will descend from heaven with a shout, with the voice of an archangel, with the trumpet of God. And the dead in Christ will rise first.*

This Doesn't Sound like a Silent Removal of Saints.

Pre-Mid-Post... Do you think no one would notice if millions of tombstones were being uprooted? What's that all about? Such confusion about what is supposedly being said and misunderstood by men of God.

Psalm 50.3-6 *Our God shall come, and shall not keep silent; A fire shall devour before Him, and it shall be very tempestuous all around Him. He shall call to the heavens from above, and to the earth, that He may judge His people. Gather My saints together to Me, those who have made a covenant with Me by sacrifice. Let the heavens declare His righteousness, For God Himself is Judge.* What sacrifice?

That We Would Die to Self as Jesus Did.
He Will Judge Us All and Separate the Saints
From Sinners on the Day of the Lord.

Matthew 24.30-31 *Then the sign of the Son of Man will appear in heaven, and then all the tribes of the earth will mourn, and they will see the Son of Man coming on the clouds of heaven with power and great glory. And He will send His angels with a great sound of a trumpet, and they will gather together His elect from the four winds, from one end of heaven to the other.* We will all see Him coming - saints and sinners; some with joy and some with sorrow and regret. On this glorious Day of the Lord we will be gathered unto Him for eternity.

Matthew 24.26-*27 Therefore if they say to you, Look, He is in the desert! do not go out; or Look, He is in the inner rooms! do not believe it. For as the lightning comes from the east and flashes to the west, so also will the coming of the Son of Man be.* [No secret here].

Revelation 22.12-14 *And behold, I am coming quickly, and My reward is with Me, to give to every one according to his work. I am the Alpha and the Omega, the Beginning and the End, the First and the Last.*

This Is the Day of the Lord. All Will Receive Their
Just Reward for Eternity - With Him or Not!
Here's what will happen as per Scripture...

Acts 1.9-12 Now *when He had spoken these things, while they watched, He was taken up, and a cloud received Him out of their sight. And while they looked steadfastly toward heaven as He went up, behold, two men stood by them in white apparel, who also said, Men of Galilee, why do you stand gazing up into heaven? This same Jesus, who was taken up from you into heaven, will so come in like manner as you saw Him go into heaven.*

Revelation 1.7 *Behold, He is coming with clouds, and every eye will see Him, even they who pierced Him.*

So People Will See Him Coming Back
In the Same Manner He Left.

Notes from my Scofield Bible say... 'The return of Christ is an event, not a process, and is personal and corporeal' [means a physical tangible body, same as He appeared to His disciples after His resurrection]. [But then this second Scofield note tells us] 'He will come for His saints at one time and then come again on the Day of The Lord.' KJV

So Which Truth Is Correct –
A Process or a One Time Event?

It is ludicrous to try to declare when Jesus will come back. There is so much confusion concerning the day of the Lord. We can only find truth in the Word of God. To reiterate...

Matthew 24.23-29 *Then if anyone says to you, Look, here is the Christ!' or 'There!' do not believe it. For false christs and false prophets will rise and show great signs and wonders to deceive, if possible, even the elect. See, I have told you beforehand. Therefore, if they say to you, Look, He is in the desert!' do not go out; or Look, He is in the inner rooms!'* [Or He's in the sky rapturing us], *do not believe it. For as the lightning comes from the east and flashes to the west, so also will the coming of the Son of Man be.*

So, don't look to be 'raptured' out in secret before the great Day of the Lord. He is coming with all His angels and trumpets blaring to gather in His elect for all eternity.

Revelation 1.8 *And all the tribes of the earth will mourn because of Him. Even so, Amen. I am the Alpha and the*

Omega, the Beginning and the End, says the Lord, who is and who was and who is to come, the Almighty.

So, do we know 'who, where or what we are'? This is the gift we have been given - the knowledge that...

"Christianity is the self-disclosure of Jesus Christ".
Ravi Zacharias

Do you know Jesus and does He know you? Remember the 5 virgins...*I never knew you.*

Romans 10:6 *For whoever calls on the name of the Lord shall be saved.*

He Is the Way, the Truth and the Life; He Is The Word of God in Flesh. Would He Lie to Us? Do We Have Theory or Do We Have Reality?

Oh hallelujah! Job 19:25-27

For I know that my Redeemer lives, And He shall stand at last on the earth; And after my skin is destroyed, this I know, that in my flesh I shall see God, Whom I shall see for myself, and my eyes shall behold, and not another. How my heart yearns within me!

Thank You Jesus,

Thank You For Showing Me Your Truth.

TWO WITNESSES - REVELATION CHAPTER 11

And again, I write some words from a previous chapter.

Remember that Scripture is verified in the mouth of two or three witnesses; Old and New Testament.

Deuteronomy 31.25-27 *Moses commanded the Levites, who bore the ark of the covenant of the Lord, saying take this Book of the Law, and put it [inside] the ark of the covenant of the Lord your God, that it may be there as a witness against you;* This is the Old Testament.

Hebrews 10.15-16 *But the Holy Spirit also witnesses to us; This is the covenant that I will make with them after those days, says the Lord I will put My laws into their hearts, and in their minds, I will write them,* [Jeremiah 31.31]. And 1 John 5.6-7 *It is the Spirit who bears witness, because the Spirit is truth.*

Acts 1.8 *And you shall be witnesses unto me...*

We Testify to the New Covenant, The New Testament. The Word and the Spirit witness - The Old and the New Testament come together to witness the same God, the same Word, a continuation of the truth of the Gospel of 'Who is Jesus and who we are in Him'. This is the Gospel of the Kingdom of God that forms one witness.

The Christian and the Word of God are proclaiming now and till the end of time, The Gospel of the Kingdom. God is reaping His world. We Are Filled with the Holy Spirit

So We Have the Mind of Christ. We Are His Witnesses as We Share the Good News.

But will there be these witnesses only in Jerusalem? Or will the whole world be bursting with the truth of the God of our salvation, wanting to bring everyone into His eternal Kingdom.

Matthew 24:14 And *this gospel of the Kingdom will be preached in all the world as a witness to all the nations, and then the end will come.* Yes, there are witnesses of the Kingdom living right now all over the world, sharing the life of Jesus with their neighbors.

1 Timothy 2.3-4 *For this is good and acceptable in the sight of God our Savior, who desires all men to be saved and to come to the knowledge of the truth.*

Acts 2.20-21 The *sun shall be turned into darkness, and the moon into blood, Before the coming of the great and awesome day of the Lord. And it shall come to pass That whoever calls on the name of the Lord shall be saved.'*

This Message Will Be Proclaimed All Over the World.

Romans 10.14-15 *How then shall they call on Him in whom they have not believed? And how shall they believe in Him of whom they have not heard? And how shall they hear without a preacher? And how shall they preach unless they are sent? As it is written How beautiful are the feet of those who preach the gospel of peace, who bring glad tidings of good things!*

We are His 2 witnesses, The Believer and the Word.

Read Zechariah 4 especially verses 3&14.

Zechariah 4:2-4 *So I said, I am looking, and there is a lampstand of solid gold with a bowl on top of it, and on the stand seven lamps with seven pipes to the seven lamps. Two olive trees are by it, one at the right of the bowl and the other at its left.* [and see Revelation 11.4]

Zechariah 4:11-12 *Then I answered and said to him, "What are these two olive trees — at the right of the*

167

lampstand and at its left?" And I further answered and said to him, "What are these two olive branches that drip into the receptacles of the two gold pipes from which the golden oil drains?"

Zechariah 4:14 So he said, "These are the two anointed ones, who stand beside the Lord of the whole earth."

The Word of God is Symbolized by the Two Olive Trees Old and New Testament. The True Church is Symbolized By the Two Candlesticks, Jew and Gentile.

Rev 1:12-14 Then I turned to see the voice that spoke with me. And having turned I saw seven golden lampstands, and in the midst of the seven lampstands One like the Son of Man, clothed with a garment down to the feet and girded about the chest with a golden band.

Seven - the word for perfection. Jesus is here searching for His Bride within His churches, to bring correction where needed, and to make them ready for His return.

God has always had His witness in the world; but now in these times it is imperative that we, Go into all the world and preach the gospel. God is sending His witnesses into the world right now. We have a mandate to share the power, the good news of the Kingdom where ever we are; at work, at home, in the supermarket, on the bus. Time is getting short my sister, my brother.

Here's another witness...

Joshua 24.21-22 And the people said to Joshua, No, but we will serve the Lord! So, Joshua said to the people, you are witnesses against yourselves that you have chosen the Lord for yourselves, to serve Him. And they said, we are witnesses! Always confess Jesus is Your Lord!

Number 1 is the Believer in Christ -

Number 2 The Testimony of Jesus - the Word.

Jesus Is Revealed In Every Chapter Of The Bible.

And the fire of the truth of the Word will burn in the hearts of them who believe; but unbelievers will burn because they will not believe.

Here's a repeat...Fire will burn paper, and wood - it'll burn your house down and fire burned San Francisco to the ground ... But it didn't burn those three boys that were thrown into the burning fiery furnace.

Daniel 3.28 Delivered *His servants who trusted in Him so they might not serve nor worship any god, except their own God.*

Jeremiah 5.14 *Therefore thus says the Lord God of hosts Because you speak this word, Behold, I will make My words in your mouth fire, and this people wood, and it shall devour them.*

Some people believe Elijah and Moses are the two witnesses. *Elijah must come first.* - Please read Mt 11.7-15. Jesus Himself said about John the Baptist, *'this is Elijah, who was to come'.* And why, because John brought the people back to God. Moses and Elijah both brought the people back to God, and on the Mount with Jesus, they were symbolic of the Law and the Prophets, which Jesus was about to fulfill.

Revelation 19.9-10 *Then he said to me, "Write 'Blessed are those who are called to the marriage supper of the Lamb!'" And he said to me, "These are the true sayings of God. And I fell at his feet to worship him. But he said to me, see that you do not do that! I am your fellow servant, and of your brethren who have the testimony of Jesus. Worship God! For the testimony of Jesus is the spirit of prophecy.*

Jesus fulfilled those prophesies about Himself recorded in the Old Testament. The Gospel of Matthew shows us what will happen when this soon coming King comes for His Bride. It is revealed in the parable of the wheat and the tares.

He who has ears to hear, let him hear! So, we know first the wicked are taken out, and the righteous are left on the earth. Remember... When He returns *will He find faith on the earth*?

He will find no faith in the unrighteous. If the body of Christ is raptured out ahead of time, why would He look for faith among the unrighteous?

No... He's coming for Us, The Body of Christ, His Bride; Still Here - and Waiting For His Return.

TRUSTING IN GOD

Trusting in God Is the Foundation of Our Faith
And Is the Highest Form of Worship
Because You Are Literally
Putting Your Life into God's Hands.
He Is Trustworthy and Will Never Fail Us.

I have heard that the very center of all Scripture verses in the Bible is Psalm 118. 8. Could there be any words more appropriate, in a book of instructions by our God, than this one It *Is Better to Trust in the Lord Than to Put Confidence in Man*.

It would be a blessing to all who would meditate on the following verses and PRAY them into your life. Here is an example. Psalms 2.12

Blessed are all those who put their trust in Him.

PRAYER Lord, cause me to trust in You more every day, that I may receive Your blessings. Forgive me for trusting in anyone before You. Thank You for Your gift of salvation'.

If you don't understand the meaning of any verse then do James 1.5, and may God pour out His grace on you, as you search for a deeper relationship with your Lord.

So Now, Pray These Scriptures into Your Life;
Own Them as Promises from Your Heavenly Father,

As He Always Intended It to Be So.

Here are some starter verses and the beginning if your search for total dependence and trust on God for your life. There are many more. See a Concordance. And take up a journal. Write them down for your remembrance. You can refer to the ones that touched deep in your heart and experience the love and caring of the Lord Who loves you so much.

Psalm 5.11 *But let all those rejoice who put their trust in You; Let them ever shout for joy, because You defend them; Let those also who love Your name Be joyful in You.*

Psalm 7.1 *O LORD my God, in You I put my trust; Save me and deliver me,*

Psalm 9.10 And *those who know Your name will put their trust in You; For You, LORD, have not forsaken those who seek You.*

Psalm 11.1 *Faith in the LORD's Righteousness. In the LORD I put my trust.*

Psalm 25.2,20 O *my God, I trust in You; Let me not be ashamed; Let not my enemies triumph over me, for I put my trust in you.*

Psalm 13.1 *Trust in the Salvation of the LORD.*

Psalm 16.1 Preserve me, O God, for in You I put my trust.

Psalm 18.30 As *for God, His way is perfect; The word of the LORD is proven; He is a shield to all who trust in Him.*

Psalm 31.14 But *as for me, I trust in You, O LORD; I say, 'You are my God.'*

Psalm 31.19 Oh, *how great is Your goodness, Which You have laid up for those who fear You, Which You have prepared for those who trust in You In the presence of the sons of men!*

Psalm 34.22 The *LORD redeems the soul of His*

servants, and none of those who trust in Him shall be condemned.

Psalm 36.7 *How precious is Your lovingkindness, O God! Therefore, the children of men put their trust under the shadow of Your wings.*

Psalm 37.5 Commit *your way to the LORD, trust also in Him, And He shall bring it to pass.*

Psalm 37.40 *And the LORD shall help them and deliver them; He shall deliver them from the wicked, and save them, because they trust in Him.*

Psalm 40.3 He *has put a new song in my mouth Praise to our God; Many will see it and fear, and will trust in the LORD.*

Psalm 40.4 *Blessed is that man who makes the LORD his trust.*

Trusting in God is a transition from depending on yourself because no one else was ever there for you. I know all about this, for it was my story. One day God touched me to do this study on trusting Him. It revolutionized my life. Please Get a Concordance and Study the Scriptures on Trusting in God. There Are So Many.

> "Earth is crammed with heaven, and every bush is aflame with the fire of God! But only those who desire to see - will take off their shoes. The rest will just pick the berries".
> [Elizabeth Barrett Browning]

Revelation 12.11 *And they overcame him by the Blood of the Lamb and by the word of their testimony, and they did not love their lives to the death.* The word of their testimony was 'Never to deny Jesus as their Lord'. They have the testimony of Jesus, and His covenant of life and grace.

Revelation 19.10 ...*and of your brethren who have the*

testimony of Jesus. Worship God! For the testimony of Jesus is the spirit of prophecy.

The testimony of Jesus is the prophetic Word that reveals Who He is, written on the timeless pages of Bible history, and written indelibly in the hearts of all believers in Christ Who delivered them from darkness into His glorious light. Does this portray your heart?

I try so hard to surrender
All I have, all I am
But fear can have a front seat
To decide if I can
I want to live Your life,
I want to walk Your way
But every time I try Lord,
My imagination takes sway
If I could learn to trust You,
If I only could feel safe
Then my heart would truly give to You
All of me - all of me in sweet release.

One day I was feeling like I never do anything right and have so many regrets... but God in His grace and mercies said to me...

Don't go back there honey
To that dark and dismal place
I've made a way for you
To walk in My grace
Every tear you shed
Was for guilt and shame
But I've taken over your life
You're not the same
The Blood I shed on the cross for you
Has banished your shame and guilt
Remember when at prayer one night
I told My Father - 'Whatsoever You Will'.
I died so you could walk free of regret
So you don't have to go back there
Walk by My Spirit, die to your flesh
And never have any fear
So let Me dry your tears,
And stay with Me a while
I know how you are hurting,
You've been defiled
If you will trust Me, I'll show you how
You may become all you were created to be -
And we can start right now!

HALLELUJAH!

DECEPTION

For all the Scripture I've laid down here, I admonish you to investigate these in context; for the whole truth.

2 Thessalonians 2:9 *The coming of the lawless one is according to the working of Satan, with all power, signs, and lying wonders, and with all unrighteous deception among those who perish, because they did not receive the love of the truth, that they might be saved.*

If we don't want to know truth, what else can we expect.

Jeremiah 37:9 *Thus says the Lord: 'Do not deceive yourselves,*

We can fantasize many things in our own head and think they must be truth.

Jeremiah 29:8-9 *For thus says the Lord of hosts, the God of Israel: Do not let your prophets and your diviners who are in your midst deceive you, nor listen to your dreams which you cause to be dreamed. For they prophesy falsely to you in My name; I have not sent them, says the Lord.*

Too many take it on themselves to speak for God to earn notoriety, but all is deception.

Matthew 24:5 *For many will come in My name, saying, 'I am the Christ,' and will deceive many.*

Some 'pastors' have not been called of God, do not speak for God; and they do not preach the truth, for they are not anointed to know the truth. They are in 'business' for themselves, not... 1Timothy 3.9 *Holding the mystery of the faith with a pure conscience.*

Matthew 24:11-13 *Then many false prophets will rise up and deceive many. And because lawlessness will abound, the love of many will grow cold. But he who endures to the end shall be saved.*

We must bring our Bibles to Church and see if what we hear is truth; and learn to study the Word, not just read it; compare verses, OT/NT.

1 John 2:26-27 *These things I have written to you concerning those who try to deceive you. But the anointing which you have received from Him* [God's Holy Spirit John 14.26] *abides in you, and you do not need that anyone teach you; but as the same anointing teaches you concerning all things, and is true, and is not a lie, and just as it has taught you, you will abide in Him.*

Knowing the truth will make you free to worship God with a pure heart. Study the Word. Compare Scripture with Scripture.

Hebrews 5:14 *But solid food belongs to those who are of full age, that is, those who by reason of use have their senses exercised to discern both good and evil.*

Be diligent to allow the Holy Spirit to teach you and bring correction to any lies you have previously believed.

1 Corinthians 3:18-19 *Let no one deceive himself. If anyone among you seems to be wise in this age, let him become a fool that he may become wise. For the wisdom of this world is foolishness with God.*

There's too much at stake here to play games with truth/lies. Make up your mind - God or ...

1 John 1:8-10 *If we say that we have no sin, we deceive ourselves, and the truth is not in us. If we confess our sins, He is faithful and just to forgive us our sins and to cleanse us from all unrighteousness. If we say that we have not sinned we make Him a liar, His word is not in us.*

Hold steady for Holy Spirit correction. He will make things right *for* you and *in* you.

1 Corinthians 6*:9 Do you not know that the unrighteous will not inherit the Kingdom of God? Do not be deceived.*

Be quick to respond, because

Galatians 6:7 *Do not be deceived, God is not mocked; for whatever a man sows, that he will also reap.*

2 Thessalonians 2:2 *Let no one deceive you by any means; for that Day will not come unless the falling away comes first.*

Right now, many people and even pastors are leaving the church. Some because of disillusionment, some because the same dish is becoming old. 'OK I'm saved, what's next'?

Daniel 12:1-4 *At that time Michael shall stand up, the great prince who stands watch over the sons of your people; And there shall be a time of trouble, such as never was since there was a nation, Even to that time.*

And at that time your people shall be delivered, everyone who is found written in the book. And many of those who sleep in the dust of the earth shall awake, Some to everlasting life, Some to shame and everlasting contempt. Those who are wise shall shine Like the brightness of the firmament, and those who turn many to righteousness Like the stars forever and ever. But you, Daniel, shut up the words, and seal the book until the time of the end; many shall run to and fro, and knowledge shall increase."

'Knowledge shall increase'. Oh yeah... We have become very knowledgeable. Trips to the moon, atomic energy, iPhones... But where is the knowledge of the Lord. It behooves us to get in close to the Holy Spirit 'cause He's our teacher. He will show us all things.

John 14:26 *But the Helper, the Holy Spirit, whom the Father will send in My name, He will teach you all things, and bring to your remembrance all things I said to you.*

When Was The Last Time You Asked Him For Help?

2 Corinthians 2:9 *Lest Satan should take advantage of us; for we are not ignorant of his devices.*

1 Thessalonians 4:13 *But I do not want you to be ignorant, brethren...*

Paul only taught us truth, and in all his teaching, he would not have us ignorant. He did a lot of comparisons of good/evil. He wanted us to be able to discern when deception was taking place. But we wouldn't know it if we don't study the Word. If you know the truth, the moment you hear error, your spirit will reject it as not truth.

Romans 2:21 *You, therefore, who teach another, do you not teach yourself?*

1 Timothy 1:3-4 *that you may charge some that they teach no other doctrine, nor give heed to fables and endless genealogies, which cause disputes rather than godly edification which is in faith.*

If you are not able to question the teaching, then maybe it's time to leave that place and find a more reliable teacher.

Galatians 1:6-8 *I marvel that you are turning away so soon from Him who called you in the grace of Christ, to a different gospel, which is not another; but there are some who trouble you and want to pervert the gospel of Christ. But even if we, or an angel from heaven, preach any other gospel to you than what we have preached to you, let him be accursed.*

Of course, there is a church whose founder claims an angel told him all other religions were wrong and only he can build the correct one. The true church is built on Jesus the Messiah, not on a man destitute of reality; terrified and in denial.

2 Timothy 2:2-3 *And the things that you have heard from me among many witnesses, commit these to faithful men who will be able to teach others also.*

Men and women who know how to divide the Word of

truth/lies and are consistent in a Spirit led life style. They live humbly before their Lord.

Hebrews 5:12-14 *For though by this time you ought to be teachers, you need someone to teach you again the first principles of the oracles of God; and you have come to need milk and not solid food. For everyone who partakes only of milk is unskilled in the word of righteousness, for he is a babe. But solid food belongs to those who are of full age, that is, those who by reason of use have their senses exercised to discern both good and evil.*

That is, Their Spiritual Senses.
There Is Only One Foundation to Build Your Life On,

1 Corinthians 3:11 *For no other foundation can anyone lay than that which is laid, which is Jesus Christ.*

Proverbs 10:25 But *the righteous have an everlasting foundation...*

Isaiah 28:16 *Therefore, this is what the Sovereign Lord says: "Look! I am placing a foundation stone in Jerusalem, a firm and tested stone. It is a precious cornerstone that is safe to build on. Whoever believes need never be shaken.* [New Living Translation].

1 Corinthians 3:11 *For no one can lay any foundation other than the one we already have—Jesus Christ.* [Holy Bible, New Living Translation ®].

Ephesians 2.19-22 *Now, therefore, you are no longer strangers and foreigners, but fellow citizens with the saints and members of the household of God, having been built on the foundation of the Apostles and prophets, Jesus Christ Himself being the chief cornerstone, in whom the whole building, being fitted together, grows into a holy temple in the Lord, in whom you also are being built together for a dwelling place of God in the Spirit.*

I think these verses say it all as to what foundation we need. It is a rock under our feet and we will never slip.

1 Corinthians 10.4 IT'S JESUS!

Hebrews 8:11-12 *None of them shall teach his neighbor, and none his brother, saying, 'Know the Lord,' for all shall know Me, from the least of them to the greatest of them. For I will be merciful to their unrighteousness, and their sins and their lawless deeds I will remember no more.*

A repentant heart goes a long way with the Lord. Every day, be washed by the water of the Word.

What does that mean? As you read the Word, the Holy Spirit may focus on a selected one. As He does, you sense that this may be a part of your life that you need to pray about and washed clean of it. God will help you every time. Oh yes.

1 John 2:26-27 *These things I have written to you concerning those who try to deceive you. But the anointing which you have received from Him abides in you, and you do not need that anyone teach you; but as the same anointing teaches you concerning all things, and is true, and is not a lie, and just as it has taught you, you will abide in Him.*

We come together in fellowship to confirm the Word with each other - the Word we have been studying to share with others, and affirm that we have heard is truth. God does not want us ignorant of the devil's wiles; but God especially wants us to know Him personally and what does He require of you?

Micah 6:8 *He has shown you, O man, what is good; And what does the Lord require of you but to do justly, to love mercy, and to walk humbly with your God?*

Luke 10:27-28 *So he answered and said, you shall love the Lord your God with all your heart, with all your soul, with all your strength, and with all your mind,' and your neighbor as yourself. And He said to him, you have answered rightly; do this and you will live.*

2 Timothy 3:13-14 *But evil men and impostors will grow worse and worse, deceiving and being deceived.*

Titus 3:3-7 *For we ourselves were also once foolish, disobedient, deceived, serving various lusts and pleasures, living in malice and envy, hateful and hating one another. But when the kindness and the love of God our Savior toward man appeared, not by works of righteousness which we have done, but according to His mercy He saved us, through the washing of regeneration and renewing of the Holy Spirit, whom He poured out on us abundantly through Jesus Christ our Savior, that having been justified by His grace we should become heirs according to the hope of eternal life.*

I cannot say this enough...1 John 4:19

We love Him because He first loved us.

James 1:16-18 *Do not be deceived, my beloved brethren. Every good gift and every perfect gift is from above, and comes down from the Father of lights, with whom there is no variation or shadow of turning. Of His own will He brought us forth by the word of truth, that we might be a kind of firstfruits of His creatures.*

Two Of The Greatest Gifts We Can Receive Are
Learning To Forgive And Learning To Love.
Have You Yet Learned to Love the Unlovable?

2 Corinthians 6:11-7:1 *O Corinthians! We have spoken openly to you; our heart is wide open. You are not restricted by us, but you are restricted by your own affections. Now in return for the same (I speak as to children), you also be open. Do not be unequally yoked together with unbelievers. For what fellowship has righteousness with lawlessness? And what communion has light with darkness? And what accord has Christ with Belial? Or what part has a believer with an unbeliever? And what agreement has the temple of God with idols?*

For you are the temple of the living God. As God has said: I will dwell in them and walk among them. I will be their God, and they shall be My people. Therefore, come out from among them and be separate, says the Lord. Do not touch what is unclean, And I will receive you. I will be a Father to you, and you shall be My sons and daughters, Says the Lord Almighty. Therefore, having these promises, beloved, let us cleanse ourselves from all filthiness of the flesh and spirit, perfecting holiness in the fear of God [Amplified Bible].

1 John 3:2-3 *Beloved, now we are children of God; and it has not yet been revealed what we shall be, but we know that when He is revealed, we shall be like Him, for we shall see Him as He is. And everyone who has this hope in Him purifies himself, just as He is pure.*

We must be very careful of who it is we allow to teach us the Word. We are very capable of comparing words we hear and what the Word says, and what God's Holy Spirit is teaching us.

John 10:26-31 *My sheep hear My voice, and I know them, and they follow Me. And I give them eternal life, and they shall never perish; neither shall anyone snatch them out of My hand. My Father, who has given them to Me, is greater than all; and no one is able to snatch them out of My Father's hand. I and My Father are one.*

Do you hear the voice of God? He speaks to His people all the time. It is a promise to all of God's people. There are actually three voices we hear in our head. 1. Our own thoughts. 2. The voice of God. 3. the voice of the deceiver. But see John 10.27 My *sheep hear my voice...*

Hebrews 5:14 *But solid food belongs to those who are of full age, that is, those who by reason of use have their senses exercised to discern both good and evil.*

When I hear something, I always check with God. 'Is this my Jesus that hung on the cross for me'? The liar cannot admit to this so the thought will leave. If it is Jesus, He will confirm the message.

Romans 8:5-7 *For those who live according to the flesh*

set their minds on the things of the flesh, but those who live according to the Spirit, the things of the Spirit. For to be carnally minded is death, but to be spiritually minded is life and peace.

If your life's intention is to live for God, He will lead and guide you into all truth. Speak to Him on a daily basis, waiting on Him for the fellowship that is promised to you, then you will naturally hear His voice of comfort and love.

Father, Jesus, and the Holy Spirit So Long to Fellowship with You. The Cross of Jesus Made this Possible. We Serve a Good God and He Is a Good Father. Now...

May the God of Peace Fill You to Overflowing -
And be Sure to Thank Him

Martin Luther - Table Talk [quote].
"No greater mischief can happen to a Christian people than to have God's word taken from them or falsified, so that they no longer have it pure and clear. God grant we and our descendants be not witnesses of such a calamity".

John 5.19 & 12.49 God wants face to face with us, an open heaven for those of whom will choose to say what they hear the father saying, and do what they see the father doing. Jesus did what he saw His Father doing and said what His Father was saying. Can we hide behind the cross of Jesus where the darkness of our life is brought into the glorious light of the Kingdom of God? Jesus will hide us under the blood.

We Must Stop Taking Scripture out of Context. It Only Subscribes to Pretext. Pretext: a Motive Assumed - in Order To Conceal the True Purpose. Sorry to say this is done by too many 'men of God'.

A good example is what I heard the other day on YouTube, using Luke 21.31-32 and Matthew 24.3,34-35 to tell his people that the generation Jesus is talking about is the one right then - at the disciple's generation. He tears these verses out of the context of these chapters where Jesus is talking about the end time generation when He comes back. Of course, this 'pastor' also claims that Jesus is not coming back and that all these things have already happened. He fails to read the whole chapters - of Matthew 24 & Luke 21. TAKE HEED THAT NO MAN DECEIVE YOU.

Obviously, his congregation does not read the Bible for themselves. Please Read the Whole Context of These Verses.

Hebrews 10:35-39 *Therefore do not cast away your confidence, which has great reward. For you have need of endurance, so that after you have done the will of God, you may receive the promise: For yet a little while, And He who is coming will come and will not tarry. Now the just shall live by faith; But if anyone draws back, my soul has no pleasure in him. But we are not of those who draw back to perdition, but of those who believe to the saving of the soul.*

Do You Believe to the Saving of Your Soul?
If You Do...

John 14:27-28 *Peace I leave with you, My peace I give to you; not as the world gives do I give to you. Let not your heart be troubled, neither let it be afraid. You have heard Me say to you, 'I am going away and coming back to you.'*

Jesus Always Keeps His Promises

What is God saying here,
That your heart cannot agree
Are you troubled by your past?
You're afraid God can see
God is omniscient, omnipresent,
He Knows it all
There's nothing you can hide from Him
He sees you rise and fall
He saw you in your Mother's womb
He saw you being birthed
He really did create you
To walk upon His earth
He wants you for His very own,
Forever at His side
So give Him all your heart and soul
Forever to abide.

You Sent down Your Love
In the Form of a Man
Two Arms That Reached Out,
Two Feet That Walked My Path,
A Heart That Was Broken
And Tears That Were Shed,
With the Love
That You Sent down to Man.

WHAT DO WE KNOW?

There is no knowledge concerning the things of God that does not come from God; and so we must acknowledge this gift, (John 5.19 & 12.49). this treasure.

Psalm 145.16 *You open Your hand and satisfy the desire of every living thing. The Lord is righteous in all His ways, Gracious in all His works. The Lord is near to all who call upon Him, To all who call upon Him in truth. He will fulfill the desire of those who fear Him*

So, When Was the Last Time You Told God
How Grateful You Are for His Mercy and Grace?

God sees each of us as an individual. we are separate and unique to Him, and He has a wonderful plan to work out in each of our lives. Thank You Jesus, that You are the rock of my salvation and my ark of safety. The gates and walls of our city have been trampled by the enemy of our soul, but our God is in the business of rebuilding. Remember He was a carpenter.

He's Looking for Apprentices.

If we want God to correct our course we must be open to his 'interference', and choose to do it his way. Oh Lord, how You love Your creation, You have made us the focus of Your attention, that You have determined to share Yourself with us, no matter how many times we have failed You.

You've always been faithful to me,
I've learned time after time
To trust in You Lord, to rest in You Lord,
You've always been faithful to me.
Please live in me, Lord - And keep my heart true,
And I'll always be faithful to You.

The faithfulness of God is wrapped up in His integrity. It will never fail. His word is forever settled. My God, thank You for calling me into Your purpose. Please cause me to live in You. [Psalm 145]. Thank You God for making me Your temple, Your dwelling place. Thank You God, that You consider Your people worthy to partake of Your plans to harvest the earth for Your glory. Cause us to walk in Your compassionate love for the lost.

We Can Only Plant Seeds.
It Is the Lord Who Brings the Harvest.

The Most Valued Treasure on the Earth Is the Redeemed Restored Soul, and of These Will Be Built the City of God. For in Christ Jesus, Is All That the Father Has Planned.

Robert B. Thompson, Trumpet Ministries, Escondido, CA. has published several eye-opening books on the Kingdom of God. His conclusive evidence declares -

> Our life in this present world is almost exclusively a time of preparation. If we make our pilgrimage upon the earth the focus of our ambitions and joys, we shall have made the greatest mistake which it is possible for a human being to make. We are being prepared to live with God and serve Him forever and ever. And what will we be like

after a billion years have rolled by? GOD!! [1John 4.17].

Then from the throne there came a voice saying, praise our God, all you servants of His, you who reverence Him, Both small and great! After that I heard what sounded like the shout of a vast throng, Like the boom of many pounding waves, and like the roar of terrific and mighty peals of thunder, exclaiming hallelujah, praise the Lord! For now, the Lord our God the Omnipotent, the all ruler, reigns. Let us rejoice and shout for joy, exulting and triumphant!

Let us celebrate and ascribe to Him glory and honor, For the marriage of the lamb at last has come, And His bride has prepared herself. She has been permitted to dress in fine radiant linen Dazzling and white - for the fine linen is - signifies - represents the righteousness, the upright, just and godly living, deeds and conduct, and right standing with God, of the saints, God's holy people. The angel said to me, write this down; Blessed, happy, to be envied, are those who are summoned, invited, called, to the marriage supper of the Lamb. [Revelation 19. 5-9 Amplified Bible].

Dedicated to the Bride,
The Mirror Image of Our Gracious Lord
Who Shed His Blood That She Might
Come Forth Pure and Holy,
Clothed in Righteousness,
Grace and Love to Rule and Reign
At His Side Forever.

Jesus Living in His People, His Temple; and this Is What He Wants. God Wants Face to Face with Us, that we die to our own agendas as did Jesus, and live for Him only.
An Open Heaven to Those of Whom Will Choose to Say

What They Hear the Father Saying, and Do What They See the Father Doing [John 5.19 & 12.49].

Jesus Did What He Saw His Father Doing
And Said What His Father Was Saying.
WHAT WOULD HAPPEN IF WE DID THE SAME?

Ah Lord God, cause me to come to your river of life, that I may receive all you have for me; a tree planted by these waters that I will never thirst, always manifesting life, and being a resource to those around. Cause me to love others as you have loved me; to see them as You see them; not as they would appear to me. Thank You that You love them just as You love me

God Persisted Until - Chiseled out of Stone,
There Stepped this Man of Faith
To Be the Father of All Who Believe.
If We Truly Have a Heart for the Lord,
We Will Be Tested.
There Is the Proving of Mt Moriah
In Every Life That Would Follow Jesus.
Moriah - Seen of Yah. Who Will Separate unto Him?
Is There Nothing That He May Not Require of Us?
If His Love Counted No Sacrifice Too Great,
What must He Ask of Us?

Kingdom history is most severely intriguing. So all in God's time, He performs His will. If we can understand that from Genesis, the beginning of the creation of man in the image of God, there has been a supernatural progression all the way through to John's Revelation of the consummation of all things. It is the unbroken testimony of a most gracious and loving God Who is restoring His people back to Himself. The rebuilding of Jerusalem was in preparation for the revealing of our Father God through Jesus His Son, and the unconquerable love He has for the people of His heart.

John 17.3 *This is life eternal, that they might know you, the only true God; and Jesus Christ whom you have sent.*

We must never forget our first love. His desire is to live deep within us so that we never forget to put Him first. Make Him the cause of all you do; that place in your heart that runs to Him for every dream and every decision. We are indeed His tabernacle; He has made us holy and He dwells in the Holy Place.

Leviticus 11.45 *You shall therefore be holy, for I am holy.*

Peter 1.16 *because it is written, be holy, for I am holy.*

And Now His Temple, His Place of Habitation
Within His People; Manifesting His Love,
His Life and Compassion for All Eternity,
For the People of His Heart.
Never Be Weary of Worshiping
The Lover of Your Soul.

PERFECT LAW OF LIBERTY

There Are Two Keys to Living
In the Perfect Law of Liberty.

James 1.22-*25 But he who looks into the perfect law of liberty and continues in it, and is not a forgetful hearer but a doer of the work, this one will be blessed in what he does.*
#1 KEY. OBEDIENCE TO HIS WORD.
John 14.15 If *you love Me, keep My commandments.*
#2 KEY. LOVE FULFILLS THE ROYAL LAW [OF LIBERTY.
James 2.8 *If you fulfill the royal law according to the Scripture, you shall love your neighbor as yourself.*
ROYAL: From a Foundation of Ruling Power to Walk in This Liberty. Does Christ Rule in Your Heart?
James 2.9-13 *but if you show partiality, you commit sin, and are convicted by the law as transgressors. So, speak and so do as those who will be judged by the law of liberty. For judgment is without mercy to the one who has shown no mercy. Mercy triumphs over judgment.*
Matthew 6.14-16 For *if you forgive men their trespasses, your heavenly Father will also forgive you. But if you do not forgive men their trespasses, neither will your Father forgive your trespasses.*
Luke 7.23 *Blessed is he who is not offended because of me.* Offenses will come but it is useless to hold onto them. Forgive all, live in harmony with all, and the peace

of God that passes all understanding will fill your heart. There is so much more to live for.

Galatians 5.13-14 *For you, brethren, have been called to liberty; only do not use liberty as an opportunity for the flesh, but through love serve one another. For all the law is fulfilled in one word, even in this You shall love your neighbor as yourself.*

Ephesians 4.30-32 *And do not grieve the Holy Spirit of God, by whom you were sealed for the day of redemption. Let all bitterness, wrath, anger, clamor, and evil speaking be put away from you, with all malice. And be kind to one another, tenderhearted, forgiving one another, even as God in Christ forgave you.*

The first commandments have to do with honoring God, the last ones have to do with our relationships with our Brothers & Sisters; our neighbors.

2 Corinthians 3.17 *Now the Lord is that Spirit; and where the Spirit of the Lord is, there is liberty.*

Romans 8.2 *For the law of the Spirit of life in Christ Jesus has made me free from the law of sin and death.*

Where do we get the power and grace to live and walk in the Perfect Law of Liberty? Only from the Spirit of God. But we must choose to yield our own agendas and prefer this higher calling.

Romans 13.10 *Love does no harm to a neighbor; therefore, love is the fulfillment of the law.*

Colossians 3.14-15 *But above all these things put on love, which is the bond of perfection.*

Galatians 5.1 *Stand fast therefore in the liberty by which Christ has made us free, and do not be entangled again with a yoke of bondage.*

Bondage to What? God has set us free from having to function in our old nature; to the way the old man lived. We are the New Man in Christ. The prison door has been opened. It's up to each of us to choose to walk out into

The Perfect Law of Liberty.

Matthew 5.17 *Jesus came not to destroy the law, but to fulfill it.* Even if heaven and earth pass away the law will not be done until it is fulfilled; and Jesus did just that! It has been replaced by the New Covenant

Mark 14:*24 This is My blood of the new covenant, which is shed for many.* Jew and Gentile - all become new.

Acts 15.19-29 There are two things missing from Paul's admonition concerning the Gentiles - Keeping the Sabbath and Tithing. Look it up. *Only abstain from idols, fornication, blood and from things strangled.* Seems simple enough. because Jesus fulfilled the law and it is now obsolete. And now set free from the law of the 10% tithe, we are free to give freely as He leads us [2Corinthians 9.7].

Galatians 2.21 *I do not set aside the grace of God; for if righteousness comes through the law, then Christ died in vain.*

Galatians 3.11 *But that no one is justified by the law in the sight of God is evident, for the just shall live by faith.*

John 8:31-32 *Then Jesus said to those Jews who believed Him, If you abide in My word, you are My disciples indeed. And you shall know the truth, and the truth shall make you free.*

Made Free By The Blood of Jesus.

GRACE

Jesus Is the Indescribable Favor of God. His Marvelous Grace Has Appeared to All, Bringing Salvation.

Ephesians 2.6 By *grace are you saved through faith.*
He did this for a people to gladly receive that He might surround us with a grace that brings everlasting life. This grace allows us to accept that other people are different, not like us; and not try to make them like us. They need to be like Jesus. All this because His extravagant mercy and love will fill our heart if we will receive it.

Or we can live with the trauma of offenses, stress, and isolation. Yes, that's what we bear when we don't forgive. But our Life-Giver has come to surround us with His grace, mercy and love because He is God, our Savior, and asks us to share this grace and love.

The law was our master and we had no way to escape this prison of rules and regulations that was a burden we could not carry. But God, He watched and waited for His perfect time. And in His fulness. Galatians 4.4-5.

Saul, arrogant defender of the law, invaded homes to drag out those rebels of the law who wanted to be free.

Acts 8.3-4 *As for Saul, he made havoc of the Church, entering every house, and dragging off men and women, committing them to prison.* He was well on his way to Damascus to bring them bound to Jerusalem; on his way to expand his 'business', God would intervene, Oh Yes!

In explosive brightness, Yahshua, the Lord of those

who Saul was tormenting, arrested him in his path [Acts 9].

I am Yahshua, who you are persecuting. Don't resist Me!

Now he would listen but he could not see; struck as blind as he was to seeing that Jesus was the Messiah, he would now find truth for himself. Like Jesus in the tomb, in darkness for 3 days, so Saul lay in darkness, but then resurrection - new life.

Ananias - 'Khananyah' in Hebrew, his name means 'grace of God'. The first thing Saul saw when he opened his eyes was grace. It's only grace that opens our eyes to see Yahvahshua our Messiah, and walk in our calling. It was the grace of God that brought Saul to his senses. And it was the pure revelation of grace given for the first time, since David. Yes David, the only Old Testament 'prophet, priest and king', [a picture of our Redeemer], who walked in God's grace. Others may have but it's not recorded. Now it would be shed abroad for all who would listen.

Ephesians 2.8-10 For *by grace you have been saved through faith, and that not of yourselves; it is the gift of God, not of works, lest anyone should boast.*

God prepared beforehand that we should walk in them.

Saul, his Hebrew name means 'to inquire, to ask'.

Acts 9.1-2 went *to the high priest and asked letters from him to the synagogues of Damascus, But* now!

Acts 9.5 And *he said, Who are You, Lord?*

Acts 9.6 Lord*, what do You want me to do?*

Now He's Asking the Right Questions.

When grace opened his eyes, He was saved, baptized and verse 20, knew what he had to do. But please know that his name was changed as was his intentions and attitude toward His new Law Giver Who would write His laws on Saul/Paul's heart as He does ours. His new name - Paul- means 'little'. Yes, God would humble Paul before people who would reject and even kill him

[Acts 14.19-20]. But up again. He wrote the letter to the Galatians exchanging the law for the abundant grace of God. No one is saved by keeping the law [Galatians 2.16].

Acts 14.22-23 *Strengthening the souls of the disciples, exhorting them to continue in the faith, and saying, we must through many tribulations, enter the Kingdom of God;*

Paul Was the Apostle of Grace.

Yes, God's grace led Paul through every trial you can imagine, only to come out victorious and knowing the heart of unbelievers. He knew where they were coming from.

Acts 28.26 *'Go to this people and say 'Hearing you will hear, and shall not understand; And seeing you will see, and not perceive;* but it didn't deter him. See verses 30-31. He still believed in God's grace and so do I, as I pray his prayer...

Philippians 3.7-11 *But what things were gain to me, these I have counted loss for Christ. Yet indeed I also count all things loss for the excellence of the knowledge of Christ Jesus my Lord, for whom I have suffered the loss of all things, and count them as rubbish, that I may gain Christ and be found in Him, not having my own righteousness, which is from the law, but that which is through faith in Christ, the righteousness which is from God by faith; that I may know Him and the power of His resurrection, and the fellowship of His sufferings, being conformed to His death, if, by any means, I may attain to the resurrection from the dead.*

Paul laid his heart bare for all to understand that unless we leave all our stuff behind, the Kingdom of God will not come in its fullness for those who would pursue the things of the world. [I too have suffered the loss of many things but I have released them into the hands of my Lord].

Philippians 2.12 *Not that I have already attained, or am already perfected; but I press on, that I may lay hold of that for which Christ Jesus has also laid hold of me. Brethren, I do not count myself to have apprehended; but one thing I do, forgetting those things which are behind and reaching forward to those things which are ahead, I press toward the goal for the prize of the upward call of God in Christ Jesus. Therefore, let us, as many as are mature, have this mind; and if in anything you think otherwise, God will reveal even this to you. Nevertheless, to the degree that we have already attained, let us walk by the same rule, let us be of the same mind.*

The Only Place of God's Rest
Is in His Grace.

Paul's credentials were of the highest recommend. To be known in the temple, the pharisees would have given him anything. His zeal for the law surpassed even them. He was adamant that the Jews would obey the law no matter what he had to do; if kill them he must; but God had other plans. Paul's determination would be used to conquer grace. His fierce anger against Jesus and His followers would be turned to love/compassion, and those things he was so proud of would be humbled on his knees of prayer.

When he left that bed of blindness, he forever closed the door to his accomplishments. He would now embrace the Kingdom of God in righteousness, peace and joy. Now on the other side of the fence, he would experience what he had poured out on those he hated, and he would learn the power of forgiveness. No longer Saul but now Paul; small in his own eyes but great in the eyes of the Jesus he came to die for.

God gave me a determination to keep going in the face of failure. Before Jesus came into my life, I was always disappointed and so therefore turned away from accomplishing anything. But Now God! I am determined to push through to what God has for me.

How about you? Are you ready to close forever, the door to your past; all your accomplishments, fame or fortune; and I speak also to those of whom had no accomplishments. These are the 'are nots, the has been's,' the failures, the unloved, abandoned, cast out, those who walk in fear of being tagged useless'. Well, believe it or not, I fit into most of these categories. My accomplishments were anger and unforgiveness. Yet Jesus found me on the road to nowhere. He grabbed me and pulled me out of darkness as He did Saul. He changed my name. Isaiah 62.12 You *shall be called Sought Out, A City Not Forsaken.*

And He Gave Me This Scripture...

Ephesians 2:19-22 *Now, therefore, you are no longer strangers and foreigners, but fellow citizens with the saints and members of the household of God...*

He Pulled out That Spirit of Rejection;
Opened the Door to the Kingdom
And I Ran Through.

Jeremiah 30.17 For *I will restore health to you and heal you of your wounds, says the Lord, because they called you an outcast...*

This is not only for me, but for any who will leave all behind and serve the God of love, grace and peace. You may have been a believer for a long time, but have you laid all your past, good or bad, on the altar of sacrifice to be burned in the fire of God's love?

God brought the fulness of grace through Paul; but David also knew God's grace as tearful repentance threw him on his face before God. Grace is for the repentant heart, it is divine power to walk in righteousness; the power to walk in confidence in the New Covenant with the law written in our heart, so we know the difference between the holy and the profane. It is not a license to sin willfully and then keep asking for forgiveness. It just doesn't work that way.

The Word of God gives so many keys to the Kingdom of God that in reading and studying the Word, one will have a positive sense of wisdom and acknowledgment of what it means to walk in the Kingdom with trust and faith in the God Who brought them in; and grace to do it.

May the Fire of God's Love and Grace
Burn in Your Heart Forever.

So, what is there explained how-to walk in faith and trust and experience the fulness of such;

Habakkuk 2.4, Hebrews 11.39 *The just shall walk by faith*.

Colossians 2.9-10 *For in Him* [Christ] *dwells all the fullness of the Godhead bodily; and you are complete in Him, who is the head of all principality and power.*

So How Do We Experience the Kingdom
To Be Blessed and Content?

Jesus taught us the principles of the Kingdom.

You're blessed when you've lost it all. I have lost many things in my life, I gave them all to the Lord, I'm ready for Him to give me what He knows I need [Matthew 6].

You're blessed when you're hungry for the Word; then you're ready for God to teach you.

You're blessed when the tears flow freely. God will heal your broken heart.

You're blessed every time someone offends you, and you immediately forgive them.

So, Give Away Your Life.
Your Task Is to Be True, Not Popular.

Love your enemies, yes! No matter what they've done. Forgiveness is a major principle in the Kingdom of God. Don't be poisoned by anger and bitterness. You will never regret living in this kind of freedom. As the Father is gracious and loving, so walk by His Spirit and *let this peace that passes understanding rule in your heart.* And we know that also...

He is the God of hope [Romans 15.13],
He is the God of patience [Romans 15.5; 16.20]
He is the God of peace [Heb 13.20]
He is the God of grace [1 Pet 5.10]
He is the God of love [2 Cor 13.11]
He is the God of comfort [Rom 15.5]
The God of truth [Psalm 31.5]

He Fills Our Life With Everything We Need.
Matthew 1.16 And Jesus said, *Blessed is he who is not offended because of Me.*

It's who you are; who you are becoming that counts. Born again lovers of God are being transitioned into the nature and character of God. The nature of sin no longer rules over your life. It was left in the pit, to shrivel up and die. So let His peace, love and joy rule over your mind, your heart and your soul.

Seems to me that God sends his blessings down through the generations for all of whom will obey him. look up the verses on 'blessed'. You will be surprised to know what God has in store for you.

Jeremiah 17.7-8 *Blessed is the man who trusts in the*

Lord, and whose hope is the Lord. For he shall be like a tree planted by the waters, which spreads out its roots by the river, and will not fear when heat comes; But its leaf will be green, And will not be anxious in the year of drought, Nor will cease from yielding fruit.

The Blessing of His Presence Has Been Passed Down to All Lovers of God. But We Know the Age of Grace Will Soon Come to Close, as Our Messiah Comes to Earth Once Again; This Time to Rule and Reign with a New Purpose; So Totally Embraced by the Living God.

Now We Have the Foretaste; Then the Reality –HABITATION.

COVENANT

Before Christ, covenants were modified with animal's blood, but then...

Mark 14:24 *This is My blood of the new covenant, which is shed for many.*

It is adamant - set in stone that we understand the power of covenant and who can make it, revise and modify it.

Man's covenant - shake hands.

But God's Covenants are Ratified by Blood.

Leviticus 26.9-13 *For I will look on you favorably and make you fruitful, multiply you and confirm My covenant with you. I am the Lord your God, who brought you out of the land of Egypt, that you should not be their slaves; I have broken the bands of your yoke and made you walk upright.* [Upright: to establish, to succeed].

God's Covenants All Began with Noah.

Genesis.6.18-19 *But I will establish My covenant with you; and you shall go into the ark — you, your sons, your wife, and your sons' wives with you.*

Genesis 9.12-17 *And God said This is the sign of the covenant which I make between Me and you, and every living creature that is with you, for perpetual generations I set My rainbow in the cloud, and it shall be for the sign of the covenant between Me and the earth. It shall be, when I bring a cloud over the earth, that the rainbow shall be seen in the cloud; and I will remember My covenant which is between Me and you and every living creature of all flesh; the waters shall never again become a flood to destroy all flesh.*

The rainbow shall be in the cloud, and I will look on it to remember the everlasting covenant between God and every living creature of all flesh that is on the earth. And God said to Noah, this is the sign of the covenant which I have established between Me and all flesh that is on the earth.

Genesis 8:20 *Then Noah built an altar to the Lord, and took of every clean animal and of every clean bird, and offered burnt offerings on the altar.* The sacrifice of blood to thank God for keeping them safe, and to acknowledge the covenant God had just promised. We still see the rainbow after the rain. God remembers and so do we; that He is a faithful God.

Genesis 11.10 tells us Shem was 100 years old when they came out of the ark. It took Noah 120 years to build the ark. They were in the ark for one year. So was Noah building the ark by himself for 30 years, before his sons could help him? I'm just wondering. I also think the animals in the ark were young and small to get use to their new environment and...

God's Covenant Is for Life for All His Creation.
That We Would Be Fruitful and Multiply.
Now it Is Renewed with Abraham.

Genesis 15.7-8 God's covenant with Abraham for the land of Israel. 15.4 covenant for a son.

Chapter 17 covenant to be father of many nations.

Verses .9-14 the covenant of circumcision.

Genesis 17.9-10 *And God said to Abraham As for you, you shall keep My covenant, you and your descendants after you throughout their generations. This is My covenant which you shall keep, between Me and you and your descendants after you. Fear not Abraham, I am your shield and exceedingly great reward.*

God's Covenants are Ratified with Blood.

Genesis 15.7-21 please read it. The Lord made these covenants with Abraham with blood and for every one after with blood. For He said, *The Life is in The Blood.*

Genesis 15.9-10 He *said to him, Bring Me a three-year-old heifer, a three-year-old female goat, a three-year-old ram, a turtledove, and a young pigeon. Then he brought all these to /Him and cut them in two, down the middle, and placed each piece opposite the other; but he did not cut the birds in two.* He took from the great to the small... In Behalf of the Rich and the Poor.

And it came to pass, when the sun went down and it was dark, that behold, there appeared a smoking oven and a burning torch that passed between those pieces.

It was the Shekinah glory. Nothing less could have made these promises that we know all came to pass. *On the same day the Lord made a covenant with Abram...*

First a Man - Now a Nation.

Israel, Set Free by the Blood of the Lamb.

Exodus 12.7 *You will take of the blood and strike it on the two side posts and the upper door posts of the houses.* Israel walked out of Egypt.

Exodus 7.20-21 *And Moses and Aaron did so, just as the Lord commanded. So, he lifted up the rod and struck the waters that were in the river, in the sight of Pharaoh and in the sight of his servants. And all the waters that were in the river were turned to blood. The fish that were in the river died, the river stank, and the Egyptians could not drink the water of the river. So, there was blood throughout all the land of Egypt.*

This Was the First Plague by the Blood
To Affirm Those That Came After.

Ten plagues destroyed Egypt, their gods, their cattle, and finally their first-born sons. Retribution for Israel's sons. Psalm 105.23-38 tells the story.

Now they are free from slavery, but not free to go their own way. The grace and love of God wants to show them Who it was that set them free and to understand covenant. The law set in stone was their covenant with the God that brought them out slavery into His Kingdom.

Exodus 23.31-33 *And I will set your bounds from the Red Sea to the sea, Philistia, and from the desert to the River. For I will deliver the inhabitants of the land into your hand, and you shall drive them out before you. You shall make no covenant with them, nor with their gods.*

Exodus 24.7-8 *Then he took the Book of the Covenant and read in the hearing of the people. And they said, all that the Lord has said we will do, and be obedient. And Moses took the blood, sprinkled it on the people, and said, this is the Blood of the Covenant which the Lord has made with you according to all these words* [because God's covenants are binding].

Psalm 105.9-10 *The covenant which He made with Abraham, And His oath to Isaac, and confirmed it to Jacob for a statute, To Israel as an everlasting covenant.*

Psalm 89.27-29 *Also I will make him My firstborn, The highest of the kings of the earth. My mercy I will keep for him forever, And My covenant shall stand firm with him. His seed also I will make to endure forever, And his throne as the days of heaven.* [Covenant with David].

1 Chronicles. 15-16 tells the story of what David did. He set up a tent on Mt Zion and after a glorious parade he set inside the tent, the Ark of Covenant and appointed praisers and worshipers just outside the tent

to continuously acknowledge the holiness of the God of Israel. Vs 1-2 *And they offered burnt sacrifices.*

Psalm 89.34-*36 My covenant I will not break, nor alter the word that has gone out of My lips. Once I have sworn by My holiness; I will not lie to David. His seed shall endure forever...* [And it did, right up to Jesus].

Acts 15.16 *After this I will return And will rebuild the tabernacle of David, which has fallen down; I will rebuild its ruins, And I will set it up; So that the rest of mankind may seek the Lord, Even all the Gentiles who are called by My name, Says the Lord who does all these things.* [God wants covenant with 'whosoever will].

The tabernacle David set up was the definition of New Testament worship to the God of all creation. He tore the curtain from top to bottom; He did it so we could come in. Praise and worship before coming into His presence, for God is holy and wants us to be holy [Colossians 1.22] And the sacrifice of Blood has already been made by Jesus for an everlasting covenant with His New Man creation.

Psalm 103.17-*18 But the mercy of the Lord is from everlasting to everlasting on those who fear Him, And His righteousness to children's children, To such as keep His covenant, And to those who remember His commandments to do them.*

Isaiah 55.2-3 *Listen carefully to Me, and eat what is good, and let your soul delight itself in abundance. Incline your ear, and come to Me. Hear, and your soul shall live; And I will make an everlasting covenant with you — The sure mercies of David.*

2 Chronicles 6.10-11 *So the Lord has fulfilled His word which He spoke, and I have filled the position of my father David, and sit on the throne of Israel, as the Lord promised; and I have built the temple for the name of the Lord God of Israel. And there I have put the ark, in which is the covenant of the Lord which He made with the children of Israel* [this was Solomon]

Psalm 50.4-6 *He shall call to the heavens from above, and to the earth, that He may judge His people. Gather My saints together to Me, those who have made a covenant with Me by sacrifice. Let the heavens declare His righteousness, For God Himself is Judge.*

So, you say what about this new covenant? This new one is a revised edition. The new Everlasting Covenant is this; He wrote His new covenant laws on our heart, as it was prophesied and declared in former chapters of His Book. No more bound by a law they, or us, could not keep. It is important to know how this new covenant was established. Proof text in His Word.

Malachi 3.1-*3 Behold, He is coming, [the messenger of the covenant] Says the Lord of hosts. But who can endure the day of His coming? Who can stand when He appears? For He is like a refiner's fire and like launderers' soap.*

Matthew 26.27-29 *Then He took the cup, and gave thanks, and gave it to them, saying, Drink from it, all of you. For this is My blood of the new covenant, which is shed for many for the remission of sins.*

Mark 14.23-24 *Then He took the cup, and when He had given thanks, He gave it to them, and they all drank from it. And He said to them,* <u>*this is My blood of the new covenant, which is shed for many*</u>.

Jeremiah 31.31 This is the New Covenant verified in...

Hebrews 8.7-13 *For if that first covenant had been faultless, then no place would have been sought for a second. Because finding fault with them, He says Behold, the days are coming, says the Lord, when I will make a new covenant with the house of Israel and with the house of Judah — not according to the covenant that I made with their fathers in the day when I took them by the hand to lead them out of the land of Egypt; because they did not continue in My covenant, and I disregarded them, says the Lord.*

For this is the covenant that I will make with the house

of Israel after those days, says the Lord I will put My laws in their mind and write them on their hearts; and I will be their God, and they shall be My people. None of them shall teach his neighbor, and none his brother, saying, 'Know the Lord,' for all shall know Me, from the least of them to the greatest of them. For I will be merciful to their unrighteousness, and their sins and their lawless deeds I will remember no more. In that He says, A new covenant, He has made the first obsolete. Now what is becoming obsolete and growing old is ready to vanish away.

Hebrews 9.13-19 *For if the blood of bulls and goats and the ashes of a heifer, sprinkling the unclean, sanctifies for the purifying of the flesh, how much more shall the blood of Christ, who through the eternal Spirit offered Himself without spot to God, cleanse your conscience from dead works to serve the living God? And for this reason, He is the Mediator of the new covenant, by means of death, for the redemption of the transgressions under the first covenant, that those who are called may receive the promise of the eternal inheritance.*

The Mediator's Death is Necessary

For where there is a testament, there must also of necessity be the death of the testator. For a testament is in force after men are dead, since it has no power at all while the testator lives. Therefore, not even the first covenant was dedicated without blood. And More Confirmation...

Hebrews 10.16-18 *This is the covenant that I will make with them after those days, says the Lord I will put My laws into their hearts, and in their minds, I will write them, then He adds, their sins and their lawless deeds I will remember no more. Now where there is remission of these, there is no longer an offering for sin.* The Blood of Jesus Was Final...

So How Far Does this New Covenant Extend?

Remember This One...

Psalm 103.17-18 *But the mercy of the Lord is from everlasting to everlasting On those who fear Him, And His righteousness to children's children, To such as keep His covenant, And to those who remember His commandments to do them.*

Covenant is always Linked to Obedience.

This new covenant became reality as the good news of the Kingdom was spread first in Judea, then to all parts of the world. With the Holy Spirit living within us, it is easy to remember to worship God and love our brother.

These next Verses Concern Circumcision. It's Important to Understand How the Hebraic Law Does Not Apply to Gentile Converts. Be Sure to Understand Verse 18 and What Was Left Out of this New Covenant.

Acts 15.6-11 *Now the Apostles and elders came together to consider this matter. And when there had been much dispute, Peter rose up and said to them Men and brethren, you know that a good while ago God chose among us, that by my mouth the Gentiles should hear the word of the gospel and believe. So God, who knows the heart, acknowledged them by giving them the Holy Spirit, just as He did to us, and made no distinction between us and them, purifying their hearts by faith. Now therefore, why do you test God by putting a yoke on the neck of the disciples which neither our fathers nor we were able to bear? But we believe that through the grace of the Lord Jesus Christ we shall be saved in the same manner as they.*

Acts 15.12-21 *Then all the multitude kept silent and listened to Barnabas and Paul declaring how many* miracles and wonders God had worked through them among the Gentiles. And after they had become silent, James answered, saying, Men and brethren, listen to me. Simon has declared how God at the first visited the Gentiles to take out of them a people for His name. And with this the words of the prophets agree, just as it is written - Leviticus 11.45 *You shall therefore be holy, for I am holy.*

1 Peter 1.16 *Because it is written, Be holy, for I am holy.*

Acts 15.18 *Known to God from eternity are all His works. Therefore, I judge that we should not trouble those from among the Gentiles who are turning to God, but that we write to them to abstain from things polluted by idols, from sexual immorality, from things strangled, and from blood.* No tithe and no Sabbath laws;

2 Corinthians 9:7-8 So *let each one give as he purposes in his heart, not grudgingly or of necessity; for God loves a cheerful giver.* Yes, now Gentiles have come under this new covenant because of Romans 11. 7-32. Gentiles were grafted in to the 'olive tree' of Israel to become ...

Ephesians 2:1-14-17 *Therefore remember that you, once Gentiles in the flesh — who are called Uncircumcision by what is called the Circumcision made in the flesh by hands, that at that time you were without Christ, being aliens from the commonwealth of Israel and strangers from the covenants of promise, having no hope and without God in the world. But now in Christ Jesus you who once were far off have been brought near by the blood of Christ. For He Himself is our peace, who has made both one, and has broken down the middle wall of separation to create in Himself one new man from the two, thus making peace, and that He might reconcile them both to God in one body through the cross, thereby putting to death the enmity* [differences between us.].

The law of Moses became saturated with the pharisees'

rules and regs that no one could possibly endure. The straight commandments were hard enough because at that time the grace of God had not been available. But Now...

Romans 11.6-8 *And if by grace, then it is no longer of works; otherwise grace is no longer grace. But if it is of works, it is no longer grace; otherwise work is no longer work. What then? Israel has not obtained what it seeks; but the elect have obtained it, and the rest were blinded.*

The law of Moses was obeyed by works of the flesh and not possible to keep for a lifetime; that's why God had mercy, but only at the appropriate time

Galatians 4.3-*5 Even so we, when we were children, were in bondage under the elements of the world. But when the fullness of the time had come, God sent forth His Son, born of a woman, born under the law, to redeem those who were under the law, that we might receive the adoption as sons.*

Isaiah 45.4-5 *For Jacob My servant's sake, And Israel My elect, I have even called you by your name; I have named you, though you have not known Me. I am the Lord, and there is no other; There is no God besides Me.*

Isaiah 65.22-23 *And My elect shall long enjoy the work of their hands. They shall not labor in vain, nor bring forth children for trouble; For they shall be the descendants of the blessed of the Lord, And their offspring with them.*

Christians Are the Elect Descendants of Israel. God Has Covered Us Christians Also Under His Covenant That We May Inherit Their Blessings. One New Man in Him, Jew and Gentile.

We are each and every one
A reflection of God's glory,
Not a copy of another
A facsimile to ponder,
We're a one-time gift
A one-time wonder.
Faces made and character blend,
For only God to apprehend.

AND...

We Are Not of this World,
We Are Just Passing Through.
So Remember....
It's in the journey we come to know
The God of all creation
He didn't just come for us
He came for every nation
Though separated from each other
We're living on His earth
And we should learn they have His worth
And treat them as a brother
The love of God, not just for us
Was shed abroad for them
That they would also come to know
The presence of Ha Shem
So pray we must though they are strange
He died for all who lives
Because of love He has arranged
Eternal life to give.

WHO ARE THE ELECT?

Isaiah 45.4 *For Jacob My servant's sake, And Israel My elect, I have even called you by your name; I have named you, though you have not known Me.*

God also knew us before we were born and knows exactly who we are and where we are. We didn't know Him until the day He called us to His side. And to get ahead of myself, He knew when we would say yes to His call; His perfect timing. Romans 4 & 11 tell the story of why Gentiles are also called the elect. Abraham was called righteous because of his faith, and if we walk by faith as He did and believe God, then we are the righteousness of God in Christ.

2Corinthians 5.17-21 *For He made Him who knew no sin to be sin for us, that we might become the righteousness of God in Him.*

Isaiah 65.9 *I will bring forth descendants from Jacob, and from Judah an heir of My mountains; My elect shall inherit it.*

Romans 11.19-20 *You will say then, Branches were broken off that I might be grafted in. Well said. Because of unbelief they were broken off, and you stand by faith.*

We can also walk in the high places of God because us Gentiles have been grafted in to the vine. We inherit the blessings of Israel.

Romans 11.7-8 *What then? Israel has not obtained what it seeks; but the ELECT have obtained it, and the rest were blinded.*

Romans 11.16-18 *For if the roots of the tree are holy, the branches will be, too. But some of these branches from Abraham's tree—some of the people of Israel—have been broken off. And you Gentiles, who were branches from a wild olive tree, have been grafted in. So now you also receive the blessing God has promised Abraham and his children, sharing in the rich nourishment from the root of God's special olive tree. But you must not brag about being grafted in to replace the branches that were broken off. You are just a branch, not the root* [New Living Translation].

Colossians 3.12 *Elect of God holy and beloved.* Israel is still God's people, His ELECT, He will never abandon them; and He includes Gentiles. He sent Paul after us.

Isaiah 65.22-23 *And My elect shall long enjoy the work of their hands. They shall not labor in vain, nor bring forth children for trouble; For they shall be the descendants of the blessed of the Lord, And their offspring with them.*

God Deeply Cares for His People and Their Descendants.

Isaiah 45:4 *For Jacob My servant's sake, And Israel My elect, I have even called you by your name;*

2 Timothy 2:10 *Therefore I endure all things for the sake of the elect, that they also may obtain the salvation which is in Christ Jesus with eternal glory.*

Matthew 24.23-25 *Then if anyone says to you, 'Look, here is the Christ!' or 'There!' do not believe it. For false christs and false prophets will rise and show great signs and wonders to deceive, if possible, even the elect. See, I have told you beforehand.*

Mark 13.22-23 *For false christs and false prophets will rise and show signs and wonders to deceive, if possible, even the elect. But take heed; see, I have told you all things beforehand.*

God Always Warns Us When Trouble Is Coming.

Matthew 24.21-*22 For then there will be great tribulation, such as has not been since the beginning of the world until this time, no, nor ever shall be. And unless those days were shortened, no flesh would be saved; but for the elect's sake those days will be shortened.*
You See, the Elect, the Lovers of God
Are Still Here When Jesus Comes Back.
Please read 1John 4.10-21 We must never deny His name. The mark of the beast is a religious symbol; that is 1John 2.22 *Who is a liar but he that denies that Jesus is the Christ. He is antichrist that denies the Father and the Son.* [The spirit of antichrist lives in them].

Read this again, see if you missed anything.

Daniel 3:14 *Is it true, Shadrach, Meshach, and Abed-Nego, that you do not serve my gods or worship the gold image which I have set up? Now if you are ready at the time you hear the sound of the horn, flute, harp, lyre, and psaltery, in symphony with all kinds of music, and you fall down and worship the image which I have made, good! But if you do not worship, you shall be cast immediately into the midst of a burning fiery furnace. And who is the god who will deliver you from my hands*
Worshiping this image meant to worship the king and his belief system. This is what worshiping any image actually means. In Jeremiah 44 they worshiped the queen of heaven; this image was associated with molech, the idol to which they sacrificed their babies. They lived in Egypt, where once they were delivered from. In 42.19 they were warned not to go into Egypt but they went anyway; and were seduced by their gods.
Is anyone aware there is a giant statue of molech at the entrance of the colosseum in Rome.

So, let's look at the verses that speak of worshiping the beast, and/or his image. Revelation 13.4,12,15; 14.9,11; 16.20. In all these verses, worshiping the image means that you agree with his doctrine and you will believe his lies.

The image of any person is portrayed by our nature and character. That's how people know us. The image of the beast is portrayed by the nature of the antichrist; anyone who denies the Deity of Christ as it says in 1John 2.22.

He makes himself a god and demands that the unbeliever lives by his rules.

It Is Sad to Know Many People Will Do This.

There's only one way to break free from this deceiver, and that is by the Blood of Jesus. Repent and turn your heart around to worship the living God Jesus, Who gave His life for your salvation.

Matthew 24.30-*31 And they will see the Son of Man coming on the clouds of heaven with power and great glory. And He will send His angels with a great sound of a trumpet, and they will gather together His ELECT from the four winds, from one end of heaven to the other.*

So, His Elect are Still Here When He Comes Back.

Mark 13.26-27 *Then they will see the Son of Man coming in the clouds with great power and glory. And then He will send His angels, and gather together His ELECT from the four winds, from the farthest part of earth to the farthest part of heaven.*

Here again. Yes! Two witnesses, #1 Matthew, #2 Mark

God Wants Us to Know We Are Safe in Him.

Revelation 14.1 The Elect Are Marked by God and it Is Because We Worship Him Who Saved Us by His Blood.

Romans 8.31-36 *What then shall we say to these things? If God is for us, who can be against us? He who* did not spare His own Son, but delivered Him up for us all, how shall He not with Him also freely give us all things? Who shall bring a charge against God's ELECT? It is Christ who died, and furthermore is also risen, who is even at the right hand of God, who also makes intercession for us. Who shall separate us from the love of Christ? Shall tribulation, or distress, or persecution, or famine, or nakedness, or peril, or sword?

Nothing Shall Separate Us from God's Hand.
Colossians 3.12-17 The Character of the New Man.

Therefore, as the ELECT of God, holy and beloved, put on tender mercies, kindness, humility, meekness, long-suffering; bearing with one another, and forgiving one another, if anyone has a complaint against another; even as Christ forgave you, so you also must do. But above all these things put on love, which is the bond of perfection. And let the peace of God rule in your hearts, to which also you were called in one body; and be thankful. Let the word of Christ dwell in you richly in all wisdom, teaching and admonishing one another in psalms and hymns and spiritual songs, singing with grace in your hearts to the Lord. And whatever you do in word or deed, do all in the name of the Lord Jesus, giving thanks to God the Father through Him.

2 Timothy 2.9-10 But the word of God is not chained. Therefore, I endure all things for the sake of the ELECT, that they also may obtain the salvation which is in Christ Jesus with eternal glory.

God has not given up on Israel. The same salvation message pertains to Israel as it does to Gentiles. Both are His Elect.

Titus 1.1-3 Paul, a bondservant of God and an apostle of Jesus Christ, according to the faith of God's ELECT and the acknowledgment of the truth which accords with godliness, in hope of eternal life which God, who cannot lie, promised before time began, but has in due time manifested His word through preaching, which was committed to me according to the commandment of God our Savior.

In this day and time, the message of the gospel, the power of God is running through the earth, capturing the hearts of those who want truth and love in their lives. And here it is, freely given... JUST ASK.

1 Peter 1.1-2 Greetings to the ELECT Pilgrims

To the pilgrims of the Dispersion in Pontus, Galatia, Cappadocia, Asia, and Bithynia, ELECT according to the foreknowledge of God the Father, in sanctification of the Spirit, for obedience and sprinkling of the blood of Jesus Christ. Grace to you and peace be multiplied.

God's people *have* been dispersed all over the earth; running from tyranny and persecution. Many He has brought home to Himself, to others He grants perseverance. But He never takes His eyes off us.

Jeremiah 17.10 *I, the Lord, search the heart, I test the mind, even to give every man according to his ways, According to the fruit of his doings.*

2 Chronicles 16.9 *For the eyes of the Lord run to and fro throughout the whole earth, to show Himself strong on behalf of those whose heart is loyal to Him.*

And He Never Forgets.

1 Peter 1.1-2 *To the pilgrims of the Dispersion in Pontus, Galatia, Cappadocia, Asia, and Bithynia, ELECT according to the foreknowledge of God the Father, in sanctification of the Spirit, for obedience and sprinkling of the blood of Jesus Christ.*

Grace to You and Peace Be Multiplied.

1 Peter 2.1-6 *Therefore, laying aside all malice, all deceit, hypocrisy, envy, and all evil speaking, as newborn babes, desire the pure milk of the word, that you may grow thereby, if indeed you have tasted that the Lord is gracious.*

Coming to Him as to a living stone, rejected indeed by men, but chosen by God and precious, you also, as living stones, are being built up a spiritual house, a holy priesthood, to offer up spiritual sacrifices acceptable to God through Jesus Christ.

The Chosen Stone and His Chosen People

2 John 1-4 Greeting the ELECT Lady

The Elder, To the ELECT lady and her children, whom I love in truth, and not only I, but also all those who have known the truth, because of the truth which abides in us and will be with us forever Grace, mercy, and peace will be with you from God the Father and from the Lord Jesus Christ, the Son of the Father, in truth and love. Walk in Christ's Commandments.

John is writing to the Church, the ELECT of God.

2 John 13 *The children of your ELECT sister greet you.*

3 John *Greeting to Gaius the Elder, To the beloved Gaius, whom I love in truth Beloved, I pray that you may prosper in all things and be in health, just as your soul prospers. For I rejoiced greatly when brethren came and testified of the truth that is in you, just as you walk in the truth. I have no greater joy than to hear that my children walk in truth.*

The name Gaius means 'earth man'; that's all of us.

John, the apostle of love sent his letters to all the lovers of God.

John wrote most often to the Elect - The natural man - not just Israel, but ones who have chosen to walk with Jesus the Messiah; to encourage those to walk in truth and encouraging along the way.

The Elect - God's Chosen - to Walk in Holiness Day by Day
To Be Restored to the Image of God.
We love Him because He first loved us. 1John 4

I Am Loved by the God Who Created the Universe
And All There Is in It.
I am so Grateful to Him.

You've Taken the Broken Pieces
Of a Heart e'er Longed to Love
You Knew How Lonely and Lost I Was,
You Chose Me from Millions of 'Are Nots'.
You Put Your Arms Around Me
And Made Me Your Child
You Took Me as a Baby
And Brought Me Through Day by Day
You Gave Me the Courage to Pursue
Those Things I Never Knew Existed.
Now I Know It's You I Am Seeking
Cause You Are All I Will Ever Need
And You Will Always Be Enough.

One day I asked the Lord,
"Why are You called Holy?"
He said to me...
I Am called Holy because I Am unique -
Set apart from all creation.
All of creation is useless and of no value
But for what I give it.
I Am high above all else.

He said...
You are called holy
Because you are set apart
From all creation.
You are a son of God
Set apart to be My bride
High above all other creation for eternity
Your value is established in Me.

Malachi 3.16-17
Then they that feared the Lord spoke often
one to another and thought upon His name...
And the Lord heard it; ...They shall be Mine,
says the Lord of hosts, On the day that I make
up my jewels. And I will spare them as a man
spares his own son who serves him. NKJV

HIS REST

Exodus 16:*23 Then he said to them, "This is what the Lord has said: 'Tomorrow is a Sabbath rest, a holy Sabbath to the Lord* [means an intermission]. The Sabbath rest is repeated in 23.24 and 39. Even God rested when He finished the work of creation.

And slaves were to be given a day of rest. It was an insult to God when they did not take His Sabbath rest. Remember Israel went into 70 years of captivity because they would not rest on the seventh day nor the Sabbath year for the fields to rest. The bottom line is they would not trust God to take care of them for that year. They didn't do the feast of booths either; the Feast of Tabernacles; seven days of living in a flimsy makeshift tent and trust God to protect them from their enemies. In their disobedience they were constantly overrun by their enemies to steal their harvest and came to fear they would not have enough. [See Gideon's story]

The whole reason God created man was He wanted personal relationship with us; so, we would learn that in His great love for us, He would take care of us; that we would learn to trust Him in all our endeavors, and rest in that love. But the people He set apart for His own witness to the world that He is a good God, became rebellious and would not. Of course, we understand now that this rebellion came down the line from Adam. All we knew was to live in the flesh. And laws of do's and don'ts - well, it got too hard.

223

Of course, God knew we were just flesh and it would be too hard; but in fact, these rules are what make up the Kingdom of God. 'Love God and love your neighbor'. But there was a lot of regulations that seemed to make this too hard. And of course, the pharisees had to stick their nose in and make it even harder. But God already had a plan and now puts it into motion. This flesh thing had to die, but certainly we didn't know how to do that nor did we have the ability. So, God began to implement the whole process. He would show us by example.

Hebrews 3.7-11 Today, *if you will hear His voice, do not harden your hearts as in the rebellion, In the day of trial in the wilderness, where your fathers tested Me, tried Me, and saw My works forty years. Therefore, I was angry with that generation, and said, 'They always go astray in their heart, they have not known My ways.' So, I swore in My wrath, 'They shall not enter My rest.'*

Hebrews 3.15-16 Today, *if you will hear His voice, Do not harden your hearts as in the rebellion.*

Hebrews 3.18-19 *but to those who did not obey? So we see that they could not enter in because of unbelief.*

What it boils down to is this - they would not trust in God. Coming into His rest would be the same as the feast of Tabernacles; building booths out of palm, and myrtle tree branches, living in them for 7 days. But they would not believe nor trust in the God Who gave them such a wonderful land of their own. After four generations of slavery. I guess they forgot about all that but now God gives us understanding in these verses of how to climb into his rest. We should realize that God's rest is for every day of trusting Him for everything; not just one day a week.

Matthew 6:33-34 *But seek first the Kingdom of God and His righteousness, and all these things shall be added to you. Therefore, do not worry about tomorrow, for* tomorrow will worry about its own things. Sufficient for the day is its own trouble.

Isaiah 30.15 *For thus says the Lord God, the Holy One of Israel in returning and rest you shall be saved; In quietness and confidence shall be your strength.*

Jeremiah 6.16 *Thus says the Lord, stand in the ways and see, and ask for the old paths, where the good way is, and walk in it; Then you will find rest for your souls.*

Now God gives again the invitation in His New Covenant

Matthew 11.28-30 *Come to Me, all you who labor and are heavy laden, and I will give you rest. Take My yoke upon Me and learn from Me, for I am gentle and lowly in heart, and you will find rest for your souls. For My yoke is easy and My burden is light.*

Hebrews 3.14-15 we *have become partakers of Christ if we hold the beginning of our confidence steadfast to the end,*

Hebrews 4.3-4 *We who have believed do enter that rest, for the works were finished from the foundation of the world. God rested on the seventh day from all His works.*

This small nation of Israel was so indoctrinated into slavery, perhaps they saw God as just another slave master. They would not trust in Him nor would they keep His commandments. Miracles do not produce long lasting faith. They just saw each miracle as a way to satisfy their immediate need. So, God begins again with a generation that knew not slavery. Joshua rehearses their history and they swear they will serve the Lord [Joshua 24]. *You are witnesses against yourself that you have chosen to serve the Lord.*

Now a hundred years has passed, Moses and Joshua are gone, so God sent Judges to lead them in battle against their enemies, but finally ...

Judges 21.25 *In those days there was no king in Israel; everyone did what was right in his own eyes.*

225

And so there came great rebellion to God's ways so that finally they were taken captive to Babylon for 70 years. Their sin... They would not come into God's rest nor did they let the land have its Sabbath rest. In the seventh year they were to let the land lay dormant; but their fear of no harvest for a year, took precedent over God's word.

Hebrews 4.1-14 *Therefore, since a promise remains of entering His rest, let us fear lest any of you seem to have come short of it. For indeed the gospel was preached to us as well as to them; but the word which they heard did not profit them, not being mixed with faith in those who heard it. For we who have believed do enter that rest, as He has said So I swore in My wrath, 'They shall not enter My rest,' although the works were finished from the foundation of the world.*

For He has spoken in a certain place of the seventh day in this way And God rested on the seventh day from all His works; and again, in this place They shall not enter My rest. Since therefore it remains that some must enter it, and those to whom it was first preached did not enter because of disobedience, again He designates a certain day, saying in David, Today, after such a long time, as it has been said

Today, if you will hear His voice, Do not harden your hearts.

For if Joshua had given them rest, then He would not afterward have spoken of another day. There remains therefore a rest for the people of God. For he who has entered His rest has himself also ceased from his works as God did from His.

We must lay down our self-life if we are to inherit God's Kingdom and His promises. His rest brings our righteousness, peace and joy in the Holy Spirit.

Romans 14.17-18 *for the Kingdom of God is not eating and drinking, but righteousness and peace and joy in the*

Holy Spirit. For he who serves Christ in these things is acceptable to God and approved by men.

The Word Discovers Our Condition.

Let us therefore be diligent to enter that rest, lest anyone fall according to the same example of disobedience. For the word of God is living and powerful, and sharper than any two-edged sword, piercing even to the division of soul and spirit, and of joints and marrow, and is a discerner of the thoughts and intents of the heart. And there is no creature hidden from His sight, but all things are naked and open to the eyes of Him to whom we must give account.

God Knows Exactly Where We Are and How Much
We Trust Him. We Have A Compassionate High Priest.

Hebrews 4.14 *Seeing then that we have a great High Priest who has passed through the heavens, Jesus the Son of God, let us hold fast our confession. For we do not have a High Priest who cannot sympathize with our weaknesses, but was in all points tempted as we are, yet without sin. Let us therefore come boldly to the throne of grace, that we may obtain mercy and find grace to help in time of need.*

Psalm 24.7 *Lift up your heads, O you gates! And be lifted up, you everlasting doors! And the King of glory shall come in. Who is this King of glory? The Lord strong and mighty, The Lord mighty in battle.* Our King/Priest.

Thank You Lord, For Your Great Love
You've Brought Me to Your Rest,
I'm No Longer Second Hand
You've Given Me Your Best.

REDEMPTION

Father grieved when He lost touch with His son, but holiness demanded judgment, no matter what the price. The prodigal son took after our Prodigal Father. His wasteful expenditure of finances, extravagant love and spendthrift ways of dealing with compassion and mercy is what draws wayward children back home.

Romans 2:4-5 *Or do you despise the riches of His goodness, forbearance, and longsuffering, not knowing that the goodness of God leads you to repentance?*

But all this had to be done in a legal process that according to the law, was settled before time.

Esther was brought to the king's palace for such a time as this. She had a mission. When she discovered the plot to annihilate her people, she worked with the legal plan set down by her king, the laws of the land that could not be changed; but could there be an alternative? She was three days in prayer to know what was God's will; three days of preparation for the banquet to reveal the enemy's intentions, and in prayer again, three days to find the answer for her people to overcome what was set against them. The people took a stand against their enemy and won.

Jesus was sent from the Father in the fulness of time. He had a mission to accomplish, to overcome the plot to annihilate His people. He subjected Himself to the King's law that could not be changed, only fulfilled. He was 3½ years in prayer to know the Father's will;

Matthew 14.23 *And when He had sent the multitudes away, He went up on the mountain by Himself to pray.*

Luke 6.12-13 *Now it came to pass in those days that He went out to the mountain to pray, and continued all night in prayer to God.*

He was these years revealing to us our enemy's plans to destroy us and how we could overcome; and three days in the tomb to *be* the answer for His people to be overcomers. But when that 3½ years were over, the prophecy of Daniel 9.27 could be completed. *He shall confirm the covenant for one week.* There was still 3½ more years until it would be fulfilled. The first 3½ years He reminded them of what was written.

Jeremiah 31.31-35 *Behold, the days are coming, says the Lord, when I will make a new covenant with the house of Israel and with the house of Judah according to the covenant that I made with their fathers in the day that I took them by the hand to lead them out of the land of Egypt, My covenant which they broke, though I was a husband to them, says the Lord. But this is the covenant that I will make with the house of Israel after those days, says the Lord I will put My law in their minds, and write it on their hearts; and I will be their God, and they shall be My people* [Malachi 3.1]..

No more shall every man teach his neighbor, and every man his brother, saying, 'Know the Lord,' for they all shall know Me, from the least of them to the greatest of them, says the Lord. For I will forgive their iniquity, and their sin I will remember no more [See Ezekiel 36.26; 37.26].

Now for the last 3½ years to be fulfilled.

Acts 1.8 But *you shall receive power when the Holy Spirit has come upon you; and you shall be witnesses to Me in Jerusalem, and in all Judea and Samaria, and to the end of the earth.* And here comes the power...

Acts 2:1-4 *When the Day of Pentecost had fully come,*

they were all with one accord in one place. And suddenly there came a sound from heaven, as of a rushing mighty wind, [Father once again breathed on His creation], *and it filled the whole house where they were sitting. Then there appeared to them divided tongues, as of fire, and one sat upon each of them. And they were all filled with the Holy Spirit and began to speak with other tongues, as the Spirit gave them utterance.*

The very first evidence of the power was Peter speaking with boldness, not overcome with fear as at the arrest of Jesus. Now V.41 *Then those who gladly received his word were baptized; and that day about three thousand souls were added to them.* The power of the true gospel will change men and women to receive the New Covenant, the Word written in our hearts and minds and being filled with God's Holy Spirit.

Acts 2.46-47 So *continuing daily with one accord in the temple, and breaking bread from house to house, they ate their food with gladness and simplicity of heart, praising God and having favor with all the people. And the Lord added to the Church daily those who were being saved.*

Acts 5.42 *And daily in the temple, and in every house, they did not cease teaching and preaching Jesus as the Christ.*

Jesus Fulfilled the Law. Remember 'It Is Finished'. And Now The New Covenant Is Written in Our Heart Too Bad about Ananias and Saphira - but the Infant Church Could Not Start out with Deception.

Peter's second sermon. Theme; The covenants will be fulfilled. Read the rest... The priests were not happy...but then... the Apostles did not deter from their assignment. [to reiterate] ....

In prophecy, it is a day for a year, so this one week, [Daniel 9.27] 7 days - 7 years. 3½ years were fulfilled in Jesus teaching, then He 'was cut off' - crucified. Now for the last 3½ years, Jesus' instructions would be carried out by the disciples [Acts 1.8]. First go to Jerusalem and Judea, then to Samaria and then to uttermost parts of the earth. And how would this be accomplished; for 3½ years they stayed in Jerusalem [Acts chapters 3-7]. Much persecution was endured and Stephen was the first martyr in Christ. But how would they know those days were finished. Well...

Acts 8.1-4 At *that time a great persecution arose against the Church which was at Jerusalem; and they were all scattered throughout the regions of Judea and Samaria, except the Apostles.* [Most of them stayed in Jerusalem for a while]. *As for Saul, he made havoc of the Church, entering every house, and dragging off men and women, committing them to prison. Therefore, those who were scattered went everywhere preaching the word.*

These Last Years Were Now Being Fulfilled
According to Daniel 9.27.

And Guess Where Philip Went, Yes, Samaria and to the eunuch; and Peter went to the Centurion. Now this New Covenant was sent forth to the whole earth that we may be reconciled with the Father Who created us to be His very own family. He reminds us again of His promise to redeem us and cause us to know His Father's heart. And this is exactly what He did.

Hebrews 8.10-12 *For this is the covenant that I will make with the house of Israel after those days, says the Lord I will put My laws in their mind and write them on their hearts; and I will be their God, and they shall be My people.*

Because of his great love for us who have believed in him. Thank you, Jesus, for your great sacrifice, to lay down your life for such a rebellious people to bring us back to that for which we were created.

Galatians 2:7-9 *When they saw that the gospel for the uncircumcised had been committed to me,* [Paul] *as the gospel for the circumcised was to Peter; that we should go to the Gentiles and they to the circumcised.*

How do we Escape His Wrath?

Romans 5.1-12 *For when we were still without strength, in due time Christ died for the ungodly. For scarcely for a righteous man will one die; yet perhaps for a good man someone would even dare to die. But God demonstrates His own love toward us, in that while we were still sinners, Christ died for us. Much more then, having now been justified by His Blood, we shall be_saved from wrath through Him. For if when we were enemies we were reconciled to God through the death of His Son, much more, having been reconciled, we shall be saved by His life. And not only that, but we also rejoice in God through our Lord Jesus Christ, through whom we have now received the reconciliation.*

Colossians 1.27 Christ *in you, the hope of glory.*

Matthew 4:15-16 *The land of Zebulun and the land of Naphtali, By the way of the sea, beyond the Jordan, Galilee of the Gentiles: The people who sat in darkness have seen a great light, And upon those who sat in the region and shadow of death Light has dawned."*

Our Father Longs for Each of Us
to Receive the Salvation
For Which Jesus Gave His Life. So Great a Sacrifice
For the People Who Lived in Darkness -
To Bring Us into His Light.

You are an original, I made you like you are
I set aside all others, and made for you a start
The beginning of a perfect you,
So, we could become one
I birthed you and re-birthed you,
So, you would never be alone
Each and every one of you, Fills a place in my heart
And I will never leave you, we'll never be apart
I made each one individual, Never like another
But I brought you all together,
So you could be brothers
Your spirit, soul and body
Are different in time
And when I gather all of you together -
You will be mine
So, remember I made you
Exactly as you are.
Be At Peace.

233

THE LORD'S TIMING

Daniel 12.7 and Revelation 12.14 speak of 'times, time and half a time.' How do we determine exactly what this means? And who has determined just exactly what this means.

How do we know it speaks of years?

Let's investigate what this word 'thousand' really means.

Psalm 90.4 *A thousand years in thy sight are but as yesterday when it is past.*

2 Peter 3.8 *Beloved be not ignorant of this one thing, one day is with the Lord as a thousand years, and a thousand years as one day.*

> The Use of the Word Thousand in
> *Prophecy* Is a Metaphor,
> A Concept, Not Literal.

Psalm 105.8 *He remembered his covenant forever, the word which he commanded to a thousand generations.* Has His covenant only lasted a thousand generations? Some of us may be out of the loop!

Revelation 14.1-5 *There stood on Mt Zion one hundred forty-four thousand having his Father's name written in their foreheads.* So in the end, will there be only 144,000 with Him for eternity? Or is this actually a metaphor for the government of the Kingdom of God and for the complete Elect, The Bride of Christ?

Revelation 20.4 *Souls who have not received the mark of the beast lived and reigned with Christ a thousand years.* What happens to us after a thousand years is over?

Revelation 20.6 *Those who take part in the first resurrection shall reign with Christ a thousand years.*

Again, What Happens to Believers After the Thousand Years Are Over?

Jude 14 *Enoch prophesied the Lord cometh with ten thousand of His saints.* Is He only partial to 10,000?
He owns the cows on a thousand hills.

Is There Only A Thousand Hills On The Earth?

There are 10 centuries in a thousand years, approximately 20 generations; and so, these thousand years is a metaphor, a figure of speech for a long time. God wants us to know He will never quit on us, even to everlasting.

There was only one of Jesus' parables that could be taken literally and that was because the story was about Lazarus in Paradise, and He named him. There are no names mentioned in His other parables.

A Parable Is a Short Story Which Illustrates a Moral Lesson.

It behooves us to ask for wisdom and understanding for what is prophecy and what is literal. [James 1.5] God wants us to understand what He has promised for the people of His heart. And please notice Revelation 1.3...

Revelation Is a Book of Prophecy.

Total reliance on God is the doorway into the Kingdom realm. The poor in spirit have only one remedy, That Is Trusting in God, just as all of God's people.

If I have been repetitive it is because I am trying to convey all that God has caused me to understand.

Everything Is Unfolding in God's Time.

There Had to Be a Temple and a City Finished and His People Living in the Land, For the Day of Messiah Is Come for Him To Enter the Earth Realm for His Mission,

Prepared from the Foundation of the World.

Our Mighty God of Creation has drawn up His plans. He has chosen to build His dwelling place within His people. The architecture must be perfect with no spot or wrinkle; cleansed unto holiness; sound unto righteousness, yet no hammering will be heard in this Temple. Now for this Temple - built without hands; each brick will be laid with tears of repentance. Each column is held fast on the humble knees of prayer. The ceiling will be constructed of praise and worship. The foundation is built upon no less than the Rock, Our Redeemer, Our glorious Lord and King,

JESUS MESSIAH - Our Chief Cornerstone.

The anointing which you have received of Him abides in you, and you need not that any man teach you; but as the same anointing teaches you of all things and is truth, and is no lie, and even as it has taught you, you shall abide in Him.

God Is Really Looking to Establish
His Foundation in Our Lives.

God's hand had been heavy on Israel. Zerubbabel's Temple had to be restored and rebuilt. The City of Jerusalem had to be restored - rebuilt - for their Messiah was soon to come to His Temple. And now - Israel must be rebuilt - restored - for the Messiah of the world is soon to come to His people. These things must be in place. And now His people - His true Temple, He is rebuilding - restoring;

Restoring His people - Maturing His Bride...
FOR MESSIAH IS SOON TO COME TO HIS TEMPLE.

How do you feel about your Temple being under reconstruction? Are you cooperating? [OUCH!]
Thank You God for Writing Your Laws on My Heart That I Might Not Sin Against You, And Please Forgive Me for Allowing the Idols of the World to Ever Influence Me.

Sin Doesn't Hurt Us Because It's Wrong;
Sin Is Wrong Because It Hurts Us.
Our Human Love Wants Reward.
God's Love Asks for Nothing.

Proverbs 1.33 *But whosoever hearkens unto me will dwell safely and shall be secure without fear of evil.*
God wants to dwell in us and live with us seated at the right hand of God. When He said 'It is finished', the joy that was set before Him is the omnipresence of Christ dwelling in man.

The angels were amazed at creation - they saw the glory covering the man. They were amazed that man cast off the covering to seek his own way. They were amazed at Jesus - to see the glory covered by flesh. They were amazed at Pentecost to see again the flesh covered by the glory - The glory in and around earthen vessels.

Oh, What Love the Father Has for His Own! And We Will Dance Before the Throne Of Our Glorious God and Savior, To Worship and Praise Him Throughout All Eternity.
Time - Is it Running out for Us. Should We Run into the Caves? Or Does God Have a Place for Us to Hide?
Isaiah 24.20 Come, *my people, enter your chambers, and shut your doors behind you; Hide yourself, as it*

were, *for a little moment, Until the indignation is past. For behold, the Lord comes out of His place to punish the inhabitants of the earth for their iniquity; The earth will also disclose her blood, and will no more cover her slain*.

Yes, the Scripture says we will all be caught up with the Lord, but carefully research WHEN!

1 Thessalonians 4.13-18. When the Lord comes back, *we who are alive* [the lovers of God] *and remain unto the coming of the Lord... - With a shout and the voice of the archangel and the trump of God* - This does not sound like a silent shwooshing rapture. It seems that at this same time verses 5.2-4 will happen. *Sudden destruction on the unbeliever and they shall not escape*. Now see verses 4-6 Please read the whole passage.

1 Thessalonians 5:4-6 *But you, brethren, are not in darkness, so that this Day should overtake you as a thief. You are all sons of light and sons of the day. We are not of the night nor of darkness*. That's Us!

Remember the Five Faithful Virgins.

This Is from David Wilkerson's Book on How God's People Should Respond in The Times Ahead.

Many believers have put their eternal destiny into the Lord's hands—but not all have done the same with their earthly destiny. God is about to take His Church into a wilderness of testing, to strip away our human resources and make us wholly dependent on Him and to bring us into His rest! Tragically, God's rest remains largely unclaimed by His people today. Rest is total trust in God for all things. How do we prepare for the storm? Our place of safety is our secret closet of prayer! The darker things get, the brighter our Lord's light will shine.

We are going to witness the greatest miracles of any past generation. If you live in His presence, you're going to see His creative power manifested in your life. Crave His presence, not merely His provision. His presence is your protection. If you will watch out for your heart, He will watch out for your provision. By not fully trusting God, we literally put other people's lives at risk. Get alone with Jesus and seek His face and develop a loving relationship with Him in prayer; and praying for others [Isaiah 26.20].

If we as Christians live in fear, how can we hope to give assurance and hope to the unbeliever in such a time as this. The Gospel is the story of hope and trust in the God Who loves us so much, He gave His life for us.

Romans 1:16-17 *For I am not ashamed of the gospel of Christ, for it is the power of God to salvation for everyone who believes, for the Jew first and also for the Greek. For in it the righteousness of God is revealed from faith to faith; as it is written, "The just shall live by faith."*

The 'Thousand' of Prophecy Is a Metaphor, Symbolic for Fulness and Eternity.
The Only Concept We Can Have Of Eternity Is To Totally Trust And Rest In God.

All the sins of the world
were paraded there
before the Christ hanging
on the Cross. The soldiers
representing what an
oppressive government
lays on the shoulders of a conquered people; all
the sins committed against humanity and yes,
the sins of the people themselves. Of course,
there also were the scoffers, the phony religious,
the betrayers; the wicked, the strong
and the weak. And then,
the darkness of man and
devil tried to envelope Him
in their ghastly embrace
only to be overwhelmed
by love for His creation
and brought to its knees
before a sinless Lord;
its strength broken
by His Blood, its power
and force coming to a
standstill before this Man,
clothed in humility.
And even death himself
made a mockery of -
in the wake of
mercy and grace.

My God, My God, How Can it Be
That Thou My Lord Would Die for Me.

THE HABITATION OF GOD REVEALED

1 Corinthians 1-3...God intended that we be established in the wisdom of God; *for the wisdom of this world is foolishness*. We must understand the story of the cross, for it is the power of God released in us; the mystery revealed for resurrection and eternal life; released to those who will look to the cross for salvation.

God takes great delight in the simple preaching of the cross because to those who believe comes salvation from darkness into His light. He has taken the 'are-nots', the powerless, to reveal the power of the cross to lift them into the heavenlies [Ephesians 1].

You are the temple of God, and the Spirit of God dwells in you. If any man defiles the temple of God, him shall God destroy, for the temple of God is holy, which temple you are. [Be careful of what you share with others].

The revelation of the mystery of the cross brings us to the true inner sanctuary, redeemed man, the habitation of Jesus, our Messiah [John 14.20-23; 17. 13-23] for this was always His prime motivation. *I will put my laws into their minds and write them in their heart, and I will be to them a God, and they shall be to me a people* [Hebrews 8].

The first tabernacle was revealed as the Garden of Eden, the presence of God. Adam built his tabernacle right outside the door he could no longer enter. There was a gate, angels with sword, [metaphor for the law, the word in the Ark], The law Adam broke, the altar of sacrifice, and the tree of life, the presence of Jesus. This was the infant tabernacle maturing into Solomon's temple.

We see that Moses built the second tabernacle in a tent in which Moses worshiped and the third was the tent David placed on Mt Zion, the mountain on which David conquered the Jebusites, [means threshing place]. The very Ark of Covenant, the presence of that Holy God that David worshiped with all His heart and soul, was manifested again in a tent, yet still God's habitation for more than 20 years.

David left Asaph and his brethren before this tent of His Presence, that his God would be honored and worshiped continuously. His 'presence' actually means 'face to face'. Zadok the priest, offered burnt offerings morning and evening. David went in there continuously to pray and worship. His desire was to build God a house to dwell in, but he was a man of war with blood on his hands. The only blood that would be allowed in the temple is the blood of the innocent lamb. His son would be a man of peace and would carry out David's vision.

Now Solomon built the fourth tabernacle, the stone temple in Jerusalem. This habitation of God lasted for 7 centuries. Israel brought captive to Babylon, was set free by King Cyrus to go back to Jerusalem and rebuild their temple. The restoration in the 5th century BC of this one that Nebbie destroyed, would be the fifth tabernacle [See Nehemiah and Ezra].

As a result of this 70-year captivity, they lost track of much of the temple furniture; foremost was the Ark of Covenant. Though there was no Ark present behind the veil in this fifth tabernacle, the temple Zerubbabel restored; Israel still considered it the house of God.

John 2:16 *Do not make My Father's house a house of merchandise!*

They had no idea that the real Ark of Covenant would appear to bring to life all that was only a figure, the shadow, the foretaste of His intention; Jesus, the Real Ark of Covenant.

This last one perhaps reminds us of the stony heart we were delivered from. He brought us gently into the final achievement of His dream, destined before the foundation of the world. So it was for the fifth temple of Grace,

Zechariah 4.5-10 God spoke to Zechariah about Zerubbabel finishing the temple in the fifth century, so that our Redeemer, the real Ark of Covenant would come to fulfill all of what was prophesied, in spite of their rejection.

Grace, Grace unto it. But His own received Him not.

That beautiful paradise garden is now hidden from our sight, but the Tree of Life, the presence of our Redeemer will reveal it as we choose to walk and talk with Him. He has always meant for beauty to surround His people, and He will restore, when He gathers His jewels and make us His own.

Malachi 3.16-17 *Then those who feared the Lord spoke to one another, And the Lord listened and heard them; So, a book of remembrance was written before Him For those who fear the Lord And who meditate on His name. They shall be Mine, says the Lord of hosts, On the day that I make them My jewels. And I will spare them as a man spares his own son who serves him.*

All this is so encompassing that there is no longer needed a manmade 'sanctuary or tabernacle'. God has taken us from Adam's altar, to a tent, to a stone building which was finally smashed again [and were just the progressive images and shadows of His intention].

243

The final habitation of God would be His 6th temple. The sixth tabernacle is us, a tent of flesh, the lovers of God, the people that God has chosen to dwell in. In every tabernacle there presided the God of creation; His habitation. And of course, the number six is the number of man. Has God set up his habitation in the heart of every believer? Are we the tabernacle of God? *Know ye not that ye are the temple of God, and that the Spirit of God dwells in you*? [1 Corinthians 3.16].

And in the Fulness of Time, The Son of God Stepped out of Eternity To Become the Habitation of Man.

The all-encompassing heart of God has such love for His creation, it is beyond our imagination. We are living a life not our own, for we now live in Him and He lives in us. *He that loves me will be loved by my Father and I will love him, and will manifest myself to him...And we will come and make our abode with him* [John 14]. By grace do we stand in Christ, created to be the habitation of God, to live forever in His glorious presence. He had it all planned out from before the foundation of the world [Revelation 13.8].

He is the Cornerstone of our Faith.
From Visitation to Habitation.
The Ark of Covenant Has Made His Home
In the Tabernacle of Man to Come to fulness
When Jesus Comes Back to the Earth,
The Seventh Tabernacle.

He crossed through the barrier
From death to life
And He lives forever more
He shared with us truths we could never know
Until the New Man was restored
It all began with Adam, he strayed too far
He wanted to be free
But freedom has a price to pay
It cost you and me
Born in darkness, afraid of the light
But Spirit took flight and captured me
From darkness - so I could see
Now escaped from death to walk with God
No more barrier, I am free.

TRUTH/REALITY

Ephesians 2.19-31 *So now you Gentiles are no longer strangers and foreigners. You are citizens along with all of God's holy people. You are members of God's family. Together, we are his house, built on the foundation of the Apostles and the prophets. And the cornerstone is Christ Jesus himself. We are carefully joined together in him, becoming a holy temple for the Lord. Through him you Gentiles are also being made part of this dwelling where God lives by his Spirit.*
Holy Bible, New Living Translation.

Psalm 68.5-6 *A father of the fatherless, a defender of widows, Is God in His holy habitation. God sets the solitary in families; He brings out those who are bound into prosperity...*

What love is this cannot be ignored
It penetrates the heart and soul
No question as to where it comes
But needs our all in all
It's only Him - the One Who died for me
His name is Jesus - only Jesus
Whose love can penetrate
The heart and soul -
Oh, how He loves.

John 10.27-30 *My sheep hear My voice, and I know them, and they follow Me. And I give them eternal life, and they shall never perish; neither shall anyone snatch them out of My hand. My Father, who has given them to Me, is greater than all; and no one is able to snatch them out of My Father's hand. I and My Father are one.*

Sometimes it Will Be Only a Whisper
The Glory of God Is Awaiting Your Answer -
Will You Tun Your Face Toward Him
And Bow Your Knee in Worship.

Isaiah 15.1-2 *Lord, who may abide in Your tabernacle? Who may dwell in Your holy hill? He who walks uprightly, And works righteousness, And speaks the truth in his heart;*

Psalm 25.4-5 *Show me Your ways, O Lord; Teach me Your paths. Lead me in Your truth and teach me, For You are the God of my salvation; On You I wait all the day.*

Jesus - the Way, the Truth and the Life
Has Come to His Temple,
To Dwell in His People, to Bring Us
To the Fulness of His Plan for All of Creation,
To Be His Habitation.

Proverbs 2:3-5

Life is like a waterfall
It thunders deep in our soul
As it rambles on toward the sea
It conquers all in all
The rocks and debris are carried along
For a space and then let go
It settles down to be forgotten
As the river continues to flow
So all the sorrows of time gone by
Can be taken into God's arms
Carried along by His sweet love
That they shall no longer harm
So the waters of life flows over me
And the love of God prevails
They were hammered into
His hands and feet
By those old rusty nails
To conquer every sin and shame
In the glory of His name.

It's all about transition
Can You handle the change?
No - we can't
That's why we need the Lord.
Nothing is a surprise to Him.

Yes, if you cry out for discernment,
And lift up your voice for understanding,
If you seek her as silver,
And search for her as for hidden treasures;
Then you will understand the fear of the Lord,
And find the knowledge of God.

BE ENCOURAGED

Read the story of Elijah in 1 Kings 18-19

He is challenging Ahab but most of all his wicked queen.

And he answered, I have not troubled Israel, but you and your father's house have, in that you have forsaken the commandments of the Lord and have followed the Baals. Now therefore, send and gather all Israel to me on Mount Carmel, the four hundred and fifty prophets of Baal, and the four hundred prophets of Asherah, who eat at Jezebel's table.

Now here on Mount Carmel comes the time of the evening sacrifice. The Lord is about to show Himself to all of backslidden Israel.

1 Kings 18:38-40 *Then the fire of the Lord fell and consumed the burnt sacrifice, and the wood and the stones and the dust, and it licked up the water that was in the trench. Now when all the people saw it, they fell on their faces; and they said, The Lord, He is God! The Lord, He is God. And Elijah said to them, Seize the prophets of Baal! Do not let one of them escape! So they seized them; and Elijah brought them down to the Brook Kishon and executed them there.*

Elijah Had Just Killed All the False Prophets
And Now Comes the Result.
Jezebel Is out to Kill Him.

1 Kings 19:1-13 *And Ahab told Jezebel all that Elijah had done, also how he had executed all the prophets with the sword. Then Jezebel sent a messenger to Elijah, saying, so let the gods do to me, and more also, if I do not make your life as the life of one of them by tomorrow about this time. And when he saw that, he arose and ran for his life, and went to Beersheba, which belongs to Judah, and left his servant there. But he himself went a day's journey into the wilderness, and came and sat down under a broom tree. And he prayed that he might die, and said, it is enough! Now, Lord, take my life, for I am no better than my fathers!*

Too Many of God's People Feel at Times, Abandoned.

But God is still on His throne and knows all about you. His angels are sent to minister to us - if we will only turn our face back to God and listen.

God sent an angel to Elijah to feed him and give instructions. God was not finished with him.

1Kings 19.5 Arise *and eat, because the journey is too great for you. So, he arose, and ate and drank; and he went in the strength of that food forty days and forty nights as far as Horeb, the mountain of God. And there he went into a cave, and spent the night in that place; and behold, the word of the Lord came to him, and He said to him, What are you doing here, Elijah?*

Is God asking you the same question?

10 So *he said, I have been very zealous for the Lord God of hosts; for the children of Israel have forsaken Your covenant, torn down Your altars, and killed Your prophets with the sword. I alone am left; they seek to take my life.*

Well surprise; all Israel had just come back to the Lord. But Elijah was exhausted and very discouraged. Too often we feel the same way. Now comes God's Revelation.

Verse 11 *Then He said, go out, and stand on the*

mountain before the Lord. And behold, the Lord passed by, and a great and strong wind tore into the mountains and broke the rocks in pieces before the Lord, but the Lord was not in the wind; and after the wind an earthquake, but the Lord was not in the earthquake; and after the earthquake a fire, but the Lord was not in the fire; and after the fire a still small voice. So it was, when Elijah heard it, that he wrapped his face in his mantle and went out and stood in the entrance of the cave. Suddenly a voice came to him, and said, what are you doing here, Elijah?

Does God have to speak to you in an earthquake or can you hear His still small voice. There are many that love God and are faithful to follow Him. It would be good to get back into fellowship with God's people. Be encouraged and be at peace. God has not left you.

Learn to Listen for His Voice.

I give you here some Scriptures that may apply to some. Please go to the Lord to clarify if you don't understand; but these may release many from shame, guilt and condemnation. These were applied to my life.

Hebrews 9:11-15 *But Christ came as High Priest of the good things to come, with the greater and more perfect tabernacle not made with hands, that is, not of this creation. Not with the blood of goats and calves, but with His own blood He entered the Most Holy Place once for all, having obtained eternal redemption. For if the blood of bulls and goats and the ashes of a heifer, sprinkling the unclean, sanctifies for the purifying of the flesh, how much more shall the blood of Christ, who through the eternal Spirit offered Himself without spot to God, cleanse your conscience from dead works to serve the living God? And for this reason, He is the Mediator of the new covenant.*

251

Hebrews 10:19-24 *Therefore, brethren, having boldness to enter the Holiest by the blood of Jesus, by a new and living way which He consecrated for us, through the veil, that is, His flesh, and having a High Priest over the house of God, let us draw near with a true heart in full assurance of faith, having our hearts sprinkled from an evil conscience and our bodies washed with pure water. Let us hold fast the confession of our hope without wavering, for He who promised is faithful.*

1 John 3:18-21 *My little children, let us not love in word or in tongue, but In deed and in truth. And by this we know that we are of the truth, and shall assure our hearts before Him. For if our heart condemns us, God is greater than our heart, and knows all things. Beloved, if our heart does not condemn us, we have confidence toward God.....* Very Important see these Verses....

Hebrews 9.12-14; 10.19-22; 1John 3.19-21.

We all have an evil conscience from our life in the world - But... *You shall know the truth and the truth shall make you free.*

FOR THOSE WHO
ARE IN CHRIST

One night in 1985, the Lord got me up out of bed to write these things down. As fast as I was able to write, He gave me the paraphrased version of the Word, the Scripture reference, and then on to the next verse. All told, I found I had written down 88 verses of God's wonderful plan for our lives as told in story form, one verse after another compiled in less than one hour. It had to be the Lord, for even though most of these Scriptures were familiar to me, I could never have produced all these, in this sequence, in less than several days, with many hours of research in the process. Since I know it was Spirit led, I am including it in the book.

He that is joined to the Lord is one spirit. [1]
Your body is the temple of the Holy Spirit in you. [2]
If any man be in Christ, he is a new creation, old things are passed away, all things become new. [3]
For in Christ Jesus neither circumcision availeth anything nor uncircumcision but a new creation. [4]
So, put on the new man which after God is created in righteousness and true holiness. [5]
Put off the old man - put on the new man that is renewed in knowledge. [6]
And we have the mind of Christ. [7]
God reveals the things of the Spirit to us by His Spirit. [8]

The same Spirit that raised Jesus from the dead
dwells in you. [9]
If you are led by the Spirit of God, you are a son of God. [10]
An heir of God, joint heirs with Christ. [11]
Because we are called to His purposes. [12]
For it is God who works in you to will and do of
His good pleasure. [13]
For Jesus is the author and finisher of our faith. [14]
And He makes us perfect in every good work to be pleasing
in His sight. [15]

Therefore, let us continually offer the sacrifice of praise
unto our God. [16]
He hath said, I will never leave thee, nor forsake thee. [17]
For the Kingdom of God is righteousness, peace and joy
in the Holy Spirit. [18]
The Kingdom of God is not in word, but power. [19]
It is the Father's good pleasure to give you the Kingdom. [20]
That we might be conformed to the image of His Son. [21]
For He is the first born.[22]
From the dead so that He might have pre-eminence. [23]
That he might bring many sons to glory. [24]
That He might bring us to God. [25]
In Him dwells all the fullness of the Godhead bodily. [26]
And we are complete in Him. [27]
The Father gives us the Spirit of wisdom and revelation
in the knowledge of Him - the eyes of our understanding
being enlightened. 28
To understand the power working in us. [29]
Resurrection power that raised Christ from the dead.[30]

For once we were dead in trespasses and sins. [31]
And He's made us alive together with Jesus and forgave
all our trespasses.[32]
Buried with Him in baptism and risen with Him, through
faith that all things are possible with God.[33]

If we confess our sins, He is faithful and just to forgive us our sins and to cleanse us from all unrighteousness.[34]
For He that knew no sin became sin for us, that we might become the righteousness of God in Christ.[35]
And we are the temple of the living God, as God hath said, I will dwell in them and walk in them and I will be their God and they shall be my people.[36]
Be ye holy in all manner of life, be ye holy for I am holy. [37]
For we shall bear the image of the heavenly.[38]
We continue to reflect the glory of the Lord as we are changed into His image more and more every day by the Spirit of the Lord living in us.[39]
As the inward man is renewed day by day.[40]
We shall all be changed.[41]
With Christ in us the hope of glory.[42]
For we are a chosen generation, a royal priesthood, a holy nation, a people of His own.[43]
He has made us a nation of kings and priests unto God.[44]
So that we may show forth the praises of Him who called us out of darkness into His marvelous light.[45]
Through the shed blood of Jesus, we have our consciences purged from dead works to serve the living God. [46]

Because we are all as an unclean thing and all our righteousness is as filthy rags.[47]
But even when we were dead in our sin.[48]
God who is rich in mercy, with His great love for us.[49]
Made us alive in Christ.[50]
And by His grace He saves us through faith.[51]
It is His gift to us.[52]
Not of works lest any man should boast. [53]
He gathers us into His household.[54]
And frames us together with each other, to be His holy temple.[55] To be the habitation of God through the Spirit. [56]
That we might be strengthened with might by His Spirit in the inner man.[57]

That is renewed day by day.[58]

That we might experience the love of Christ which is so far beyond anything we might imagine - and be filled with all the fullness of God.[59]

And be partakers:

Of Christ [60]

Of the heavenly calling [61]

Of grace [62]

Of the Holy Spirit [63]

Of the gospel [64]

Of His holiness [65]

Of His inheritance [66]

Of His promise in Christ [67]

And of Christ's suffering [68]

For the glory of the Son has been given to us.[69]
As Jesus prayed for us who were yet to believe on Him.[70]
So that we might be made perfect in one.[71]
So the world might believe and know that Jesus has come.[72]
And all that come to Jesus He will in no wise cast out.[73]
That we might have everlasting life and be raised
on that last day.[74]
And all that receive Him, He gives the power to become children of God.[75]
That we might eat of the tree of life which is in the midst of the paradise of God.[76]
We will not be hurt of the second death which is the lake of fire.[77]
And we will eat of the hidden manna and receive a new name in Christ.[78]
We will walk with Jesus in robes of righteousness, for He has made us worthy.[79]
We will be pillars in the temple of God and never leave His presence. [80]

We will sit on the throne with Jesus. [81]
And receive power to rule over the nations. [82]

And we will reign on the earth with Him.[83]
And have the privilege, with billions of other ransomed believers, of falling down before our precious Lord and Savior and worshiping Him for eternity.[84]
And the King shall say unto us, Come ye blessed of My Father, inherit the Kingdom prepared for you from the foundation of the world.[85]
And we shall inherit all things, and He will be our God and we shall be His sons.[86]
For me to live is Christ and to die is gain.[87]
Surely, I come quickly. Amen. Even so, come, Lord Jesus. [88]

Rejoice in the Lord for His Word Is True
And He Will Always Be with You
Even to the End of Time.

THOSE IN CHRIST SCRIPTURES.

1. 1Co 6:17	2. 1Co 6:19	3. 2Co 5:17
4. Ga 6:15	5. Ep 4:24	6. Co 3:10
7. 1Co 2:16	8. 1Co 2:1	9. Ro 8:11
10. Ro 8:14	11. Ro 8:17	12. Ro 8:18
13. Ph 2:13	14. He 12:2	15.e 13:21
16. He 13:15	17. He 13:5	18.o 14:17
19. 1Co 4:20	20. Lk 12:32	21. Ro 8:29
22. Co 1:15	23. Co 1:18	24. He 2:10
25. 1Pe. 3:18	26. Co 2:9	27.Col 2:10
28. Ep 1:17	29. Ep 1:19	30. Ep 1:20
31. Ep 2:1	32. Co 2:13	33. Co 2:12
34. 1Jn 1:9	35. 2Co 5:21	36.Co 6:16
37. 1Pe 1:15	38. 1Co 15:49	39.Co 3:18
40. 2Co 4:16	41. Co 15:51	42. Co 1:27
43. 1Pe 2:9	44. Re 1:6	45. 1Pe 2:9

46. He 9:14   47. Is 64:6   48. Ep 2:5
49. Ep 2:4   50. Ep 2:5   51. Ep 2:8
52. Ep 2:8   53. Ep 2:9   54. Ep 2:19
55. Ep 2:21   56. Ep 2:22   57. Ep 3:16
58. 1Co 4:16   59. Ep 3:19   60. He 3:14
61. He 3:1   62. Ph 1:7   63. He 6:4
64. 1Co 9:23   65. He 12:10   66. Co 1:12
67. Ep 3:6   68. 1Pe 4:13   69.Jn 17:22
70. Jn 17:20   71. Jn 17:23   72.Jn 17:21
73. Jn 6:37   74. Jn 6:40   75. Jn 1:12
76. Re 2:7   77. Re 20:6,14   78. Re 2:17
79. Re 3:4   80. Re 3:12   81. Re 3:21
82. Re 2:26   83. Re 5:4   84. Re 5:13
85. Mt 25:34   86. Re 21:7   87. Ph 1:21
88. Re 22:20

SMIDGENS FROM THE HEART FROM ME, GOD, AND FROM OTHER DIFFERENT SOURCES.

Our quality of life is determined, not so much by what life brings us, as by our attitude towards it. Life is not so much what has happened to us, but the way we look at it and deal with it. We decide what our attitude will be. No one else should be able to have that control over us. The offenses brought on by another can be manifested in anger and unforgiveness - or forgiveness and peace in our soul. It is our own choice. What we decide to do in any given circumstance is that which makes or mars us.

When we compromise our commitment to Christ we are left with nothing more than casual encounters with the Spirit of God [Larry Randolph].

Our spiritual fellowship with God should have no consciousness of sin because of the Blood of Jesus which made the way clear to meet with God. It is in our soul that we need cleansing and healing. Our soul and spirit are two different things; so we should have no guilt or shame or condemnation when we approach, in spirit, the throne of God; and we deal with our soul fractures as God reveals them.

Heavenly blessings defined in the Word
Given to us in the Name of the Lord
Poured out from heaven, Given as leaven
To grow and produce A true son of God.

When our identity is in Christ, we cannot be crippled by the opinions of others. We don't work to fit into other people's expectations - but we burn with the realization of who the Father says we are. The secret to life is to let your existence flow through Him.

[This next is an excerpt from Morning Star Journal, Francis Frangipane].

God's intention with us is for Him to live in the very center of our lives. Not just the focus because we can look elsewhere - not just our goal because this can change day by day. For Him to be in the very center of our life means that everything pertaining to our life emanates from Him. All our decisions, our attitudes, our motives, ideas, imaginations, our heart, our intentions will be bound up in His glorious grace, plans and purposes for our life.

Christ dwells within us, but is He standing behind our walls? The walls between our Savior and us is primarily the work of unrenewed minds and hardened hearts. We have barricaded ourselves behind fears and carnal attitudes and we are held hostage by sin and worldly distractions; yet these barriers can be eliminated. To the degree they are removed, we possess oneness with Christ and experience true spiritual advancement. Is shame of failure a wall, is fear a barrier? If Jesus were in the next room, and His holy presence flooded your senses - would you enter that room?

We have been given the *mind of Christ*. What shall we do with it? Do we examine all our options, or do we seek wisdom from God [James 1]? So, I would ask...

How would you enter? What about the garment of Praise? Would you fall face down as a dead man before

Him? Approach with great trembling? I do believe that His overwhelming love and grace would enrapture you. Yes, fall down to worship the One Who so gladly received you into His Kingdom and gave you the gift of eternal life.

Revelation chapters 21-22 *And I heard a loud voice from heaven saying, Behold, the tabernacle of God is with men, and He will dwell with them, and they shall be His people. God Himself will be with them and be their God. And God will wipe away every tear from their eyes; there shall be no more death, nor sorrow, nor crying. There shall be no more pain, for the former things have passed away.*

The throne of God and of the Lamb shall be in it, and His servants shall serve Him. They shall see His face, and His name shall be on their foreheads. Then He who sat on the throne said, Behold, I make all things new. And He said to me, Write, for these words are true and faithful. And He said to me, it is done! I am the Alpha and the Omega, the Beginning and the End. I will give of the fountain of the water of life freely to him who thirsts. He who overcomes shall inherit all things, and I will be his God and he shall be My son. And behold, I am coming quickly, and My reward is with Me, to give to every one according to his work.

I am the Alpha and the Omega, the Beginning and the End, the First and the Last. And the Spirit and the bride say, Come! And let him who hears say, Come! And let him who thirsts come. Whoever desires, let him take the water of life freely.

The Bible records that the greatest love ever manifested in this world was the love of God in Messiah, dying on the cross in our place, for our sins, to bear our judgment, and then rising from death to life, that we could be saved; that we could have eternal life with Him. So, how does one become born again? In the Bible it declares ...

John 1.12 But *as many as received Him, to them He*

261

gave power to become the children of God, even to them that believe in His name. Who are born not of natural birth, but of spiritual birth by the will of God.

Making Jesus Lord and Savior of Your Life,

And Love Him Enough That -

John 14.15-18 *If you love Me, keep My commandments. And I will pray the Father, and He will give you another Helper, that He may abide with you forever — the Spirit of truth, whom the world cannot receive, because it neither sees Him nor knows Him; but you know Him, for He dwells with you and will be in you. I will not leave you orphans; I will come to you.* [2 Jn 6].

The Presence of Jesus in our life and His Holy Spirit to guide us, is the most precious gift we could ever receive and all it takes is for you to say with all your humble heart; 'Yes Lord, thank you for dying on the cross for me and forgiving my sins; I want to know You and follow You. Amen - So Be It'.

A people physically taken from the nations

A people spiritually taken from the world.

Ephesians 2:14-*18 For He Himself is our peace, who has made both one, and has broken down the middle wall of separation, that He might reconcile them both to God in one body through the cross, thereby putting to death the enmity. For through Him we both have access by one Spirit to the Father.*

In the first century there had to be a temple and a people in the land for the first coming of their Messiah. Now there will be the people of God; The temple of His habitation; prepared and waiting for His second coming.

If this Book Has Caused You to See the
Truth of God's Word, Please Give Him - All the Glory.

[For me] ...To Know God -
To Know Beyond a Shadow of a Doubt
That He Is Sovereign And
That My Life Is in His Care,
This Is the Unshakable Foundation
On Which I Stay My Soul.
Unknown Author

I have a Father, He knows my name
He calls me to His side, again and again
He sees me where I am,
And where I will go
His plans for me too wonderful,
He reveals so I will know
Eternity - for at His side,
I'll rule and reign with Him
Because by His precious Blood,
He redeemed me from my sin
So I'm free to worship
With all my heart and soul
And live with Him forever,
In the Kingdom of His love.

Father God has everything in Control. He knows all His children by name and will keep us safe from the evil one as long as we trust in Him.

OTHER BOOKS BY AUTHOR Dory Robertson...You may Order any of these books from doryptl7@hotmail.com Send your address I'll give you mine and you can send a check for $14.00. Your book will be mailed to you.
$4.00 is for postage.

Several of these books are a witness to what God did in my life as I was growing up in the Lord. For 48 years God has been working diligently to set me free from a life time of fear, rejection, and self-hatred. He's still at it. It takes a lifetime for us to get all our issues dealt with. I give all glory and honor to the Most High God for causing me to come into His presence; to know that I finally have a real Father, and to know what it means to have a relationship with a family, the family of God.
And He Has Put a New Song in My Heart.

The Temple of God Restored - The Ark of Our Covenant
A Word on Wisdom and Knowledge - Kingdom Keys
The Enemies of Our Land - A Manual for Warfare
The Love of Jesus - Journey into Reality
Home Away From Home - We're Just Passing Through
He Never Came Back - Recovery From Divorce
Hope and the Will of God - Our Inheritance
The Gift of Life - His Hand Is Reaching out to You
Songs of My Life - Poetry and Prose From the Heart of God.
Freedom From the Spirit of Fear - The Law of Liberty
The Seven Churches of Revelation –
[Jesus is Looking for His Bride]
The Manifested Bride of Christ - Who is She?
Knowing Abba Father - Finding Our Real Father
The Tabernacle of God - Journal of Redemption
Notes From a Newborn - Looking Back
[Memoirs of a Baby Christian Longing for Maturity].
Habitation of God - He lives in us.

And of course, TRANSITION

Printed in the United States
By Bookmasters